The European Union and the Rise of Regionalist Parties

Rather than weakening the forces of nationalism among member states, the expanding power of the European Union actually fosters conditions favorable to regionalist movements within traditional nation-states. Using a cross-national, quantitative study of the advent of regionalist political parties and their success in national parliamentary elections over the past 60 years, along with a detailed case study of the fortunes of the pro-independence Scottish National Party, Seth K. Jolly demonstrates that supranational integration and sub-national fragmentation are not merely coincidental but related in a theoretical and predictable way.

At the core of his argument, Jolly posits the Viability Theory: the theory that the EU makes smaller states more viable—and more politically attractive—by diminishing the relative economic and political advantages of larger-sized states. European integration allows regionalist groups to make credible claims that they do not need the state to survive because their regions are part of the EU, which provides access to markets, financial institutions, foreign policy, and other benefits. His in-depth examination of the Scottish National Party—which has gained increasing popular support since the 1970s—serves as a prime example of this phenomenon. Ultimately, Jolly emphasizes, scholars and policy makers must recognize that the benefits of European integration come with the challenge of increased regionalist mobilization that has the potential to reshape the national boundaries of Europe.

Seth K. Jolly is Assistant Professor of Political Science at the Maxwell School of Citizenship and Public Affairs at Syracuse University.

The European Union and the Rise of Regionalist Parties

Seth K. Jolly

University of Michigan Press
Ann Arbor

Copyright © by Seth K. Jolly 2015
All rights reserved

This book may not be reproduced, in whole or in part, including illustrations, in any form (beyond that copying permitted by Sections 107 and 108 of the U.S. Copyright Law and except by reviewers for the public press), without written permission from the publisher.

Published in the United States of America by the
University of Michigan Press
Manufactured in the United States of America
♾ Printed on acid-free paper

2018   2017   2016   2015   4   3   2   1

A CIP catalog record for this book is available from the British Library.

ISBN 978-0-472-07259-0 (hardcover)
ISBN 978-0-472-05259-2 (paperback)
ISBN 978-0-472-12100-7 (e-book)

For Gretchen and our daughters

Contents

List of Tables • ix

List of Figures • xi

Acknowledgments • xiii

Introduction • 1

1 Regionalist Parties in Western Europe • 13
   1.1 Comparative Framework • 14
   1.2 Concepts and Definitions • 15
   1.3 Classifying Regionalist Parties • 18
   1.4 Rising Regionalists? • 29
   1.5 Discussion • 32

2 The Viability of Regionalist Parties • 33
   2.1 Regionalist Mobilization in Western Europe • 34
   2.2 European Integration and the Viability of Small States • 38
   2.3 Preferences Matter, but Which Preferences? • 45
   2.4 Alternative Theories • 48
   2.5 Research Design • 50
   2.6 Discussion • 52

3 Regionalist Political Party Success • 54
   3.1 Modeling Regionalist Party Success • 55
   3.2 Where Do Regionalist Parties Compete? • 68
   3.3 Does European Integration Affect Regionalist Party Incidence? • 72
   3.4 What Explains Regionalist Party Success? • 80

	3.5	Discussion	85
4	Euroskeptic and Europhile Regionalists		87
	4.1	Competing Hypotheses	88
	4.2	Data and Methods	92
	4.3	The Regionalists and the EU	96
	4.4	Analysis	106
	4.5	The SNP and the "Independence in Europe" Policy	113
	4.6	Discussion	119
5	Public Support for the EU and Decentralization		123
	5.1	Citizens and the Viability Theory	127
	5.2	Support for European Integration	128
	5.3	Scotland	134
	5.4	The Scottish Referenda on Devolution	136
	5.5	Similar Preferences, Different Outcomes?	138
	5.6	Discussion	147

Conclusion		149
Appendixes		163
A	Regionalist Party Vote Shares, by Country	163
B	Cultural Difference by Language Families	167
C	Incidence and Success	187
	C.1 Incidence	187
	C.2 Success	194
	C.3 Combined Incidence and Success Models	201
	C.4 Discussion	202
D	Survey Questions	204
References		207
Index		225

List of Tables

1.1	Regionalist Political Parties in Europe	19
3.1	Observations with Regionalist Political Parties	70
3.2	Logistic Regression of Regionalist Party Incidence	75
3.3	Robustness Tests, by Different EU Specifications	77
3.4	OLS Regression of Regionalist Party Electoral Success	83
4.1	Peak and Average National Vote Shares of Regionalist Parties (1984–2006)	94
4.2	OLS Analysis of Party EU Positions, 1984–1996	107
4.3	OLS Analysis of Party EU Positions, 1984–2006	110
5.1	OLS Regression of EU Support in 2000	130
5.2	Scottish Perceptions of EU as a Good Thing	135
5.3	Attitudes and Actual Voting Positions on Devolution in 1979 and 1997	138
5.4	Expected and Actual Voting Positions on Devolution in 1979 and 1997	141
5.5	Preference Ordering on Devolution in 1979	142
5.6	Referendum Support in 1979, by Preference Ordering	144
5.7	Constitutional Attitudes in 1979 & 1997	145
5.8	Referendum Positions in 1979 & 1997, by Class	146
C.1	Robustness Checks for Incidence—Variables	190
C.2	Robustness Checks for Incidence—Specifications (1)	192
C.3	Robustness Checks for Incidence—Specifications (2)	193
C.4	Robustness Checks for Incidence—Excluding Countries	195
C.5	Robustness Checks for Success—Variables	196

C.6	Robustness Checks for Success—Specifications (1) . . .	198
C.7	Robustness Checks for Success—Specifications (2) . . .	199
C.8	Robustness Checks for Success—Excluding Countries . .	200
C.9	Heckman Selection Model (2-step)	202

List of Figures

1.1	Regionalist Party Incidence	24
1.2	Regionalist Party Peak Vote Share	25
1.3	Regionalist Party Incidence, 1950s–1960s	26
1.4	Regionalist Party Incidence, 1970s–1980s	27
1.5	Regionalist Party Incidence, 1990s–2000s	28
1.6	Observations with Regionalist Parties, by Country and Year	30
1.7	Regionalist Party Votes and Vote Shares, over Time	31
3.1	Language Difference in Western Europe	59
3.2	Observations with Regionalist Parties, by Country	71
3.3	Observations with Regionalist Parties, by Decade	72
3.4	Predicted Probability of Regionalist Party Incidence, by European Integration	78
3.5	Expected Vote Share, by European Integration	85
4.1	Support for European Union, by Party Family	97
4.2	Average Support for European Union, by Party	98
4.3	Regionalist Support for the EU, across Left/Right	99
4.4	Regionalist Support for the EU, across GAL/TAN	101
4.5	Trends in EU Support and Salience, by Party	102
4.6	Support for European Union in 2006, by Party and Issue	104
4.7	Predicted Support for EU, by Party Family	111
5.1	Expected Support for the EU	131
5.2	Party Cue Coefficient, over Time	133

A.1	Regionalist Support in Countries with Large Regionalist Parties (1)	164
A.2	Regionalist Support in Countries with Large Regionalist Parties (2)	165
A.3	Regionalist Support in Countries with Small Regionalist Parties	166
C.1	Predicted Vote Shares, by European Integration	203

Acknowledgments

THIS BOOK BEGAN MANY YEARS AGO at Duke University, combining my interests in nationalism, party politics, and European integration. It is the result of years of guidance and support from colleagues, friends, and family in Louisville, Durham, Chicago, Syracuse, and elsewhere scattered across the US and Europe. This book could not have been completed without them.

At Duke, I learned how to be a scholar and academic from the amazing faculty there, especially Herbert Kitschelt, Scott de Marchi, Steven Wilkinson, and Robert Keohane. I was also fortunate enough to attend classes next door in Chapel Hill at the University of North Carolina and learn from Gary Marks and Liesbet Hooghe. With their guidance, these mentors at Duke and UNC helped shape my research agenda in graduate school and beyond. In addition, several of my graduate school peers at Duke have been a constant source of support, feedback, and encouragement throughout this project, but I especially want to thank Michael Tofias, Michael Ensley, Ari Kohen, Dennis Rasmussen, Gerald DiGiusto, Jennifer Merolla, and Laura Stephenson.

My adviser Herbert Kitschelt deserves particular praise. In addition to his mentoring and friendship, his wide-ranging and insightful work provides an inspiring example for me.

While on a post-doctoral fellowship at the University of Chicago, I benefited from attending and presenting my work at the PIPES and Comparative Politics workshops. I am especially grateful to Dan Slater who helped me rethink the theory and cases in this book project.

At the Maxwell School of Syracuse University, this project has benefited from attention and criticism of several of my colleagues, particularly Matt Cleary, Brian Taylor, Shana Gadarian, and Jon Hanson who read drafts, discussed organization and strategy, helped solve methodological issues, and provided general advice and support. Also at SU, Sibel Oktay and Michael Beckstrand provided excellent research assistance at various stages of the project; I thank them for their hard work. I am also grateful to the Moynihan Center for hosting a book manuscript workshop in the fall of 2010, where Bonnie Meguid and Lieven de Winter reviewed the entire manuscript. Along with my Syracuse colleagues, many of whom read the entire draft at that time, Bonnie and Lieven provided crucial feedback that helped me revise the manuscript for submission.

Beyond Syracuse, I thank Ryan Bakker, Jonathan Polk, Jim Adams, Marco Steenbergen, Donald Horowitz, Catherine de Vries, Chris Anderson, Jae-Jae Spoon and Bonnie Meguid for offering constructive feedback on this project. In particular, my frequent co-authors Jon Polk and Ryan Bakker have not only helped me learn more about party competition in Europe with our ongoing collaboration, but they also provide just the right amount of levity and criticism when I ask them for help on my solo projects. I would also like to thank the panels and discussants at meetings of the Political Science Research Workshop at Syracuse University, the ECPR Summer School on parties in Friesland, Netherlands, the PIPES and Comparative Politics seminars at the University of Chicago, the Duke Graduate Student Colloquium, the Workshop on the Politics of Change at Vrije Universiteit Amsterdam, the European Consortium for Political Research's Fifth Pan-European Conference on EU Politics in Porto, Portugal, and annual meetings of the American Political Science Association, Midwest Political Science Association, International Studies Association, and European Union Studies Association.

I thank series editor Michael Laver for his guidance and Melody Herr at the University of Michigan Press for all her work throughout the review and publication process. It was a pleasure working with everyone at Michigan.

Material in Chapters 4 and 5 was previously published as "The Europhile Fringe? Regionalist Party Support for European Integration," *European Union Politics* 8.1 (March 2007): 109–130; and "Strange Bedfellows: Public Support for the EU Among Regionalists," in *Europe's Contending Identities: Supranationalism, Ethnoregionalism, Religion, and New Nationalism*, ed. Andrew C. Gould and Anthony M. Messina (New York: Cambridge University Press, 2014), and is

Acknowledgments

reprinted here with permission of SAGE and Cambridge University Press, respectively.

I gratefully acknowledge the financial support of the National Science Foundation's Graduate Research Fellowship, the Katherine Stern Dissertation Fellowship at Duke University, and the Appleby-Mosher Award from the Maxwell School at Syracuse University.

Finally, I owe one group more than any other—my family. My parents are a source of inspiration and encouragement. They taught me the value of education, perseverance and hard work. Without them, I would never have been exposed to or enjoyed so many opportunities.

My three amazing daughters, Brennan, Caroline, and Anna, have moved across the country with me on my academic adventures and are a constant reminder to try to be my best self. And last but certainly not least, I thank my wife, Gretchen, who is my best friend and my biggest fan. Without Gretchen's encouragement, humor, and joy in life, this project would never have become a book. I dedicate this book to Gretchen and our daughters.

Introduction

FOR MANY OF ITS FOUNDERS, the creation of the European Economic Community foreshadowed the end of national and ethnic divisions with the advent of a universalistic European identity. German Chancellor Konrad Adenauer saw supranational integration as "the modern antidote to nationalism ..." (Haas 1958, 32). Optimally, in the famous words of Jean Monnet (1962), integration would create a "silent revolution in men's minds" to finally "go beyond the concept of nation." In other words, with European integration, old loyalties and identities will simply fade away, leaving a more peaceful Europe.

Modernization theorists also predicted that Western capitalist development would diminish intra-national cultural differences, leaving a more homogeneous population unmotivated for social action (cf. Nielsen 1980, 1985; Ragin 1979, 1987; Keating and McGarry 2001). Marx, for example, foresaw the demise of many minority nations under the pressure of capitalism and a global cosmopolitan culture, a vision shared by many Enlightenment thinkers such as Condorcet (Moore 2001). Even as late as 1990, Eric Hobsbawm (1990, 192) argued that the "phenomenon [of nationalism] is past its peak." Regional integration theorists, such as Ernst Haas, also envision this identity shift. As Haas (1958, 16) notes, political integration can be seen as "the process whereby political actors in several distinct national settings are persuaded to shift their loyalties, expectations and political activities toward a new centre ... " The more loyalties shift to the new center, naturally, loyalties to the old identities weaken.

And yet, contrary to expectations, regionalist or sub-state nationalist movements, as found in the Basque country, Flanders, and Scotland, continue to gain strength vis-à-vis the central state, while European integration continues to deepen and extend multi-level governance in the

EU arena (Hooghe and Marks 2001). To clarify terminology, regional integration refers to the process of political and economic integration by European states, formalized in the European Union. The European Union project has some parallels in other regions, such as Mercosur in South America, the African Union in Africa, and ASEAN in Asia. But in no other region is regional integration as extensive or deep as it is in Europe, meaning that the EU's rules and influence reach into more national policy arenas, such as trade, monetary policy, and foreign policy, than any other regional organization. In contrast to this broader geographic grouping, regionalism refers to a form of nationalism within established states. Regionalist movements in Europe have goals ranging from ethnic or linguistic rights to decentralization to independence.

Within the last 20 years, these regionalist movements have achieved notable successes. In 1997, the citizens of Scotland and Wales voted to support the decentralization of political power to regional parliaments. In 2005, the Catalan regional parliament supported a constitutional statute granting Catalonia the right to be called a "nation" as well as an independent legal system and tax-raising authority (*The Economist* 2005). In 2010, a Flemish separatist party, the New Flemish Alliance, became the largest party in Belgium (*The Economist* 2010); with every new election, Walloon-Flemish coalitions become harder to form and the Belgian federation seems ever closer to fragmentation.

Beyond these notable examples, many scholars argue that both minority nationalism in general and regionalist parties in particular are on the rise (Esman 1977a; Lynch 1996; de Winter and Cachafeiro 2002), as voting for regionalist parties in national elections has increased in recent decades (Lancaster and Lewis-Beck 1989; Gordin 2001; Pereira, Villodres, and Nieto 2003).

This apparent contradiction between theory and practice yields the question that motivates this book: does European integration actually encourage regionalist mobilization within European Union member states?

The EU and Regionalist Mobilization

European integration is rarely considered a factor when discussing domestic elections and regionalist parties. Scholars are just beginning to understand the influence of European integration on the structure

Introduction

of political contestation at the national level (Marks and Steenbergen 2004), let alone the sub-state level. But I argue that deeper European integration, or the process of extending the EU's policy reach into more issue areas, should in fact increase support for regionalist political parties because it enhances the viability of smaller, more homogeneous political units in Europe.

The European Union makes smaller states more viable, and politically attractive, by diminishing the advantages of larger state size, such as market size, economies of scale, and defense (Bolton and Roland 1997; Keating 1995, 2001a; Alesina and Spolaore 2003; Becker 2005). Quite simply, European integration has created conditions under which regionalist groups (e.g., the Scottish) may not need the status quo state (e.g., United Kingdom) to thrive internationally. As Mark Leonard, the director of the European Council on Foreign Relations, argues, "The whole development of European integration has lowered the stakes for separation, because the entities that emerge know they don't have to be fully autonomous and free-standing.... They know they'll have access to a market of 500 million people and some of the protections of the E.U." (qtd. in Erlanger 2012). The European Union decreases regional dependency on the nation-state in both economic (e.g., international trade and monetary policy) and political terms (e.g., defense, foreign policy, and minority rights).

Although the presence of the EU diminishes the advantages of size for traditional states, the costs of heterogeneity remain. Not only do citizens in smaller political units have higher degrees of trust (Keating 2001a), but their governments should be more effective at providing public goods because the day-to-day lives of the citizens are more similar (Tilly 1975, 79). With greater ethnic heterogeneity, economic growth and public goods provision suffer (Easterly and Levine 1997; Posner 2004). Under the umbrella of the European Union, the optimal size of states in Europe is smaller than at any previous time (Alesina and Spolaore 1997, 2003; Alesina and Wacziarg 1998; Alesina, Spolaore, and Wacziarg 2000; Wittman 2000; Casella and Feinstein 2002).

In other words, the European Union system of multi-level governance increases the viability of smaller states. *The European Union and the Rise of Regionalist Parties* develops this Viability Theory and evaluates its explanatory power. What role does the EU play in autonomy movements in Flanders, Scotland, Catalonia, or northern Italy?

Does the Viability Theory help explain why so many European states are simultaneously threatened by fragmentation from below and integration from above?

For regionalist political elites with demands for greater autonomy, this increased viability increases the credibility of their party in electoral contests. European integration makes regionalist parties more politically attractive by improving the perceptions of the economic implications of independence as well as by increasing their bargaining leverage (Fearon and van Houten 2002, 22; Garrett and Rodden 2003, 94). Hence, the EU is an unwitting ally to regionalist movements who have the goal of more political autonomy or an independent state, even if it is only as a result of unintended consequences. Or, as Alesina and Spolaore (1997, 1042) state so clearly, "political separatism should go hand in hand with economic integration."

Regionalist Parties

While a rich literature on regionalist, or sub-state nationalist, movements in Europe exists (see, for example, de Winter and Türsan 1998), the effects of European integration on regionalist mobilization across Western Europe, and regionalist political parties in particular, remain under-tested and under-theorized, as de Winter (2001) notes. In this book, I first answer the research question posed above: does European integration actually encourage regionalist mobilization within European Union member states? Furthermore, I ask if the Viability Theory explains this relationship. For both questions, the answer is yes.

To pursue the first empirical question, I consider the electoral success of regionalist political parties as a key observable implication. When and where do regionalist parties choose to compete in Western Europe? And what explains these outcomes? In particular, does the development of the European Union affect where they compete (i.e., the incidence) and how successful they are in national elections (i.e., the success)?

Most work on regionalist parties has focused on individual countries or regions, and even less work considers the regions where regionalist parties do not compete. Thus, the literature cannot fully explain why Spain and the United Kingdom are rife with regionalist movements yet Germany and France have limited or non-existent regionalist parties

(Levi and Hechter 1985, 129). In this book, I analyze national-level elections from 1950 through the most recent elections in 2010 in 14 countries, encompassing 229 elections, one of the most extensive study of regionalist party electoral incidence and success yet undertaken. As one of the first truly comparative, cross-national studies of the incidence and electoral success of regionalist political parties using quantitative analysis, this book better evaluates the determinants of *both* regionalist party incidence and success within the Western European context.

After analyzing the effect of significant sociological and institutional variables, such as cultural preferences and political decentralization, I find that European integration significantly increases the success of regionalist political parties in national elections. I provide systematic evidence that European integration significantly influences the domestic elections and party systems of its member states, vis-à-vis regionalist movements. As the multi-level governance literature predicts, the various political arenas in Europe are "interconnected rather than nested" (Hooghe and Marks 2001, 4).

But the theoretical question remains open: why does European integration increase regionalist party success? Does the Viability Theory explain this relationship between the European Union and regionalist parties? Alternatively, do regionalist parties and partisans either ignore the EU or capitalize on Euroskepticism in the electorate? Logically, just as regionalist elites often oppose the central state, they could oppose the transfer of authority to Brussels. To test these alternative causal mechanisms, I analyze both elite and citizen behavior across Europe.

While the central empirical analysis of the book is a western Europe-wide comparative analysis of party success, party positions, and public opinion, I use the Scottish case to investigate the mechanisms at work behind the general findings. Scotland is an interesting case for many reasons, but two stand out. First, Scotland has a long history of regionalism. Nationalists founded the Scottish National Party in 1934 and the party won its first election in 1967. This history offers a chance to evaluate the evolution of elite attitudes toward the EU since the founding of the EU itself. Second, unlike other cases in Europe, the Scottish case offers the opportunity to evaluate public behavior regarding decentralization beyond opinon polls at two distinct time points when the public in Scotland voted on decentralization in 1979 and 1997. These two referendum votes in Scotland offer a unique opportunity to study the dynamics of the regionalist struggle in an evolving EU.

If the viability of small regions is enhanced by the presence of the EU, then regionalist elites should recognize and take advantage of the new political opportunity structure. For example, Alex Salmond, the leader of the Scottish National Party, uses the EU to respond to independence critics in a 2000 interview:

> People say, "What's a wee country like this going to do for an army." "Who's going to do food and drug testing? Who will issue the patents?" And people always worry about the money, you know: "We'll have a Scottish currency that nobody wants and a central bank that nobody listens to." ... [But] the whole debate on independence has been changed by a single idea, and that's the European Union. (qtd. in Reid 2000, A01)

In this book, I analyze whether and why regionalist political parties are supportive of the European Union in their party manifestos and public documents. I find that regionalist political parties are decidedly pro–European Union, suggesting that the regionalist political parties utilize the EU as an ally in their struggle for autonomy. Next, I consider the official positions of the Scottish National Party on European integration as more in-depth evaluation for the Viability Theory. I find that the Scottish National Party explicitly uses the European Union to frame independence as a more viable constitutional option to garner support for their movement, suggesting that viability lies at the heart of regionalist support for European integration.

But elites are only one part of the story. Another crucial test concerns voters, which requires analysis of multiple steps along the causal chain. For voters, I analyze whether European integration strengthens support for greater autonomy and even independence. If citizens recognize the changes in the political opportunity structure, they should not only be supportive of the EU project, but they should also find autonomy itself, whether decentralization or independence, a more viable and plausible prospect within a deeper European Union. Using Eurobarometer survey data, I find that regionalists in Western Europe support the European Union. Then I analyze the Scottish case in more detail, focusing on the 1979 and 1997 referenda to decentralize or devolve power to the Scottish region, and show that European integration

Introduction

does make an independent Scotland more viable and attractive in voters' minds. This increased perceived viability contributes to increased support for the Scottish National Party in national elections. These analyses of elite and voter attitudes support the theoretical proposition at the heart of this book: European integration encourages regionalist parties by making them and their goals more viable.

In the following pages, I sketch an outline of the book.

PLAN OF THE BOOK

REGIONALIST PARTIES IN WESTERN EUROPE

Before evaluating the determinants of regionalist party success, we must first meet the actors. Following Scheinman (1977, 67), I define regionalism to include all sub-state national movements that aim for some form of territorial autonomy within or outside the traditional state. These movements can justify their goals with a variety of ethnic, cultural, political, economic, or social claims. After identifying the regionalist parties, I then illustrate the geographic and temporal distribution of these parties in Western Europe. One of the main tasks of this book is to explain this variation in where regionalist parties compete and why they are successful in some regions, but not others.

EUROPEAN INTEGRATION AND THE VIABILITY OF REGIONALIST PARTIES

After introducing the regionalist party family, I develop the theoretical framework for the remainder of the book. Building on the political economy literature on the size of states (Alesina and Spolaore 1997; Bolton and Roland 1997; Alesina and Spolaore 2003), I argue that regional entities are more viable outside their traditional state due to the supranational structure of the EU, which allows them access to a larger market with less direct control than a traditional national government. The European Union system of multi-level governance increases the viability of smaller states, thereby increasing the scope and success of regionalist political parties. From this discussion, I argue that the Viability Theory explains why European integration leads to more sub-national mobilization.

However, a plausible alternative causal mechanism exists. Regionalist movements may utilize the threat of encroaching authority of Brussels to rally supporters to its cause. As more and more day-to-day regulatory issues are decided in Brussels rather than at either the national or regional level, some political entrepreneurs may seize the opportunity to gather electoral strength by assailing this trend. Thus, it may not be that regionalist groups embrace the EU as a means of making smaller independent countries more viable. Rather, it could simply be that some regionalist groups are the focal point for opposition to globalization and European integration (van Houten 2003, 113–118). Regionalist political parties may use this opposition as a mechanism to draw support to their movement. Fear of assimilation, potential loss of jobs, and animosity toward immigrants each could factor into supporting regionalist parties. Rather than an ally, therefore, regionalist political parties could frame the EU as yet another distant government dictating policy to the regions.

Thus, in addition to demonstrating that European integration does in fact positively affect support for regionalist parties, this book will evaluate under which conditions each of these causal mechanisms explains the relationship between European integration and regionalist mobilization.

Regionalist Political Party Success

Building on the Viability Theory and the comparative politics literature on new parties (see, for example, Kitschelt 1995, Hug 2001, and Meguid 2008), I develop hypotheses regarding the incidence and success of regionalist political parties, such as the Scottish National Party, the Plaid Cymru, and the Basque National Party. First, I review the literature on regionalist mobilization in Western Europe, paying particular attention to consistently robust findings. Explaining regionalist mobilization in Western Europe remains a topic of great interest to academics as well as politicians (Lynch 1996; de Winter and Türsan 1998; van Houten 2000; Tronconi 2006; Meguid 2008), yet much remains to be done.

On the demand or push side, cultural and economic differences drive the decisions of regionalist political parties to compete in national-level elections. But the opportunity structure for these parties, or the pull factor, matters as well. If the political marketplace is crowded or the mainstream parties incorporate these demands into their platforms, then the potential regionalist political party will not materialize.

But beyond the institutional and sociological factors, I argue that increased European integration actually encourages sub-state national autonomy movements by increasing the viability of smaller states within a broader political economic framework. Most studies focus on a variety of cultural and political economic factors, but they often neglect European integration as a relevant variable. By doing so, the previous literature omits a crucial variable that helps explain cross-temporal and cross-regional variation.

Using a dataset of all sub-national regions within the EU-14 from 1950 to 2010,[1] I demonstrate that a deeper EU has indeed encouraged more regionalist parties to compete in national elections. Using a variety of statistical techniques, I find that deeper integration has a consistent and robust effect on the incidence of regionalist political parties.

In this chapter, I also analyze the observable implication that regionalist political parties should obtain greater support from the regional electorate as the European Union deepens. I test the empirical implications of the Viability Theory with a dataset of regional electoral data along with cultural and political economic variables in the eight European Union member states where regionalist parties have competed in national elections between 1950 and 2010, which includes Belgium, Denmark, Finland, France, Germany, Italy, Spain, and the United Kingdom.

Empirically, I find evidence to support the specific contention that deeper integration positively affects electoral support for regionalist parties. As integration proceeds from a free trade area to a monetary union, deeper European integration is associated with more electoral success for the regionalist parties. Also, more distinct cultural preferences are positively correlated with electoral success for regionalist parties. With this analysis, I provide compelling evidence that European integration does in fact positively affect the electoral fortunes of regionalist political parties.

However, does this comparative large-N study justify the causal inferences drawn, namely that it is the Viability Theory that explains this relationship? The two sets of regressions demonstrate the descrip-

---

[1] The analysis focuses on the members of the European Union-15 (pre–Eastern enlargement), with the exception of Luxembourg.

tive inference: European integration affects regionalist party success at the incidence and election stages. But for the Viability Theory to be the driving force behind this relationship, both elites and citizens must recognize and acknowledge the strategic effect of European integration on the sub-state national autonomy movements. The next two chapters evaluate these connections.

Euroskeptic and Europhile Regionalists

In this chapter, I focus on the causal mechanism underlying the relationship between deeper European integration and regionalist party success. Do regionalist parties perform better as a result of deeper integration because they see the EU as an ally or as an enemy? In this chapter and the next, I adjudicate between two competing causal mechanisms, viability or fear, which may explain the finding that European integration increases support for regionalist parties.

First, I derive observable implications regarding party attitudes toward the EU from the two competing hypotheses. For regionalist political elites, European integration increases the credibility of demands for greater autonomy, ranging from independence to decentralization to cultural rights, and, therefore, their parties' credibility. In return, this factor provides incentives for regionalist political parties to be pro–European Union. Thus, the Viability Theory predicts regionalist parties to be pro-Europe.

Second, I introduce the Chapel Hill Expert Survey data and present the analysis of regionalist political party attitudes toward the European Union. Comparing the evolution of party positions on the EU from 1984 to 2006, I find that regionalist political parties are not Euroskeptic as are other fringe parties; rather, they are supportive of the European project, with a few notable exceptions such as Lega Nord. This finding is generally consistent across regions, supporting the Viability Theory.

Finally, I consider the official positions of the Scottish National Party on European integration. Using Scottish National Party manifestos from 1947 through 2010, I demonstrate that the Scottish National Party becomes more pro–European Union precisely when independence in the European Union becomes a viable alternative to remaining in the United Kingdom. The Scottish National Party explicitly uses the European Union to frame independence as a more viable constitutional option to garner support for its movement. Along with the statistical study of party positions, this evidence suggests that the Viability Theory explains why regionalists support the EU.

PUBLIC SUPPORT FOR THE EU AND DECENTRALIZATION

Going beyond regionalist party elites, I utilize public opinion data to determine whether regional citizens are more likely to support regionalist parties and greater autonomy because they find the idea of an independent region with Europe to be more feasible or because they fear assimilation within an all-encompassing European identity. This analysis of public opinion complements the evidence on regionalist political party views introduced in Chapter 4.

Public support for independence in Scotland reached 51 percent in a 2006 *Scotsman* survey, its highest level since the 1997 referendum that led to the creation of a Scottish Parliament (Mulholland and Tempest 2006). Meanwhile, Scottish public support for European integration increased 25 percent between 1979 and 1997, while support for the EU among all Europeans dropped nearly 14 percent during that same period. In this chapter, I evaluate whether these two trends are theoretically and empirically linked. Extending beyond the Scottish example, I test whether other Western European citizens with regionalist, or substate nationalist, attachments perceive the European Union (EU) as an ally in their struggle with the center. Using Eurobarometer surveys, I find that regionalists are pro-EU.

Then, using survey data from the Scottish referenda in 1979 and 1997, I show that European integration, particularly the Scottish National Party's successful framing of the EU as a mechanism to reduce the costs of secession, contributed to the dramatic increase in support for independence in the 1997 referendum. In 1979, at a relatively early stage of European integration in the United Kingdom, a slight majority voted for devolved political power, but the margin was not enough to overcome the electoral threshold set by Westminster. But in 1997, the result was overwhelmingly pro-decentralization in a much deeper European Union. I utilize public opinion data to test the observable implication that Scottish voters recognize the changes in the political opportunity structure caused by European integration, thereby yielding more support for decentralization with deeper integration. I find that voters are more likely to support independence as a viable constitutional option for Scotland, in part because the European Union provides an alternative political opportunity structure to the United Kingdom. This increased support for independence largely explains the dramatic increase in public support for a Scottish Parliament in 1997 compared to 1979. With this analysis, I provide further support for the Viability Theory.

Conclusion

In the conclusion, I first summarize the main findings and contributions of the book. Next, I briefly consider the empirical and theoretical implications to this project. The theoretical argument has implications for other levels within the European multi-level governance system, such as regional and European Parliamentary elections, and it has clear implications for other regions experiencing globalization and regional integration. Finally, I consider the effects of the Euro crisis on the European Union. The long-term future of the EU is uncertain, and that uncertainty has implications for regionalist movements within Europe.

Discussion

At its core, this is a book about party competition and the evolving relationships between the center and periphery within states and across Europe. By changing the perceived viability of small states within Europe, the EU has helped shift the balance of electoral power toward regionalist parties.

The core findings of this book have implications for both future academic work and future regional economic and political regimes. By investigating regionalist party incidence and success across Western Europe, this comparative study offers a more comprehensive understanding of why regionalist parties arise where they do. By triangulating on the question with multiple techniques and levels of analysis, I show that European integration does strengthen regionalist movements, as predicted by the Viability Theory. I also demonstrate that it is the increased viability of small states within the European Union that drives the relationship between integration and regionalist political parties. Supranational integration and sub-national fragmentation are, therefore, not merely coincidental phenomenon but are related in a theoretical and predictable way.

CHAPTER 1

Regionalist Parties in Western Europe

THE MOVEMENTS CENTRAL TO THIS BOOK go by many names: ethnoterritorial (Meguid 2008), peripheral nationalists (Gourevitch 1979), ethnic peripheral nationalist, peripheral regionalist, sub-national regionalist, sub-state nationalist, mininationalist, minority nationalist (cf. de Winter and Cachafeiro 2002), stateless nationalist and regionalist (SNRP) (Hepburn and Elias 2011), regional (Fearon and van Houten 2002; Brancati 2008), ethnoregional (Levi and Hechter 1985), ethnoregionalist (Gordin 2001; de Winter and Türsan 1998; de Winter and Cachafeiro 2002), and, simply, regionalist (Caramani 2000; Pereira, Villodres, and Nieto 2003; Caramani 2004; Fitjar 2010). As de Winter and Türsan (1998) argue, these terms are often used interchangeably and can be analogous to each other. For consistency, I use the regionalist term throughout the book. Beyond simply choosing a name, though, clarifying the concept of regionalist movements is a crucial step before starting the analysis.

In this chapter, I clarify a definition of the regionalist party family which focuses on party goals, specifically regional autonomy, building on previous work (especially de Winter and Türsan 1998, Caramani 2000, de Winter and Cachafeiro 2002, and Meguid 2008). Next, I identify the regionalist parties studied throughout this book. After classifying the parties, the chapter focuses on the geographic and temporal distribution of these parties throughout Western Europe.

1.1 Comparative Framework

Throughout this book, I focus on Western European countries in the post–World War II period.[1] This framework offers several advantages for this study.[2] First, these countries share similar levels of economic development and political freedoms. Of particular importance, there is a focus on electoral competition as the crucial mechanism to resolve political conflict. By controlling for many of these other factors, I can evaluate the effect of those variables that do vary across time and space, such as ethnic heterogeneity and depth of European integration.[3]

Second, this most similar framework offers access to a wealth of regional expertise in the form of case studies and expert surveys, without which a systematic cross-national time-series analysis of this nature would not be possible.[4]

This book focuses on political parties within Western Europe, especially their success, strategies, and supporters. Though regionalist mobilization could take multiple alternative forms, such as language revivals or even terrorism, the study of political parties has several advantages. Within Europe, political parties remain critical political actors in representing citizens and governing. In parliamentary systems, it is the political parties that form governments and "structure the political world" (Gallagher, Laver, and Mair 2011, 327). Despite considerable evidence of dealignment within European party systems, parties remain at the core of European parliamentary democracies (cf. Gallagher, Laver, and Mair 2011).

In addition, to analyze the emergence and success of regionalist

---

[1] I sometimes refer to this group of countries as the EU-14, or all members of the EU prior to the 2004 Eastern enlargement, excluding the small state of Luxembourg.

[2] In her study of the radical right, Norris (2005) considers the advantages of "most similar" and "most different" comparative frameworks, and this section clearly owes much to the logic of that discussion.

[3] As Norris (2005, 36) argues, this design helps alleviate "the common problem of too many variables and insufficient cases."

[4] Of course, this approach does not come without its own set of limitations. For instance, there is limited variation in wealth and electoral systems in Western Europe, relative to broader geographic studies of regionalist and secessionist parties, such as Sorens (2004, 2005) and Brancati (2014), making it more difficult to evaluate the effects of these variables on regionalist party success. Also, I should be cautious in generalizing these findings beyond Europe, as other structural conditions and institutions may interfere with the causal mechanism; nevertheless, there are lessons to be learned by studying the effects of European integration over time that may have implications for other regional integration projects.

movements across Europe over time, political parties offer another advantage. Significantly, as Levi and Hechter (1985, 130) argued twenty-five years ago, "Party organizations, members, and votes are quantifiable indicators of the probable success of a major strategy used by ethnoregionalists in advanced industrial democracies." In other words, if the goal is to compare across countries and over time, political parties have a decided empirical advantage for systematic comparative analysis.

Finally, though political parties compete in multiple levels of elections, from local to regional to European, I focus on parties that compete at the national level. While understanding the success and strategies of regionalist parties at all levels of European multi-level governance is of theoretical and empirical interest, and the interaction between success at the different levels is too poorly understood, national parliaments remain the focal point for constitutional and institutional reform. As Keating (1998, 166) so succinctly states, "For all the talk of a Europe of the Regions, the most important channel of influence is via national governments."

1.2 Concepts and Definitions

With a narrowed comparative focus on Western European political parties, I now concentrate on defining the regionalist concept itself and classifying the regionalist parties. In 1967, Lipset and Rokkan famously described party competition in Western Europe through the lens of four basic cleavages: owners-workers, urban-rural, church-state, and center-periphery. For the center-periphery cleavage, the national revolutions in some European states led to conflict between the central elites, intent on nation-state building, and the peripheral populations, often ethnically, religiously, or linguistically distinct from the center (Lipset and Rokkan 1967). At the most basic level, regionalist parties are those parties that compete mainly on this center-periphery cleavage.

The resurgence of regionalists in the 1970s, especially in the United Kingdom, refocused academic attention on explaining the phenomenon (cf. Esman 1977d; Birch 1978; Gourevitch 1979; Ragin 1979). In considering nationalism and economic growth, for instance, Gourevitch (1979) focuses on regions with "ethnic potential," or latent regionalism. In those regions with ethnic potential—or some distinctive characteristic among citizens of the region—peripheral nationalists will arise under certain economic and political conditions; however, as Levi and Hechter (1985, 131) contend, many of these early arguments tended to over-generalize from a few cases, providing little leverage on explaining the full range of variation in the success of regionalist movements across Europe.

For many authors, regionalism is a form of nationalism within established states based on two factors: ethnic distinctiveness and territorial claims (de Winter and Türsan 1998; Levi and Hechter 1985).[5] de Winter and Türsan (1998, 5), in particular, use the ethnoregionalist term to "denote ethnically based territorial movements in the Western European national states that aim to modify relations with the state." Notice the flexibility throughout the definition. Each component of the definition—ethnic, movements, and aims—is versatile, which creates space for multiple approaches and focus in their edited volume. For example, rather than narrow down "ethnically" to mean only linguistic or religious diversity, de Winter and Türsan (1998) simply state the need for an exclusive group identity. Echoing the "imagined communities" concept of Anderson (1983), de Winter and Cachafeiro (2002) go further, noting that what separates ethnoregionalist parties is that the parties represent a population *they claim* constitutes a culturally distinct category.[6]

Further, the goals are not specified and can include cultural autonomy or even separatism.[7] Similar to "ethnic parties," which are "iden-

---

[5] In contrast, some authors, such as Brancati (2008), focus only on the geographic basis of a party's support. A party is a regional party, therefore, if it competes in only one region of a country. While there is some overlap in the regionalist and regional party populations, of course, the conceptual differences between these terms are important.

[6] As Tronconi (2006) argues, ethnicity itself is among the most debated concepts in political science and sociology. Similar to the definitions discussed throughout this section, Tronconi (2006, 13) focuses on parties "that merge a sense of collective belonging (based on biological, historical, and cultural traits together with a capacity for self-identification) and a demand for control over a territory (which does not necessarily imply the formation of an independent sovereign state)." By focusing on political parties that contend they want to represent a particular group identity within a defined territory within a state, I leave aside the question of how ethnically heterogeneous these countries truly are, if that question could be answered. In the empirical analysis, though, I do introduce measures of latent cultural difference, using historical language in the region as a proxy.

[7] My broader definition therefore includes but is not limited to the separatist parties studied by Sorens (2004) and Brancati (2014), who also have different regional

tified with the cause of the ethnic group [they] represent" (Horowitz [1985] 2000, 296), regionalist parties "stand for the empowering of the (ethno)regionalist groups they claim to represent" (de Winter and Türsan 1998, 5). The demands of regionalist groups vary greatly depending on group and state contexts (Allardt 1979). Options for activists include traditional secession (exit), autonomy (religious, cultural, or political), access (power-sharing), and control of traditional states (Roessingh 1996, 25). Similarly, Pereira et al.'s working definition includes multiple goals, ranging from protectionist to autonomist to national-federalist to independentist (Pereira, Villodres, and Nieto 2003, 4–5). Hooghe (1992, 21–22) narrows the focus, discussing a range of policy options such as proportionality in public service posts, a veto on cultural matters, separate educational institutions, or even a complete consociational regime.

In addition to this variation in goals across parties, regionalist party demands also change over time. For instance, in the past 50 years, the Scottish National Party shifted from pursuing complete independence to independence within the British Commonwealth to "Independence in Europe." In the early twentieth century, rapid industrialization tied the Basque country to the Spanish center, leading moderate Basque leaders to shift from seeking independence to regional autonomy (Heiberg 1989, 73). More recently, Basque nationalist objectives transitioned from seeking autonomy through *fueros* to independence within the European Union (van Amersfoort and Beck 2000, 454). In summary, regionalist parties pursue both constitutional reform goals (e.g., devolution, federalism, independence) and capacity goals (e.g., political representation, cultural policy, socioeconomic projects) (Hepburn 2010, 41–48).

Thus, most of the regionalism scholars allow for a variety of autonomy goals, but Meguid (2008, 68) makes one distinction clear: while these parties can champion autonomy in varying degrees, the commonality is that the autonomy or territorial goal is a primary focus.[8] Even Gordin, who argues that ethnoregionalist parties "emerge due to

---

domains than this study. As Sorens (2004, 730) points out, theoretical arguments about globalization suggest that "globalization increases the appeal of secessionism and decentralization short of secession." Thus, it makes sense to study both types of parties in the European context.

[8]Meguid (2008) uses the regionalist term as a broader category, incorporating both ethnoterritorial and regional versions of other mainstream or niche parties.

the persistence of a separate and distinct ethnic identity linked to a particular identity, *regardless of its policy agenda*" (Gordin 2001, 150, emphasis added), acknowledges that all ethnoregionalist parties share regionalist aspirations as a focal point of their party program.

Returning to Lipset and Rokkan (1967), Caramani distinguishes regionalist parties as those parties that "stem from peripheral resistance to national integration" (Caramani 2004, 7). Similar to the definitions above, regionalist parties are "specifically created for territorial defense on the basis of linguistic, religious or economic distinctiveness" (Caramani 2004, 111).

Nevertheless, in all of these definitions, the defining characteristics of a cleavage, as opposed to a mere political issue, surfaces. A cleavage involves a division based on a sociocultural characteristics, such as socioeconomic, religious, ethnic, or linguistic. Not only must citizens be aware of this collective identity, but the cleavage must manifest itself as an organization, such as a political party (Gallagher, Laver, and Mair 2006). Thus, regionalist parties defend the interests of their collective identity groups, with particular emphasis on territorial autonomy and capacity goals.

1.3 Classifying Regionalist Parties

Building on this rich literature, Table 1.1 lists the regionalist parties included in this study, along with the national elections that the parties contested. In compiling the list of regionalist parties, I used a wide array of sources, but the initial classification was based on de Winter and Türsan (1998) and Caramani (2000), at least through 2000. In more recent elections, I investigated every new party through primary sources, such as manifestos and websites, to analyze whether they fall under the classification of regionalist parties. Given the focus on national elections, only parties that competed in one or more national elections are included.

I then compared my classification of parties with other studies of these parties, including Meguid (2008), Pereira, Villodres, and Nieto (2003), de Winter and Cachafeiro (2002), Caramani (2004), and Gordin (2001). In a few cases, these authors included parties that are excluded in Table 1.1; however, disagreements over classification are more of a matter of domain than conceptual. For instance, Pereira, Villodres, and Nieto (2003) focus on regional rather than national elections, which adds several small parties in France and Spain to their sample. In contrast, de Winter and Cachafeiro (2002, 486) concentrate on European elections and European transnational party federations like the European Free Alliance, which affects their sample.

Two parties stand out as sources of disagreement, though. Vlaams Blok (or Vlaams Belang) in Belgium and Lega Nord in Italy are often classified as Radical Right parties; however, while they hold far-right ideological positions, they fit the definition of regionalist parties laid out in this section.[9] If anything, this ideological diversity complicates the empirical analysis because the regionalist parties are so different in the non-territorial aspects of their platforms. Notice that neither my classification nor these others include regional branches of national political parties, such as the Christian Social Union of Bavaria (CSU) or the Flemish or Walloon version of mainstream party families. The classification is not based simply on whether a party only competes in a particular region, but whether it has territorial or autonomy goals based on a collective regional identity (see also Caramani 2004).

Table 1.1: Regionalist Political Parties in Europe

Region	Political Parties (English label, abbreviation)	Contested Elections
Belgium		
Flanders	Lijst Dedecker (List Dedecker, LDD)	2007–2010
	Nieuw-Vlaamse Alliantie (New Flemish Alliance, N-VA)	2003–2010
	Vlaams Blok (Flemish Bloc, VB)	1991–2003
	Vlaams Belang (Flemish Interest, VB)	2007–2010
	Volksunie (People's Union, VU)	1954–1999
Wallonia	Front Démocratique des Francophones (Democratic Front of Francophones, FDF)	1968–1991
	Rassemblement Wallon (Walloon Rally, RW)	1968–1981

Continued on next page

---

[9] See de Winter and Cachafeiro (2002, 484) for a similar logic on including these two parties.

Table 1.1: Regionalist Political Parties in Europe
(continued from previous page)

Region	Political Parties (English label, abbreviation)	Contested Elections
Denmark		
Southern Jutland	Slesvigske parti-Schleswigsche Partei (Schleswig Party, SLE)	1950–1964, 1968–1971
Finland		
	Svenske Folkpartiet (Swedish People's Party, SFP)	1951–2007
France		
Brittany	Union Démocratique Bretonne (Breton Democratic Union, UDB)	1986
Corsica	Union di u populu corsu (Union of Corsican People, UPC)	1986
Germany		
Bavaria	Bayernpartei (Bavarian Party)	1953
Schleswig-Holstein	Südschleswigscher Wählerverband-Sydslesvigsk vælgerforening (South Schleswig Voters' Union, SSW)	1953–1957
Italy		
Northern Italy	Lega Nord, including Liga Veneta and Lega Lombarda (Northern League, Lega)	1983–2008
Sardinia	Partido Sardo d'Azione (Sardinian Action Party, PSd'Az)	1983–87
Trieste	Associazione per Trieste (Association for Trieste, APT)	1979–83
Southern Italy	Lega d'Azione Meridionale (League for Southern Action, LAM)	1992
	Movimento per le Autonomie (Movement for Autonomies, MpA)	2008
South Tyrol	Südtiroler Volkspartei (South Tyrolean People's Party, SVP)	1953–2008

Table 1.1: Regionalist Political Parties in Europe

Region	Political Parties (English label, abbreviation)	Contested Elections
Italy (*continued*)		
Valle d'Aoste	Autonomie Liberté Démocratie (Autonomy Liberty Democracy, ALD)	2006–08
	Union Valdôtaine (Valdostian Union, UV)	1958–1963, 1972–1987, 1994–2008
Spain		
Andalusia	Partido Andalucista (Andalusian Party, PA)	1989, 1996–2004
	Partido Socialista de Andalucía (Socialist Party of Andalusia, PSA)	1979
Aragon	Chunta Aragonesista (Aragonese League, CA)	1996–2008
	Partido Aragones Regionalista (Aragonese Regionalist Party, PAR)	1979, 1986–1993, 2000
Balearic Islands	Progressistes per les Illes Balears (Progressives for the Balearic Islands, PIB)	2004
Basque Country	Eusko Alkartasuna (Basque Solidarity, EA)	1989–2008
	Euskadiko Ezkerra (Basque Left, EE)	1977–1993
	Herri Batasuna (United People)	1979–1996
	Partido Nacionalista Vasco (Basque Nationalist Party, PNV)	1977–2008
Canaries	Agrupaciones Independientes de Canarias (Canarian Independent Groupings, AIC)	1986–1989
	Coalición Canaria (Canarian Coalition, CAN)	1993–2008
	Union del Pueblo Canario (Union of Canarian People, UPC)	1979

Continued on next page

Table 1.1: Regionalist Political Parties in Europe
(continued from previous page)

Region	Political Parties (English label, abbreviation)	Contested Elections
Spain (*continued*)		
Catalonia	Convergència i Unió, including Pacte Democratic per Catalunya (PDC) & Unió del Centre i la Democracia Cristiana de Cataluna (UDC) (Convergence and Union, CiU)	1977–2008
	Coalición electoral esquerra de Cataluna (Electoral Coalition of Left in Catalonia, CEEC)	1977
	Ezquerra Republicana de Catalunya (Republican Left of Catalonia, ERC)	1979–1982, 1993–2008
Galicia	Bloque Nacionalista Gallego (Galician Nationalist Bloc, BNG)	1996–2008
Navarre	Unión del Pueblo Navarro (Union of the Navarrese People, UPN)	1979
	Convergencia Demócrata de Navarra (Democratic Convergence of Navarre, CDN)	1996
	Nafarroa Bai (Yes to Navarre, NB)	2004–2008
Valencia	Union Valenciana (Valencian Union, UV)	1986–2000
United Kingdom		
Cornwall	Mebyon Kernow (Sons of Cornwall, MK)	1970–1983, 1997–2010
Northern Ireland	Social Democratic and Labour Party (SDLP)	1974–2010
	Irish Independence Party (IIP)	1979
	Nationalists and Independent nationalists (N)	1950–1951, 1966
	Republican Labour (RS)	1964–1970
	Republicans (REP)	1950, 1964–1966, 1974–1979
	Republican Clubs (RC)	
	Sinn Féin	1950, 1955–1959, 1983–2010

Table 1.1: Regionalist Political Parties in Europe

Region	Political Parties (English label, abbreviation)	Contested Elections
United Kingdom (*continued*)		
Scotland	Scottish National Party (SNP)	1950–2010
	Scottish Labour Party (SCLP)	1979
	Scottish Militant Labour (SML)	1992
	Scottish Socialist Alliance (SSA)	1997–2005
	Scottish Socialist Party (SSP)	2010
Wales	Plaid Cymru (Party of Wales, PC)	1950–2010
	Mudiad Gweriniaethol Cymru (Welsh Republican Movement, MGC)	1950

Note: This list includes all regionalist parties that competed in national elections from 1950 to 2010 and either won a seat in the national parliament, won 5% of the national vote, or won at least 5% in one constituency. Through 1997, I compiled all electoral data from the data available in Caramani (2000). From 1997 to 2010, I compiled electoral data from national electoral archives and databases.

Many of these parties only competed in a single election. Several parties were later incorporated into other regionalist parties or competed as part of a coalition.[10] Others, like the Scottish National Party, the Convergència i Unió, and Südtiroler Volkspartei, have competed in nearly every election since 1950, or since democratization in Spain.

Table 1.1 introduces the simple variation in regionalist parties which demands explanation. For instance, out of 15 Western European countries, only eight have had regionalist parties active in national elections. In Figure 1.1, I mapped this geographic variation using GIS data collected from the European Union.[11] For each country, I coded the region as the highest territorial administrative body below the national level, matched to the corresponding Nomenclature of Territorial Units for Statistics (NUTS) code.[12] In Figure 1.1, I simply coded every region

---

[10] For instance, PSd'Az competed in more general elections than listed; however, they formed joint lists with the Italian Republicans in several elections, and they did not earn enough votes to be separately listed in electoral counts in other elections.

[11] I collected the geo-datafiles from *GISCO NUTS 2006*, made available from Eurostat (http://epp.eurostat.ec.europa.eu). I created the maps in *Stata* 12 using the spmap command.

[12] The region coding is discussed in more detail in Chapter 3, but a few examples

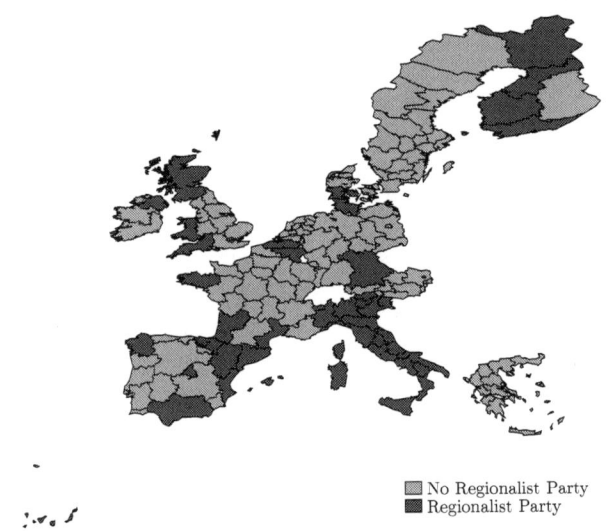

Figure 1.1: Regionalist Party Incidence

as whether a regionalist party contested a national election in any election between 1950 and 2010. Darker shading refers to those regions where regionalist parties have competed.[13]

What the map makes abundantly clear is that not only is there spatial variation across European countries, but there is also dramatic variation within states. Some states, such as Italy, are nearly entirely shaded, while the majority of France is not. Other countries, such as Greece and Austria, simply do not experience regionalist parties competing in national elections.

Beyond simply where the parties compete, though, it is of significant interest where these parties are successful. In Figure 1.2, I used the same geo-data to produce a map showing the peak regionalist party vote share between 1950 and 2010. For example, consider the United Kingdom. In the southwest of England, where Mebyon Kernow contested a few elections, the peak vote share was less than 1 percent;

---

will illustrate. For Germany, the region is the Länder, NUTS 1. For Austria, it is the Bundesländer, which is NUTS 2.

[13]In Figures 1.1–1.5, the maps show the EU-14 countries. Excluded countries, such as Luxembourg and non-EU member states (e.g., Switzerland and Norway), are simply whited out.

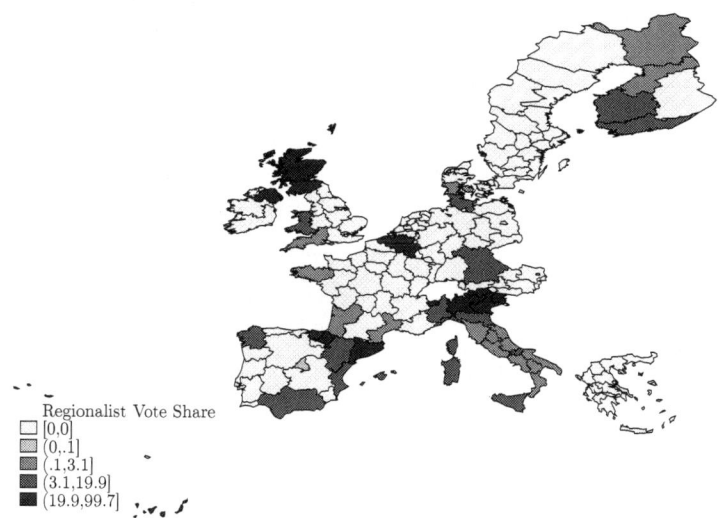

Figure 1.2: Regionalist Party Peak Vote Share

however, in Wales (14 percent), Scotland (30 percent), and Northern Ireland (42 percent), the peak vote shares are much higher. Svenske Folkspartiet achieved the highest peak vote share of 99.7 percent in the Åland region of Finland, while Union Valdôtaine won 80 percent in Valle d'Aoste in Italy. In Figure 1.2, darker shades refer to larger vote shares for regionalist parties within that region.

In contrast to Figure 1.1, this figure makes clear that regionalist parties are most successful in a few regions, while many regions host minor regionalist parties. In the case of Italy, smaller vote shares in certain areas also reflect the geographic spread of Lega Nord over time outside its traditional electoral stronghold in the north. With these two figures, the geographic variation of regionalist parties, in terms of both incidence (where they compete) and success (vote share), is apparent.

While the maps above show where regionalist parties compete, they mask any change over time. In addition to geographic distribution, it is of particular interest whether regionalist parties have spread to new regions over time. Similar to Figure 1.1, the maps in Figures 1.3–1.5 show whether a regionalist party competes in national elections within that region in any election during that decade.

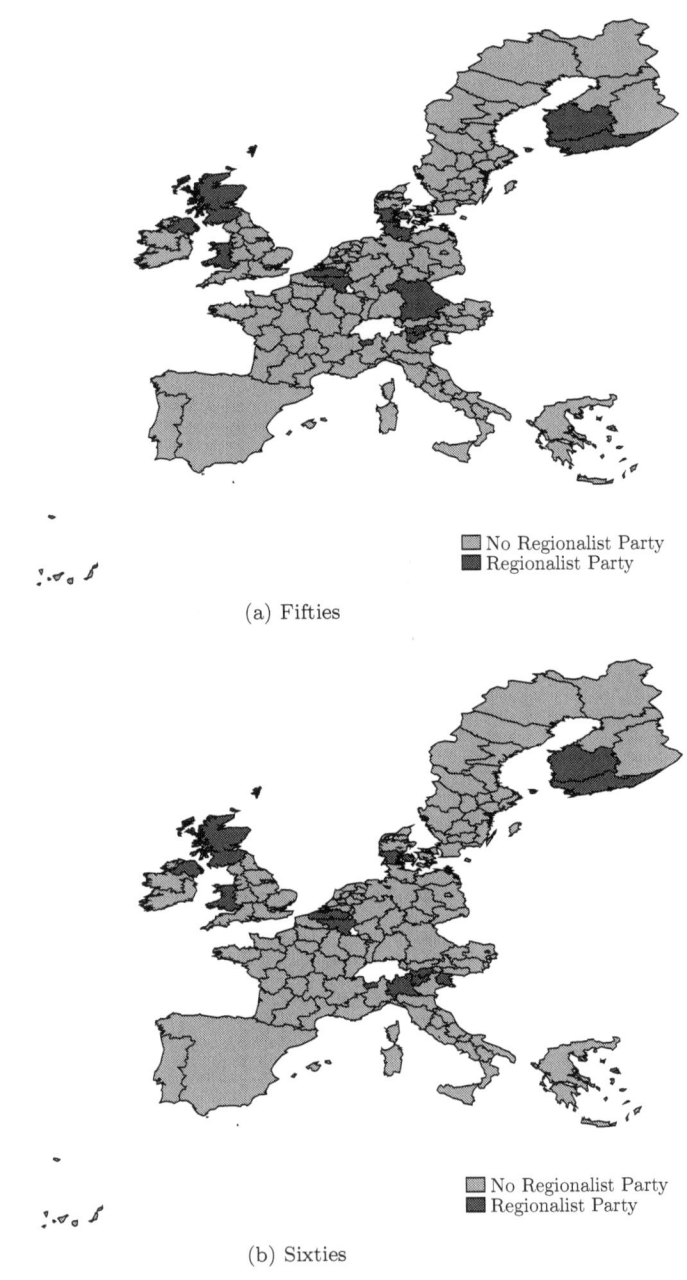

(a) Fifties

(b) Sixties

Figure 1.3: Regionalist Party Incidence, 1950s–1960s

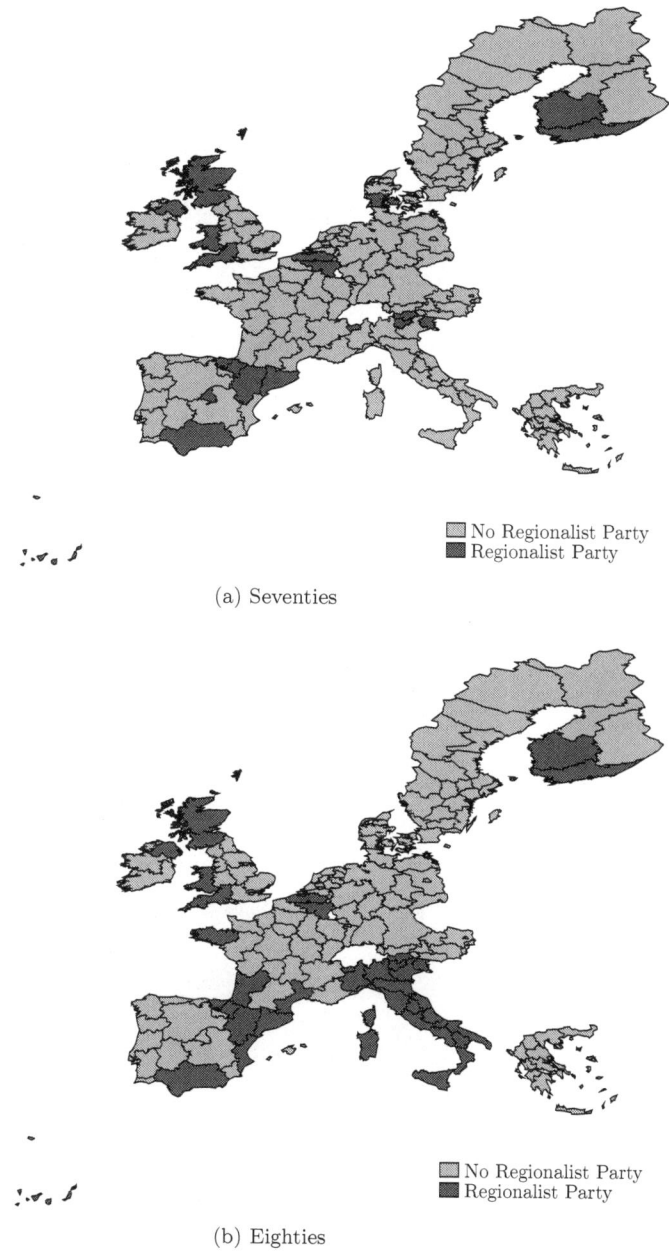

(a) Seventies

(b) Eighties

Figure 1.4: Regionalist Party Incidence, 1970s–1980s

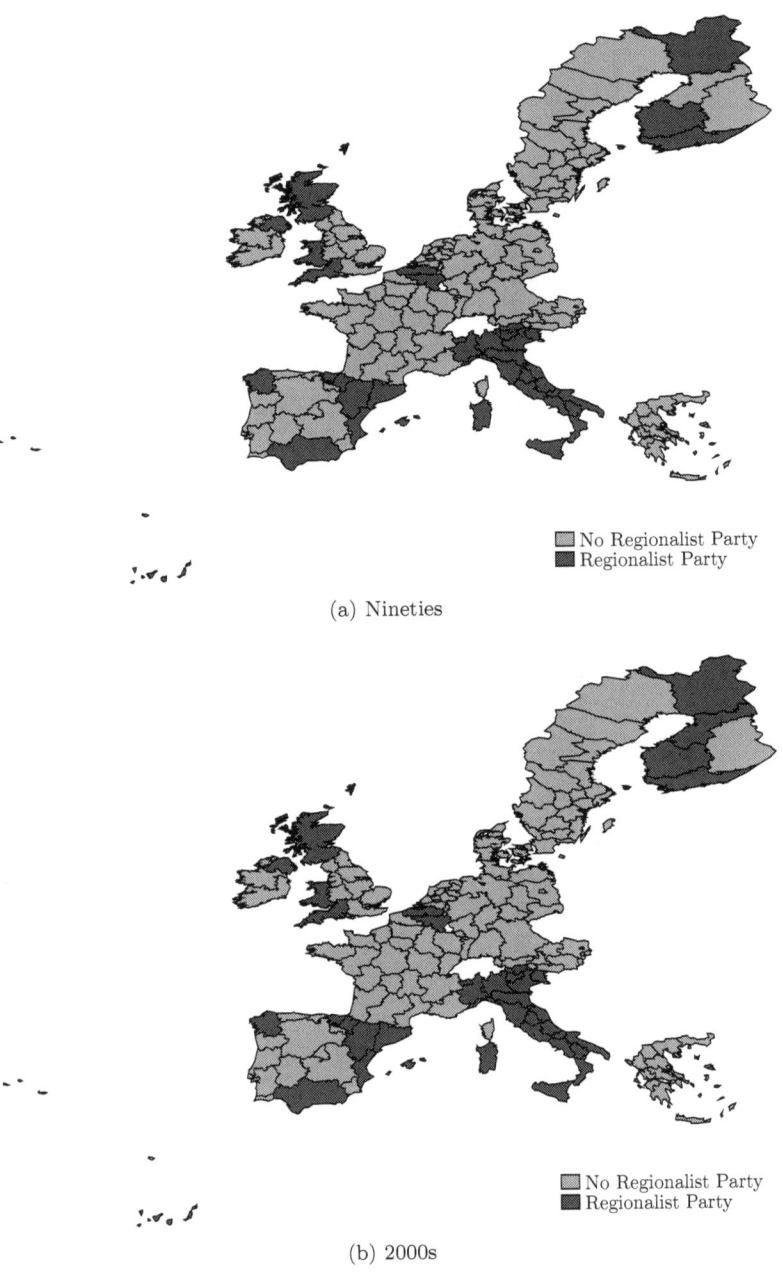

(a) Nineties

(b) 2000s

Figure 1.5: Regionalist Party Incidence, 1990s–2000s

In the first few post-war decades (Figures 1.3a and 1.3b), regionalist parties competed in a few particular regions in the United Kingdom, northern Italy, Belgium, the Schleswig regions in Germany and Denmark, Bavaria, and Finland. Figure 1.4a is similar, except for the dramatic introduction of Spanish regionalists with the first democratic elections in 1977. In the following decades as shown in Figures 1.5a and 1.5b, regionalist parties spread to most of Italy, along with more of Spain and the United Kingdom. Returning to the vote share figure, though, the spread of regionalist parties to new regions does not necessarily equate to strong success at the ballot box.

Nevertheless, in some ways, this spread of regionalism contradicts the simple frozen cleavage story, whereby the national revolution establishes political cleavages and parties compete, persistently across time. In the following chapters, especially Chapter 3, in addition to exploring the relationship of the EU and regionalist parties, I will evaluate this variation across time and space. Why do regionalist parties compete in certain regions? What explains the existence in these countries rather than others, such as Austria or the Netherlands? And what explains the timing of these regionalist parties competing in elections?

1.4 Rising Regionalists?

Are regionalist parties on the rise in Western Europe? In this section, I take a first look at this question by analyzing where they compete and their relative success in closer detail. Given the theoretical interest in the effect of European integration on regionalist parties, curious readers may simply look at Figures 1.3–1.5 and wonder whether a simple time trend explains this variation (i.e., as time passes, more parties compete). However, the evidence is not so straightforward. In Figure 1.6, I concentrate on only those eight countries where regionalist parties compete. Within each of these eight countries, Figure 1.6 presents line graphs reflecting the percentage of regions in which regionalist parties contested national elections within each country. In other words, in Belgium and Italy in several elections, regionalist parties competed in all of the regions, scoring 100 percent on the y-axis. In contrast, regionalist parties in France only enter the electoral data in 1986, thus giving a slight bump for that election. Using the percentage of a country that regionalist parties contest, a simple linear time trend is not obvious.

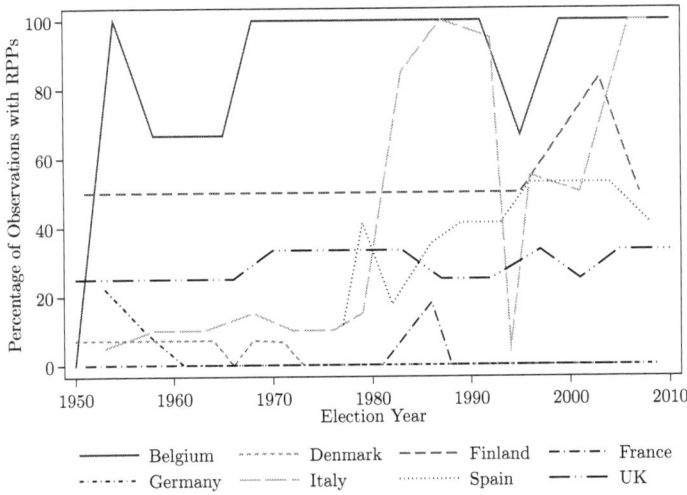

Figure 1.6: Observations with Regionalist Parties, by Country and Year

In addition to the geographic and temporal variation in where the parties compete, I also measure the electoral success of these parties. In Figure 1.7, I track electoral success for these parties over time, as measured both by the total votes for regionalist parties and by the regionalist party's share of the vote in the national election, averaged by half-decades.[14]

First, the solid line in Figure 1.7 represents the total number of votes won by regionalist parties. Certainly, this number has increased significantly over time, in large part due to the entry of Spanish regions in the late 1970s and the gradual spread of regionalist parties in Italy to compete across the entire country. However, much of this trend can simply be attributed to population growth over time, which was steeper in the immediate post-war period before leveling off in the last decade. Total votes for regionalist parties have risen steadily from less than 1 million to more than 10 million. Again, in the 1970s, there is a

---

[14] Similar charts for each individual country are provided in Appendix A, with separate figures for countries with large (Figures A.1–A.2) and smaller regionalist parties (Figure A.3).

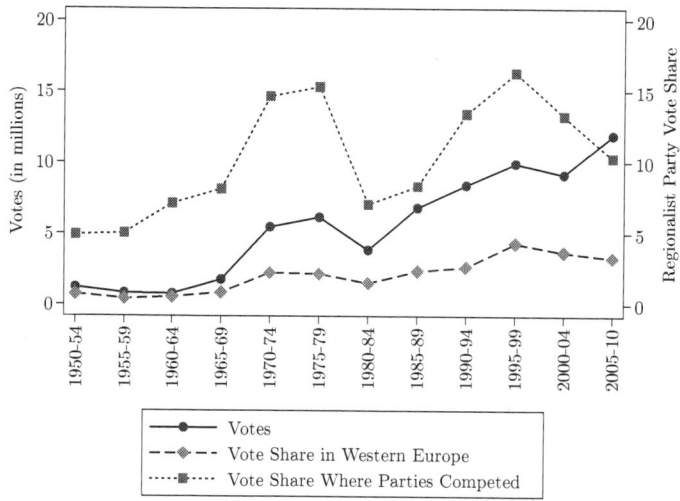

Figure 1.7: Regionalist Party Votes and Vote Shares, over Time

temporary surge in support, but the upward trend continues through the 2000s.[15]

From a long-term perspective, though, a consistent rise in regionalist vote shares is less than clear, as shown in the dotted lines in Figure 1.7. This is apparent if you consider regionalist party vote share only in those countries where regionalist parties competed (dotted line with square markers), or if you include all of Western Europe in the denominator (dashed line with diamond markers). Over the last 50 years, vote shares for regionalist parties have fluctuated between 5 and 15 percent, with a particular surge in the mid-1970s.[16]

---

[15] A simple linear regression line through these data points agrees with this analysis. The linear trend line for votes is clearly positive, while the trend line for vote share is basically flat, albeit with a slightly positive slope. This positive trend holds even if certain countries are excluded, such as Italy or Spain, which had significant institutional change during the period under consideration. As the individual country charts demonstrate, though, the spike in the 1970s for the UK and Belgium is much more dramatic than the summary chart above shows.

[16] Much of this surge can be attributed to electoral support for the Scottish National Party in the mid-1970s after the discovery of North Sea oil. I will control for these types of exogenous shocks in the empirical analysis, but the discovery of

In the individual country figures (Appendix A), the vote share lines also discourage simple stories about steady increases over time. Belgium (Figure A.1a) and the UK (Figure A.2b) do show an increase over time, but it is erratic with spikes and drops in vote share. These data support the notion that support for regionalists parties is on the rise, though the different measures suggest that the rise may be attributed to these parties competing in more districts, and more countries, rather than being more successful in any particular district. Thus, studying when and where these parties compete (and do not compete) will be just as valuable as studying how successful they are in those elections.

1.5 Discussion

In this chapter, I sought to answer a basic question: who are the regionalists? After considering various definitions and concepts, I classified the regionalist parties, which is a necessary first step in the analysis that follows. With the use of descriptive statistics and figures, I demonstrated that significant variation exists within and across countries, as well as over time. It is this geographic and temporal variation I seek to explain.

Without question, party competition is complex. Regionalist parties rise and fall in various elections, and even the most successful parties have periods of relative electoral failure. In the chapters that follow, in addition to considering institutional, economic, and cultural factors to explain this complex variation in regionalist party success, I also develop the Viability Theory to explain why European integration is a key factor in explaining regionalist party success.

---

oil, like deeper European integration, increases the viability of small states, such as Scotland, thereby making regionalist parties more viable electoral competitors. Further, de Winter (1998) argues that mainstream parties were simply unprepared for the surge in support for regionalist demands and it took some time for the mainstream parties to adjust their strategies to try to subvert these movements, an argument very much in line with Meguid (2008).

CHAPTER 2

The Viability of Regionalist Parties

WITH HIGH-PROFILE EXAMPLES such as the Scottish independence referendum in the United Kingdom and Catalonia's attempt to gain more autonomy from Spain, explaining regionalist mobilization in Western Europe remains a topic of great interest to academics as well as politicians (Lynch 1996; de Winter and Türsan 1998; van Houten 2000). Most studies focus on a variety of cultural and political economic factors, but they often neglect globalization, in general, and European integration, in particular, as a relevant variable. Following van Houten (2003), globalization is defined as a "process of economic integration, in which 'the reduction of barriers to economic exchange and factor mobility gradually creates one economic space from many.'" I argue that European integration is a similar process of economic integration, but taken to a much deeper level within Europe. Also, and significantly for regionalists, European integration adds a crucial political element that is lacking in globalization. In particular, the EU has a variety of institutions designed to protect the advances of integration against protectionism, along with various institutions designed to reduce various types of barriers to exchange and factor mobility. Thus, if globalization is expected to have an effect on nationalism because it weakens the advantages of large states, then European integration should have a far more powerful effect.

In this chapter, I first review the literature on regionalist mobilization in Western Europe, paying particular attention to potential necessary or sufficient factors. Second, I introduce the political economy literature on the optimal size of states. From this literature, I develop the hypothesis that European integration encourages higher levels of mobilization among regionalist groups. Third, I consider alternative theories, including a backlash logic based on fear of lost autonomy to Brussels or increased immigration due to deeper integration. Finally, I outline the research design to empirically test the theoretical implications, which I use to guide the remainder of this book.

2.1 Regionalist Mobilization in Western Europe

Certain regional identity groups (e.g., the Scottish, Irish, Basques, and Bretons) have increased calls for national self-determination, or at least greater autonomy, in recent years. This trend contradicts the predictions of modernization theory, which predicts that capitalist development will diminish identity conflict within states (Nielsen 1980, 1985; Ragin 1987).[1] As early as the 1970s, evidence in many Western European countries proved these theories to be "out of touch with reality" (Lane and Ersson 1999, 53). In fact, Arend Lijphart finds little theoretical value in the developmental perspective and other theories that predicted a decrease in ethnic tension in post-war Europe, contending "there were no adequate theoretical grounds for the expectation that ethnic conflict would gradually disappear" (Lijphart 1977, 55). Along similar lines, Hooghe (1992, 23) writes: "Modernization disrupts social life, causes differentiation of social roles, creates new and different modes of communication flows and transforms the political system. Nationalism can be seen as a reaction against the consequences of modernization." But, as she goes on to argue, this is a tricky causal story to untangle because modernization involves nonpolitical and individual processes, whereas regionalist or nationalist mobilization is a wholly political and collective process (Hooghe 1992, 24). In other words, political actors, such as parties, play a vital role in translating these issues into political conflict.

As it became increasingly clear that modernization would not resolve all the sub-national conflicts in Europe, scholars introduced a variety of models to explain its resurgence. In the conclusion of a 1977 edited volume on ethnic conflict in the West, Milton Esman summa-

---

[1] In contrast to this version of the developmental hypothesis, an opposing theory contends that development creates an educated elite and competitive opportunities, thereby inspiring ethnic mobilization (Ragin 1979, 622). Michael Hechter's internal colonialism model in fact predicts that development will not eliminate regional inequalities but encourage their persistence (Hechter 1975, 10).

rizes the factors that led to the resurgence of autonomy movements in Europe (Esman 1977*b*). First, the central governments expanded their scope and size while the bureaucracy became increasingly technocratic and remote. Second, a combination of industrial rationalization (centralization and concentration) and the communications revolution contributed to a period of more regional grievances and claims for autonomy. Third, security concerns decreased with détente and an associated diminished fear of the Soviet Union (Esman 1977*b*).

These factors helped create the environment in which these movements began to grow; however, they are not necessary or sufficient conditions for the politicization of the regional movements. Again, Esman illustrates several of the conditions that were necessary and sufficient, including group identity based on some objective trait; political, economic, or cultural grievances; a perception that prospects would be better under an alternative regime; a less effective central government; and political organization (Esman 1977*b*, 388–395). Each of these conditions existed in Scotland in the 1970s, thereby explaining Scotland's calls for autonomy (Esman 1977*c*, 284).[2]

Esman is not alone in focusing on grievances as a trigger for these movements. Suzanne Berger (1977, 176) contends that objective regional discrepancies in economic success heightened the salience of regional or ethnic issues. Similarly, Rudolph argues that "economic difficulty in ethnically distinct regions has tended to heighten ethnic awareness" (1977, 540). In the right context, these grievances led to demands for either autonomy or outright independence (Esman 1977*b*; McCrone 2001).[3]

---

[2] It should be noted that not all observers agree that Scotland has legitimate grievances. Birch notes that Scotland has been chronically over-represented in the House of Parliament and receives much more government expenditure per capita than England (Birch 1977, 102–105); however, he concedes that Scotland has a legitimate claim about "the inescapable evidence of mismanagement by London governments" (Birch 1977, 107).

[3] Ragin (1987) considers these factors in explicating the reactive ethnicity perspective. Under the reactive ethnicity view, a subordinated ethnic or regional group perceives an uneven distribution of resources that favors the dominant ethnic group. Urbanization and industrialization exacerbates this situation by concentrating members of the same subgroup in similar neighborhoods and social classes (Ragin 1987, 135). Nielsen (1980, 79–89) contends that despite the reactive ethnicity model's usefulness in explaining the resurgence of ethno-national mobilization, the empirical evidence, particularly from Flanders, does not support either the reactive ethnicity model or Hechter's internal colonialism model.

Though by no means complete, the theories described above represent the most popular explanations for increased regionalist demands in post–World War II Europe. Walker Connor (1977, 23–25) summarizes them nicely:

> (1) the theory of relative (economic, cultural, and/or political) deprivation; (2) anomie, resulting from a growing feeling of alienation from the depersonalized and dehumanizing modern mass society, leading, in turn, to what is alternately described as a reversion to "tribalism" or as a new, more relevant alternative; (3) a "center-periphery" series of relationships in which these newly assertive ethnic groups (the peripheral peoples) are viewed as having remained essentially outside or at the edge of the dominant society and have, therefore, been only marginally influenced by that society's principal currents; and (4) the loss of global prestige suffered by individual European states, as contrasted with their eminence in the prewar period, and a corresponding loss of pride in being viewed as British rather than Scottish, or French rather than Breton.

Alienation, economic grievances and, perhaps, a perception that the benefits of belonging to the large post-imperial states of Europe are much diminished all serve as reasons why ethnic or regionalist groups may have increased their demands for autonomy.

While grievances must exist for a group to mobilize and overcome the collective action dilemma, expectations for a brighter future after independence or autonomy is the second necessary factor in the equation. As McAdam (1982, x) writes in his classic sociology study of the American civil rights movement, "At a minimum people need to feel both *aggrieved* about some aspect of their lives and *optimistic* that, acting collectively, they can redress the problem." If group leaders cannot convince their followers that autonomy or even independence would make their lives better, then the movement would be short-lived.[4] But political theorists traditionally espouse a large state bias. Friedrich List, a German economist, contended that a country must have a large

---

[4] As shown in the 2003 SNP pamphlet, "Moving Scotland Beyond the Subsidy Myth," Scottish regionalist elites focus a lot of rhetorical attention on defending the viability of Scotland against claims of being a UK "subsidy junkie"(Wilson 2003).

population and a territory "endowed with manifold national resources" to be competitive in the world economy. Otherwise, it would have no opportunity to build viable institutions or a competitive industrial sector (Hobsbawm 1990, 30). John Stuart Mill ([1861] 1998, 395) goes further, stating:

> Nobody can suppose that it is not more beneficial for a Breton or a Basque of French Navarre to be ... a member of the French nationality, admitted on equal terms to all the privileges of French citizenship ... than to sulk on his own rocks, the half-savage relic of past times, revolving in his own little mental orbit, without participation or interest in the general movement of the world. The same remark applies to the Welshman or the Scottish highlander as members of the British nation.

According to these theorists, not only can a small state have no hope for economic or cultural success, but below some threshold, a member of such a state will revert to a "half-savage" incapable of participating or successfully competing in the larger world.

But the European Union represents another route for regionalist groups to pursue autonomy without being left behind in the global economy. In fact, some scholars contend that a true "Europe of the Regions" would be more beneficial because smaller states would be less aggressive. Further, such decentralization may create other advantages due to experimentation with public goods (Tiebout 1956). At the same time, smaller states are more viable than in previous generations due to trade liberalization and less conventional security threats (Anderson 2000, 35). Though scholars continue to debate the cause(s) of the resurgence of regionalist or ethno-nationalist movements in Europe, some ethno-nationalist groups view European integration as one means to reduce the state's dominance over their region (Cinnirella 2000). If regional groups perceive that it is no longer a choice between economic viability and independence,[5] then they may be more likely to pursue

---

[5] In a discussion of Quebec nationalism in a context of NAFTA, Meadwell and Martin (1996, 70) contend that economic integration "reduce[s] the cost of transition to independence by increasing the economic viability of small states." In linking their theoretical argument to observable implications, they further argue that "it makes sense for nationalists to be free traders," an argument I test in the European case in Chapters 4 and 5.

greater autonomy or even independence than they would otherwise.[6]

In addition to the economic viability issue, regionalist groups now have more access to the world community through European Union venues. Within the EU framework, regionalists can form trans-national groups, set up trade missions in Brussels and defend minority nationalist languages at the European Court of Justice (Hepburn 2010, 41). Regionalists use other European venues as well. For example, the Scottish National Party utilizes the European Charter for Regional and Minority Languages, a treaty adopted under the auspices of the Council of Europe, to pressure the UK government to provide support for the Scots language (Scottish National Party 2001). The Irish nationalists also demonstrate the effectiveness of external resources in challenging state borders (Anderson and O'Dowd 1999, 693).

Going further, minority nationalist parties formed groups within Europe, such as the Bureau of Unrepresented European Nations or the European Free Alliance, to pursue their political objectives (Lynch 1996, 19). By creating and enhancing these international forums, European integration may actually encourage separatism, albeit as an unintended consequence of supporting minority rights (Olzak 1983, 370). While it is apparent that most of the regionalist movements predate the European Union, the trends toward an integrated "Europe of the Regions" may exacerbate these tensions, in part by increasing hope of achieving their own independent nation-state or at least greater autonomy.

2.2 European Integration and the Viability of Small States

With international groups such as the European Union and the International Monetary Fund claiming some decision-making authority while domestic regional units seek more autonomy to control their own affairs, the existence of large traditional states is being challenged from above and below (McCrone 2001, 33). Theoretically, a variety of scholars have addressed whether regions need larger state units to thrive (Birch 1978; Horowitz 1985; Hobsbawm 1990; Alesina and Spolaore

---

[6] For instance, Alesina and Wacziarg (1998, 307) contend that several of the new small states of the former Soviet bloc would not have pursued independence if not for an environment of freer trade.

1997, 2003). Eric Hobsbawm notes that the decline of the "national economy" makes smaller states no less viable than larger ones and that it is plausible that regions make more natural sub-units of the European Union than the traditional states (1990, 185). Hooghe and Marks demonstrate that two types of multi-level governance structures, both geographic-based and policy-oriented or functional, offer alternatives to the centralized state (Marks and Hooghe 2000; Hooghe and Marks 2001, 2003). The EU, in particular, offers a new context for regionalist actors to pursue their territorial autonomy goals. As Hepburn (2010, 40–41) argues, "European integration has opened up functional and political spaces in which substate actors may operate." Within the context of the EU, regionalist actors can pursue goals such as increasing resources, controlling regional policy, and enhancing representation (Hepburn 2010, 40–41).

In recent years, economists have brought their analytical tools to bear on the question of secession or the optimal size of states (Alesina and Spolaore 1997; Alesina and Wacziarg 1998; Bolton and Roland 1997; Alesina and Spolaore 2003; Goyal and Staal 2004). In particular, Alesina and Spolaore attempt to ascertain the optimal size of states based on a trade-off between economies of scale and the "costs of heterogeneity."[7] Whereas a larger country will be able to provide public goods at a lower per capita cost (due to larger populations and economies of scale), decisions will be more politically difficult because the population is more heterogeneous (Alesina and Spolaore 1997, 2003). The formal result is a smaller optimal size of states in Europe under the umbrella of the European Union and a system of free(er) trade (Alesina and Spolaore 1997, 2003; Alesina and Wacziarg 1998; Alesina, Spolaore, and Wacziarg 2000; Wittman 2000; Casella and Feinstein 2002).

---

[7]With a similar logic but different language, Dion (1996, 272) argues that secessionist movements "are rooted in two types of perceptions: the fear inspired by the union and the confidence inspired by secession." The fear is simply the potential cost to the peripheral group if the group remains in the state the larger state, costs which are higher in region with greater levels of cultural heterogeneity. Confidence is "the sense among the group that it can perform better on its own and that secession is not too risky" (Dion 1996). Dion's rationalist approach and emphasis on perceptions as opposed to objective viability adds a more real-world political framework to the political economy models. In other words, elites in favor of devolution or secession have to persuade voters that independence is a viable and necessary goal (see Chapters 4 and 5). I argue in this chapter that European integration has affected the confidence part of the equation.

Though the political economy literature on the relationship between ethnic fractionalization and public good provision is continually expanding (Easterly and Levine 1997; Alesina and Spolaore 2003; Miguel 2003), the costs of heterogeneity still tend to be assumed in the formal models rather than empirically demonstrated; however, Charles Tilly discusses two reasons why cultural homogeneity benefits a state. First, a homogeneous population is less likely to rebel against a government of its own sub-group.[8] Second, and likely a more significant reason for economists, a government of a homogeneous population tends to be better at generating public goods because the day-to-day lives of the people are more similar (Tilly 1975, 79).[9] A third advantage to locally controlled public policy concerns accountability. Regions may achieve greater efficiency if they are able to both cater public policies to the specific area and through easier monitoring (Drèze 1993, 277).[10] Due to this comparative advantage, European regions may see themselves as more capable of providing sustained economic growth than the traditional nation-states (Newhouse 1997, 69), yielding political separatism as an unintended consequence of economic integration (Alesina and Spolaore 1997, 1042).

Yet while large states must pay the costs of heterogeneity, their advantages are numerous and worthy of reconsidering in this era of the European Union:

---

[8] Regarding the causal connection between ethnic heterogeneity and civil war, the literature has produced somewhat mixed results. Fearon and Laitin (2003) find little evidence that greater ethnic diversity makes countries more prone to civil war; however, Blimes (2006) provides compelling evidence that ethnic heterogeneity does have an indirect effect on the likelihood of civil war.

[9] In contrast with Tilly (1975), Habyarimana et al. (2007) contends that it is not that co-ethnics share similar tastes for public goods that makes homogeneous populations better at producing public goods. Rather, "successful collective action among homogeneous ethnic communities can be attributed to the existence of norms and institutions that police the defection of non-contributors" (Habyarimana et al. 2007, 724).

[10] In a critique of Drèze's model of regional autonomy, Edwards (1993, 292-293) questions whether the benefits of smallness are quite so obvious. He argues that geography and preference homogeneity may not be correlated as highly as commonly assumed; thus, any voting system would be unable to make all voters in a region happy with the public good policies. Certainly, this is an empirical question which Alesina and Spolaore (2003) simply assume away, but the recent strand of political economy literature suggests that their assumption may have validity.

> Larger political jurisdictions bring about several benefits. First, the per capita cost of any nonrival public good decreases with the number of people who finance it. . . . A second benefit of country size is related to the dimensions of markets. In a world of less than perfect free trade, the size of markets is affected by the size of political jurisdictions . . . Third, exposure to uninsurable shocks is more costly for smaller countries. A region of a large country hit by an idiosyncratic, region-specific, negative shock is compensated with redistribution from the rest of the country. . . . Last, but not least, security considerations may be a determinant of size. (Alesina and Spolaore 1997, 1028)

Nevertheless, I hypothesize that European integration diminishes these advantages of large states vis-à-vis small states, making smaller less heterogeneous states more appealing to regional elites (and citizens). Considering both globalization and regional integration, Birch (1978, 335–336) likewise concludes that the "balance of advantage" between small and large states has shifted to the advantage of the smaller state.[11] Below, I consider the advantages of large states as they pertain to European integration, focusing on how integration has diminished these advantages.

The first advantage of large states concerns public goods. Larger state size is advantageous because many public goods benefit from economies of scale. The larger a population, the less a public good will cost per capita;[12] thus, larger states have a decided advantage.

But the EU reduces this advantage as it provides certain public goods for member states (e.g., monetary policy, regulatory policy, trade authority). The EU's Solidarity Fund for Disaster Relief and the Com-

---

[11] Similarly, Fazal and Griffiths (2014, 80) argue that the post-1945 international system—with its norms against territorial conquest and institutions designed to reduce transactions cost and resolve commitment problem for all states, even small ones—has enhanced incentives for separatism by making statehood more appealing. They consider the European Union as a particularly attractive institution in this regard.

[12] Public goods of this type include: a "monetary and financial system, tax collection and fiscal institutions, a legal and judiciary system, infrastructures, communication systems, law and order, public libraries, national parks, [and] embassies" (Alesina and Spolaore 2003, 20). Admittedly, this statement is not true for all public goods because every type of public good may not benefit from economies of scale. For many public goods, though, size or scale is beneficial.

mission's Rapid Response Centre demonstrate how the EU may provide some of the collective goods for smaller countries. In addition to certain collective goods, the Union also provides regulatory policy. For smaller countries, such guidelines reduce the regulation needed for individual countries, particularly new countries. The scale advantage for larger states is diminishing as integration increases. Moreover, the economics literature is increasingly concerned about the correlations among growth problems, poor public policies, and high levels of ethnic heterogeneity (Easterly and Levine 1997). Thus, larger, more diverse states hold a smaller economies of scale advantage than they did prior to European integration, while creating effective public policies remains more difficult than it is for smaller states.

The second, perhaps key, benefit of a larger country is the size of economic markets. For countries small and large, access to a larger market is valuable in domestic economic growth. In a world of relatively large barriers to trade, the size of the state is the size of the economic market. If large barriers to trade exist, countries must expand their state boundaries to gain a larger market. A union among the nations of the British Isles certainly facilitated economic growth during the eighteenth and nineteenth centuries (Birch 1977, 41).

But in a world of (relatively) free trade, small countries may be prosperous (Alesina and Spolaore 2003, 82). And this trend of lowered trade barriers is nowhere more developed than in the European Union, which is a common market for goods, services, and labor. For small countries especially, the EU is an institution that reduces uncertainty and transaction costs and solves credible commitment problems (Keohane 1984; Moravcsik 1998). So long as a country belongs to the EU, market size is not simply the size of state.[13] The implication for sub-state nationalist entrepreneurs is clear, as Hooghe and Marks note: "The single European market reduces the economic penalty imposed by regional political autonomy because regional firms continue to have access to the European market" (2001, 166). By breaking the link between state size and market size, the European Union diminishes a significant advantage of larger states.

Further, the European Union now serves as a proxy for individual states in many international trade forums, giving smaller countries the

---

[13]The institutional structure of the EU distinguishes it from a simple free trade regime. Without the EU, small states would rightly fear trade wars or simply being shut out of large foreign markets (Meadwell and Martin 1996, 73).

advantage of the backing of a larger market (the largest internationally) to gain access to international markets abroad. In the context of an integrated Europe, the size of the state itself is less critical for economic activity because it no longer relates directly to market size (Alesina and Spolaore 1997, 1040). In fact, Keating (1998) argues that globalization has reduced the ability of national governments to manage their own territorial economy, creating pressure for regionally-based responses. Hence, it is no longer necessary to trade local autonomy for access to global or even regional markets (Birch 1978, 335–336).

The third issue is that a smaller state will be more susceptible to regional economic shocks. Usually, national policies attempt to protect regions from "asymmetric adverse shocks," such as industrial decline or weather-related disasters, through redistribution transfers and insurance schemes (Bureau 1992, 88; Alesina and Spolaore 1997, 2003). Larger states can afford transfers from prosperous areas to subsidize regions suffering from these economic shocks (e.g., industrial decline or weather related disasters). The potential loss of such subsidies actually served to diminish enthusiasm for independence among the Scottish during the 1970s. The Scottish National Party struggled to convince factory workers that seceding from the United Kingdom would not result in even more unemployment if the subsidies stopped and access to the British market was blocked (Esman 1977c, 266–267).

Increasingly, the European Union seems capable of serving in this capacity via structural or regional funds (Bureau and Champsaur 1992, 90; Allen 1996, 22), albeit in a smaller role than traditional states.[14] For example, structural funds from the European Union have six distinct goals, including assistance to areas affected by low GDP, high unemployment, sparse population, and industrial decline (Allen 1996, 225). Certainly, these European-level transfers are relatively small compared to state-level subsidies, but structural funds, among other European-level initiatives, may alleviate some of the small state disadvantages associated with asymmetric shocks.[15]

---

[14]In 1992, the EU budget grew at a faster rate than EU GDP and EU member country's budgets. This growth can be attributed, in large part, to the structural funds.

[15]Among many changes in the post-Euro and post-enlargement EU, a shift in the destination of structural funds may influence attitudes toward the EU among old member states and their regionalist groups. More significantly, in the crisis of the late 2000s, the limits of the EU's burden sharing were tested as Greece and other countries received bailouts from other member states. As stated in the main

Finally, security concerns often encourage larger state size. But for Western European countries, the fears of invasion by a foreign country are much diminished. In Anthony Birch's analysis, the interdependent international system removed this key advantage of larger "multipurpose" states vis-à-vis smaller states in Europe (Birch 1978, 335).[16] As he points out, the Scottish and Welsh nations would be just as protected by NATO, which acts to protect Europe, if they became independent as they would if they remained part of the United Kingdom. Plus, they may gain by reducing expenditures on defense spending, a relatively low priority among Scottish citizens (Birch 1978, 335). Along these lines, the Scottish National Party argues that Scotland could be as safe as Ireland or Norway with fewer per capita defense expenditures. Once the Soviet Union collapsed, this argument became decidedly more believable (Esman 1977c, 266). Though Birch referred mainly to NATO in 1978, his point would be even more convincing if the European Union formed its own multinational army.

While this brief discussion does not address all the advantages and disadvantages of size, I argue that European integration devalues critical roles of the state. Or as Marks and Hooghe (2000, 799) conclude,

> the logical implication of neoclassical theory is that national states are both too large and too small. Too large, because they encompass heterogeneous populations that are best served by local jurisdictions; too small, because they cannot encompass the territorial scope of market exchange or of policies that have international externalities.

By utilizing economies of scale to improve functionality in some issue areas, such as monetary and environmental policy, integration allows sub-national units to claim legitimate authority over other issues that could be better handled at that level. Thus, integration increases the pressure on central governments from both directions

To return to the formal economic models, the optimal size of a state "emerges from a trade-off between the benefits of scale and the costs

---

text, the EU has not and is unlikely to fully replace the role of traditional states in handling adverse economic shocks.

[16]The situation may not be quite as simple as presented. New states may be forced to provide armies or support to NATO in return for defense. This type of expenditure may eliminate any advantage gained by ending support for a larger national army.

of heterogeneity in the population" (Alesina and Spolaore 2003, 175). As discussed above, membership in the European Union diminishes the advantages of large states vis-à-vis small states. But the key cost of a larger state, namely heterogeneity of preferences, remains.

Yet, as Horowitz (1981, 167) argued, if the trade-off between large and small states has shifted so dramatically in favor of smaller states across the universe of cases, the important question then becomes "what kind of groups are likely to secede, and under what circumstances." For these questions, I focus on the second half of the Alesina and Spolaore (2003) trade-off: preferences.

2.3 Preferences Matter, but Which Preferences?

The optimal size of states has decreased due to regional integration and broader globalization trends. Based on their analysis, Alesina and Spolaore conclude that European integration has changed the incentives sufficiently to encourage independence movements; however, their model is a theoretical formalization and is not fully tested empirically. Also, the model leaves a puzzle for empirical researchers. If the advantages of smaller states (homogeneous preferences) are so great and the advantages of large states so diminished, then why are so few regionalist groups pursuing outright independence in Europe? Further, does this rational cost-benefit approach toward the optimal size of states offer any explanatory power over the regionalist movements that do not desire independence from the larger state?

I argue that a major deficiency in the formal models is a lack of full consideration on the advantages of smallness. The advantages are attributed to more homogeneous preferences, but little consideration is given to what type of preferences. The economic models are decidedly vague about whether it is cultural, economic, political or some other type of preferences. Rather, they utilize distance from the capital as a simpler proxy for different preferences to observe and model (Alesina and Spolaore 1997, 2003). If there are territorial differences in culture, political preferences, or economic interest, then a region will be more likely to pursue more autonomy from the capital. In those regions that have a combination of these different preferences, an even stronger case can be made for regionalist movements.

In the standard model, smaller states have an advantage because their preferences will be more homogeneous and, therefore, their governments will be easier to choose and monitor, making public goods better for their population. But homogeneous preferences by themselves are not enough to warrant regionalist mobilization for independence. The preferences must be distinct from nearby regions or the larger state itself. For instance, if citizens in Northern England have homogeneous preferences but they are similar to their Southern English counterparts, then there is no reason to pursue autonomy. Or a regionalist group may have homogeneous preferences on one issue (e.g., language in Brittany) but indistinct preferences on many other issues.

For example, Scotland appears to have distinct ideological preferences from the rest of the United Kingdom, particularly England. Scotland's electorate and political elite are much more sympathetic to leftist and socialist causes than those in England (Lynch 2009; Keating 2009). The population in Scotland is relatively homogeneous and their preferences are certainly distinct from the larger state, perhaps more in line with Scandinavian countries. Also, Scotland is a relatively cohesive region with a history of self-government and independence. This combination creates an environment where independence is on the agenda, with support from many of the political elite and the population. Further, independence within a deeper European Union is a viable economic option whereas full independence is not.

The Bretons in France are a second example. The Celtic language and customs are one area in which Bretons have distinct homogeneous preferences; however, ideologically and politically, Bretons do not have enough preference differences with the rest of France to actually consider independence. Thus, in Brittany, cultural autonomy is the goal rather than independence.

Theoretically, the mobility of the population, or the exit option, plays a significant role (Hirschman 1970). For instance, the issue of preferences may matter less if the population is highly mobile; however, in the case of the EU-15, at least, evidence suggests that cross-border labour mobility remains remarkably low.[17] If people have made specific investments in the region, either cultural or economic, then they will

---

[17] According to the European Commission's 2002 "Action Plan for Skills and Mobility," only 0.1 percent of the total EU-15 population changed official residence between two member countries in 2000 and only 1.2 percent moved to another region (European Commission 2002). In contrast, approximately 3 percent of the US population moves to a different state each year (European Commission 2006).

be relatively immobile. This immobility interacted with distinct homogeneous preferences may explain when regionalist movements take the incentives given by the European Union and pursue some form of autonomy. This lack of a plausible exit option also leads many citizens to exercise their voice by supporting non-established parties (Lago and Martínez 2011, 7), like regionalist parties.

In addition to homogeneous cultural preferences and labor mobility, income distribution patterns may create an advantage for being smaller (see Bolton and Roland 1997). A relatively rich region may consider autonomy worthwhile simply because their region distributes more money to the center than it receives. The Northern League is an obvious recent example. Some Northern Italians support Lega Nord because they resent subsidizing southern Italy and Rome. Ties to the region prevent fluid labor mobility to Switzerland or other neighboring regions outside Italy. As with distinct homogeneous preferences, this combination encourages autonomy movements because the advantage of being small seems clear and obvious. As the deepening of the European Union erodes some of the advantages of being a region within a large state, the cost-benefit analysis may shift to independence or at least greater autonomy.

In other words, as the advantages of a large heterogeneous state diminish, the incentives for regionalist mobilization should increase. Alesina and Spolaore (1997, 1042) agree as they discuss two empirical implications of their economic model: "First, political separatism should go hand in hand with economic integration.... The second implication is that the benefit of country size on economic performance should decrease with the increase of international economic integration and removal of trade barriers." But Alesina and Spolaore do not evaluate the empirical validity of the first of these implications in Europe. Further, as Keating (2009, 102) points out, Alesina and Spolaore (2003) neglect almost entirely the role of politics, especially the political actors most likely to translate this functional pressure into action, namely political parties.[18] Greater attention to the role of preferences and the significance of political parties will help identify the regions most likely to mobilize for greater autonomy.

---

[18] Dardanelli (2014, 215) affirms this focus on political parties as the crucial actors, when he argues that "party competition [i]s the crucial mechanism through which European integration can potentially influence state restructuring and 'rhetorical strategies' as the key tool utilized in such competition."

2.4 Alternative Theories

In many ways, the main alternative theory is simply that European integration has no effect on regionalist party success. In other words, if the evidence does not support the descriptive inference that European integration increases regionalist mobilization, then it would suggest that either integration does not affect ethno-national mobilization or integration has affected tension in a random, rather than systematic, way.[19] Countering the benefits of homogeneity, the costs of secession could be quite large, including both the transaction costs of seceding and creating a new country and the market uncertainty associated with such upheaval (Young 1992, 124). Furthermore, European monetary integration could provide some disincentive to independence because, even if secession were successful, countries would still not have autonomy over its currency or monetary policy (Lindsay 1991; Lynch 1996, 200–201). These costs may discourage some regionalists from pursuing autonomy despite the improved incentives.

Research on the interaction of globalization and regionalist autonomy suggest that while globalization may reinforce already assertive regions, it does not necessarily have a general effect on autonomy demands (van Houten 2003). However, much of the research on globalization is limited in looking at only one time period or only considering one dependent variable to measure autonomy demands. Further, I contend that while the EU may simply be an advanced form of globalization, it goes further in political and economic terms than just reducing trade barriers. Thus, I argue that it is premature to conclude that regional integration does not affect regionalist mobilization.

In direct contrast to the main viability mechanism, however, it may

---

[19] Potentially, integration may actually discourage further mobilization, which would clearly serve as disconfirming evidence. According to Ghai (1998, 158):

> This diminution of national sovereignty opens up possibilities of new arrangements between the state and its regions. The benefits work both ways: the state feels less threatened by regions in a multi-layered structure of policy-making and administration; and the region becomes more willing to accept national sovereignty, which may be the key to its participation in the wider arrangements. This trend is most developed in the European Union, where it is helping to moderate tensions and border regions previously intent on secession.

A testable observable implication of this theory is that deeper European integration should be associated with decreased electoral support for regionalist parties.

The Viability of Regionalist Parties

be Euroskepticism that drives increased regionalist mobilization. As state sovereignty transfers to the supranational level, it becomes less clear to ethno-national or regional groups how the state and the supranational entity will manage or treat them in the new situation. Groups may be wary of losing cultural identity themselves within a supranational Europe. And a deeper European Union would only serve to exacerbate these concerns. Regionalist politicians may utilize this public backlash against the EU to increase support for the movement.[20] This uncertainty might lead to diminished support for the European project rather than the symbiotic relationship predicted above. In other words, the EU may encourage regionalist mobilization, but the causal relationship may be based on Euroskepticism rather than Euro-enthusiasm.

While this alternative seems plausible, Peter Lynch finds little support for it among minority nationalist parties through the 1990s. He notes that these political parties show no concern over a potential loss of cultural identity:

> Clearly, for minority nationalists, the European Union is no melting-pot destined to turn Basques, Bretons, Catalans and Scots into hyphenated Europeans. Indeed, it seems more likely that the very plurality of European culture and identity—in which there can be no hegemonic culture promoted by the centre of the EU—actually facilitates some of the cultural and political arguments of minority nationalism. (Lynch 1996, 198–199)

Nevertheless, this theory provides an alternative to the viability model that merits systematic testing.[21]

---

[20] As de Winter (1998, 243 fn 3) points out, no party can remain immune to growing public Euroskepticism; thus, if voters in these regions become increasingly Euroskeptical, regionalist parties are likely to follow. However, this view is not necessarily inconsistent with the predictions of the Viability Theory, depending on the type of elite Euroskepticism expressed (i.e., "hard" or "soft" Euroskepticism (Taggart and Szczerbiak 2004)). In Chapter 4, I show that regionalist parties do begin expressing more soft Euroskepticism in the 2000s, especially about particular policies, but generally they remain supportive of the project, in part because of the role that the EU plays in providing credibility to the regionalists' viability arguments.

[21] As Chapter 4 discusses at length, many regionalist parties oppose European integration on particular policy issues, while supporting the general integration project, particularly how it affects the balance of power between the state center and periphery. In other words, it is possible that regionalist parties can oppose

Next, I introduce the research design that will allow me to test the descriptive inference—that European integration does encourage regionalist mobilization—and the causal inference—that this link can be attributed to the Viability Theory rather than fear or xenophobia.

2.5 RESEARCH DESIGN

The nature of this research question precludes direct and straightforward testing. So I utilize multiple approaches, such as cross-national quantitative analysis of election and survey data along with detailed analysis of party rhetoric to triangulate on the problem. This research design is not just cross-sectional, considering all Western European regions in the post–World War II period, but also, and perhaps mainly, longitudinal, focusing on various stages of European integration, including before and after the Treaty of Rome, Maastricht, and the introduction of the Euro. This design allows for variation in the key explanatory variable (integration) as well as the dependent variable (regionalist mobilization).

In this book, I divide the empirical work into several chapters, focusing on different units of analysis: political parties—in terms of when and where they compete, their relative electoral success, and their attitudes toward European integration—and individuals.

2.5.1 OBSERVABLE IMPLICATIONS

In the study of regionalist mobilization and regional integration, several observable implications present opportunities to test the Viability Theory, as well as other key alternative theories. Studying regionalist parties and individual support for the movements in a variety of ways will allow triangulation on the problem. It seems obvious that no single indicator or operationalization will be convincing by itself. Similarly, neither qualitative nor quantitative analysis is sufficient by itself to adequately investigate this research question. To increase both external and internal validity, I will use multiple methods to complement each other, both by relying on the cumulative knowledge in the literature and my own empirical research.

---

the EU for non-cultural factors. In addition, as the European Union evolves and expands into more policy arenas, the regionalists' perceptions of the EU may shift as well.

The Viability of Regionalist Parties

Based on this strategic account of elite behavior and the framing of the European Union as a mechanism to make independence more viable, the theory has clear implications for electoral support for regionalist parties. If parties utilize the European Union as described above, then more citizens will view the region as a viable independent entity within the EU. This realization should fuel more support for regionalist parties, who generally support greater autonomy for their region, either in terms of cultural autonomy, fiscal federalism, or outright independence. Using a dataset compiled from various sources, including Caramani's dataset of electoral data (Caramani 2000), Eurostat's political economic variables (Eurostat 2004), and the Comparative Manifesto Project (Budge et al. 2001; Volkens et al. 2006), I test this implication at two stages, both when and where the regionalist political parties decide to compete in national parliamentary elections and how well the parties do once they enter competition (Chapter 3).

A corollary to this implication is if regionalist parties see the European Union as an ally in their quest for autonomy, then party manifestos should reflect a greater level of support for the European project as it deepens. Similarly, the rhetoric of party leaders should reflect this rational-choice logic. Contrary to the opportunity mechanism, fear of immigration or economic dislocation associated with economic integration may diminish party support for European integration. Party elites may utilize this fear to attack the European Union. Using elite surveys of party positions, I directly address this empirical question in Chapter 4.

Some evidence already exists to support the viability hypothesis. As far back as the 1920s, the Parti Autonomiste Breton (PAB) stated its objective as political autonomy for Brittany but sought a European federation to preserve military and economic security (Lynch 1996, 87). In Catalonia, the former President of Catalonia Jordi Pujol is considered to be an enthusiastic European, in part because he perceives the EU as an ally to help distance his region from Spain (Newhouse 1997, 77).

In Scotland, many Scottish National Party (SNP) leaders have utilized exactly this type of language over the last 35 years. In 1976, for example, MP Jim Sillars made numerous linkages between European integration and devolution, justifying this link by theorizing that the European Community eliminates some of the disadvantages associated with separatism, thereby making independence a more viable option (Lynch 1996, 36). This justificatory logic supports the reasoning behind the causal mechanism.

Using Eurobarometer surveys in Chapter 5, I test whether other Western European citizens with regionalist, or sub-state nationalist, attachments perceive the European Union (EU) as an ally in their struggle with the center. Then, using individual-level survey data from Scotland, I investigate mass support for autonomy movements. If the theory is correct, as the European Union deepens, overall public support for autonomy should increase, ceteris paribus. For example, nearly a third of the Scottish population supports independence within the European Union (McMillan 1996, 80). Further, they should consider independence to be a more viable constitutional option, in part because the European Union provides an alternative to the central state.

The distribution of supporters should change as well. Traditionally in the Basque country, the middle class and the lower clergy have been the most ardent supporters, while industrialists, fearing the economic disruption that may result from independence, have been less supportive of Basque nationalism (Linz 1973; da Silva 1975, 241).[22] But capitalists or industrialists should be more supportive of autonomy if the European Union provides more economic security than independence without such a union. Thus, a new "bourgeois regionalism" should emerge in response to the changing economic context (van Houten 2003, 10). Admittedly, support for nationalism in the traditional sense is fairly limited (e.g., 15 percent in Corsica, 10 percent in the Basque country) (Crowley 2000, 98–99). Nonetheless, if public opinion data demonstrate that deeper European integration influences support for regionalist autonomy movements, particularly within the economic elites, then the evidence supports the theory. I test these observable implications in Chapter 5.

2.6 Discussion

In many of the regions, the regionalist parties are well-established, albeit niche, parties. They compete over the center-periphery cleavage

---

[22] This fear of disruption now afflicts regionalists outside of Europe (e.g., the Québécois) more than regionalists within the European Union (Young 2012). However, as Young (2012) notes, this lack of fear of disruption within the EU depends crucially on whether seceding states would be admitted easily as new members.

that dates back to the national revolutions (Lipset and Rokkan 1967). But the existence or persistence of this cleavage is not automatically translated into regionalist party success. As Brancati (2008, 136) points out, that translation depends on strategic politicians and the incentives they face. And the European Union has dramatically changed the incentives in recent decades, acting as a permissive factor to both weaken regionalist ties to the central state and the arguments made by mainstream politicians to undercut regionalist movements (Keating 2009, 61).

In her discussion of radical right parties, Pippa Norris introduces a theoretical framework of party competition with a "zone of acquiescence" (Norris 2005, 20). Voter policy preferences are typically distributed along a normal curve. Inside this curve, there lies an area that represents policy positions acceptable to the public (i.e., the zone of acquiescence). Rational politicians wish to stay within this zone because the public is far more likely to support them (Norris 2005, 21). And yet, as she points out, the zone is not static. And in the case of regionalist parties, I argue that the process of European integration has expanded the zone of acquiescence to include more regionalist parties and their territorial goals.

In this theory, European integration is not an active driver of regionalist mobilization. Rather, it creates permissive conditions conducive to regionalist party success by reducing the key advantages of large states. By increasing the viability of small states, the European Union affects the strategies of politicians and the perceptions of the public. Continuing down the causal chain, European integration therefore should affect where regionalist parties compete and their relative electoral success.

In the remainder of this book, I test this argument by investigating regionalist party success, strategies and supporters.

CHAPTER 3

Regionalist Political Party Success

ON ONE HAND, European political and economic integration threatens traditional state sovereignty from above. On the other hand, sub-state national autonomy movements, such as in Scotland and Catalonia, gather momentum with referendums and public support, threatening state sovereignty from below. Are these two phenomena coincidental or interdependent?

In this chapter, I develop hypotheses regarding the incidence and success of regionalist political parties, such as the Scottish National Party, Lega Nord, and the Basque National Party. Similar logics explain the incidence and success of these parties. Most significantly, cultural differences typically drive the decisions of regionalist political parties to compete in national-level elections as well as their success. But beyond the demand side, I argue that increased European integration actually encourages sub-state national autonomy movements by increasing the viability of smaller states within a broader political economic framework.

Thus far, much of the best work on regionalist parties in Europe focuses on particular regions or even particular parties (Lynch 1996; de Winter and Türsan 1998). While these detail-rich case studies provide insightful looks into individual parties, they do not readily lend themselves to generalizations. This analysis contributes to the literature on regionalist political parties as one of the first comparative statistical analyses of the incidence (i.e., where the parties compete) and success of regionalist political parties (i.e., how well they do in elections).[1] In

---

[1] Other authors, such as Tronconi (2006) and Brancati (2014), address electoral

this analysis, I focus exclusively on national-level parliamentary elections.[2]

In the next section, I develop a baseline theoretical model to explain the determinants of regionalist party electoral success, focusing on preferences, institutions, and strategic interactions with mainstream parties. Next, I consider a supply and demand framework for understanding the dynamics of new party entry and competition. Finally, I develop the theory connecting European integration to the incidence and success of regionalist political parties.

Using a dataset of all regions within the EU-14 from 1950 to 2010, I then test these hypotheses.[3] As the statistical models show, the demand side of the equation, in the form of preference heterogeneity, largely explains where regionalist parties compete. In particular, it is cultural heterogeneity that motivates regionalist parties.

While cultural difference remains a powerful predictor of regionalist party success, the results demonstrate that a deeper EU has indeed increased the likelihood that regionalist parties will compete and be successful in national elections. As the Viability Theory argues, a more integrated European Union creates a political environment more conducive and receptive to the electoral arguments of regionalist parties.

3.1 Modeling Regionalist Party Success

3.1.1 Preferences

Several potential factors may drive demand for niche parties. Typically, salient new issues create the "push" for new parties (Rüdig 1990). For Green parties, the controversy over nuclear energy, among other issues, created a push for alternative representation in parliaments (Kitschelt 1989). For New Radical Right parties, immigration concerns and eco-

---

success, but neglect the first stage (i.e., whether the parties compete in a region). This chapter builds on this prior work by focusing attention on both stages.

[2] Similar to other work (e.g., Brancati 2014), I focus on lower house parliamentary elections because not all countries have upper houses, complicating useful comparison and analysis.

[3] Following many cross-national studies of European Union countries, the dataset excludes Luxembourg. The electoral data from 1950 to 1997 was collected and provided by Caramani (2000). For electoral data from 1997 to 2010, I compiled election results directly from national election commissions, with the research assistance of Michael Beckstrand.

nomic insecurity often fuel support (Hug 2001, 4). For regionalist political parties, it is not surprising that regional issues drive demand for new political representation (Hug 2001, 3). However, underlying these demands must be a certain level of preference heterogeneity, either in cultural or economic terms. In other words, citizens who live in a region that is different from the rest of the country are more likely to support regionalist parties (Hearl, Budge, and Pearson 1996; de Winter and Türsan 1998). And in fact, most studies include historical language of the region, a proxy for cultural difference, as an explanatory variable and conclude that language trumps political economic variables as a causal variable (Hearl, Budge, and Pearson 1996; Gordin 2001; Fearon and van Houten 2002).

Language difference is highly correlated with regionalist party existence and success. As demonstrated in an analysis of nine advanced industrial countries, 91 percent (20 out of 22) of the regions where regionalist parties competed did have a distinct language; however, 62 percent (32 out of 52) of the regions with distinct languages did not have regionalist parties competing in elections (Fearon and van Houten 2002). These simple facts highlight the near necessity of language difference as a determinant of regionalist parties, but they also show that a different language is by no means sufficient for a regionalist party (Fearon and van Houten 2002, 20).[4] In other words, while nearly all regions that have a regionalist party also have a distinct historical language (i.e., language is a necessary condition for a party), more than half of the regions with a distinct language do not support a regionalist party (i.e., language is not a sufficient condition for a party). Cultural difference, in the form of historical language, must be considered a significant potential explanatory variable in any empirical model of regional mobilization.

Language difference also provides some leverage on the preference issue central to the viability argument elaborated in Chapter 2. Alesina and Spolaore (1997, 2003) and others tend to assume heterogeneous preferences based on distance from the center. But distance seems a poor proxy for heterogeneous preferences. In contrast, linguistic dis-

---

[4] Gordin's Boolean analysis comes to the same conclusion about language's necessary but not sufficient relationship with regionalist party success. In other words, in almost all cases where a regionalist party exists, the region has a distinct language, but the presence of a distinct language does not, by itself, guarantee a regionalist party (Gordin 2001).

tinctiveness of the region from the country's center, as a proxy for cultural differences and heterogeneous preferences, is one way to test whether heterogeneous preferences affect support for regionalist parties (Fearon and van Houten 2002).

Rather than compare the most commonly used language in the region to that of the capital, Fearon and Laitin (2000) utilize the *Ethnologue's* categorization of languages into different language families to determine how similar the region's historical language is to the capital's language (SIL International 2006). Using the historical language of the region rather than the current language allows the measure to serve as a proxy for cultural differences in a way that using current language does not because it underestimates preference differences due to linguistic but not cultural assimilation (Fearon and Laitin 2000).[5] Fearon and Laitin (2000) articulate this point clearly: "even a vague memory of an ancestral language indicates a storehouse of cultural practices and beliefs that can be mined by political entrepreneurs seeking to mobilize support along cultural lines."

By following the coding guidelines, I derived each region's Language Family from the *Ethnologue* database.[6] Following Fearon and van Houten (2002), the Language Family variable is converted to Language Difference by using the reciprocal [Language Difference].[7] For

---

[5] For example, consider Northern Ireland or Scotland. Using current spoken language would underestimate the cultural differences between Catholics in Northern Ireland or Scots and the dominant English (Fearon and Laitin 2000).

[6] The coding works as follows: Each language has a classification designated by Grimes' *Ethnologue* (SIL International 2006). The Language Family variable simply measures the level at which the region's language branches off from the capital's language. For example, English's classification is Indo-European, Germanic, West, English while Scotland's code is Indo-European, Celtic, Insular, Goidelic. The two languages branch off at the second level, so the code is two. Another example is Spanish (Indo-European, Italic, Romance, Italo-Western, Western, Gallo-Iberian, Ibero-Romance, West Iberian, Castilian) and Basque (Basque), which gives Basque a code of one. If two languages are identical, the Language Family code is ten, which is one level higher than the most similar yet still distinct languages. Examples of regions coded ten are Andalusian and Canaries (both utilize Spanish). For a more complete discussion of the coding guidelines, see Fearon and Laitin (2000) and Fearon and van Houten (2002).

[7] Language Difference is simply the reciprocal of Language Family, or $\frac{1}{Language\ Family}$. This simple conversion emphasizes the differences that are earlier in the family trees (e.g., Spanish is more different from Basque than Catalan), both because branches earlier in the family tree are more significant and because larger differences between languages are more reliably coded in the *Ethnologue*. Drawn

example, the Basque region in Spain scores 1 on the Language Difference variable, while Catalonia scores 0.125 because Catalan is far more similar to Spanish than Basque is. The Galician region is even more similar, scoring 0.111. Appendix B lists all West European regions, along with the language classification, language family, and language difference values.

In Figure 3.1, I mapped language difference using GIS data collected from the European Union.[8] Darker shading refers to more language difference. Again, the language difference variable is constructed from the historical language of the region. This map demonstrates clear variation both within and across European states. Some states, such as Greece, have little cultural difference, as measured by Language Difference. In contrast, Spain has both culturally similar and dissimilar regions, with much variation.

Next, we compare the Language Difference between regions with regionalist parties and those without. For regions without regionalist parties, the language difference score is 0.14 ($N = 2366$), a score between the same language or dialect (0.10) and a close linguistic relative, such as Napoletano-Calabrese in Italy or Aragonese in Spain (a region with 0.167). For regions with regionalist parties ($N = 374$), the language difference is 0.35, a score between Frisian vis-à-vis Dutch (0.25) and Welsh in the UK (0.50). On average, regionalist parties compete when there is far more historical linguistic difference.[9]

As Language Difference between the region and the center increases, therefore, I expect support for the regionalist political parties to increase both in terms of competing in the elections in the first place and electoral success.

Previous studies demonstrate convincingly that cultural differences are a key predictor for regionalist party support (Hearl, Budge, and Pearson 1996; Fearon and van Houten 2002), but cultural differences are not the only preferences that can affect support for regional autonomy. The dramatic rise of the Lega Nord in Italy highlights another

---

from the *Ethnologue* (SIL International 2006), the coding of the Language Family variable is provided in Appendix B.

[8] I collected the NUTS geo-datafiles from *GISCO NUTS 2006*, made available from Eurostat (http://epp.eurostat.ec.europa.eu). I created the maps in *Stata* 12 using the spmap command.

[9] The difference in means is both statistically and substantively significant. These group differences are statistically significant at the 0.001 level.

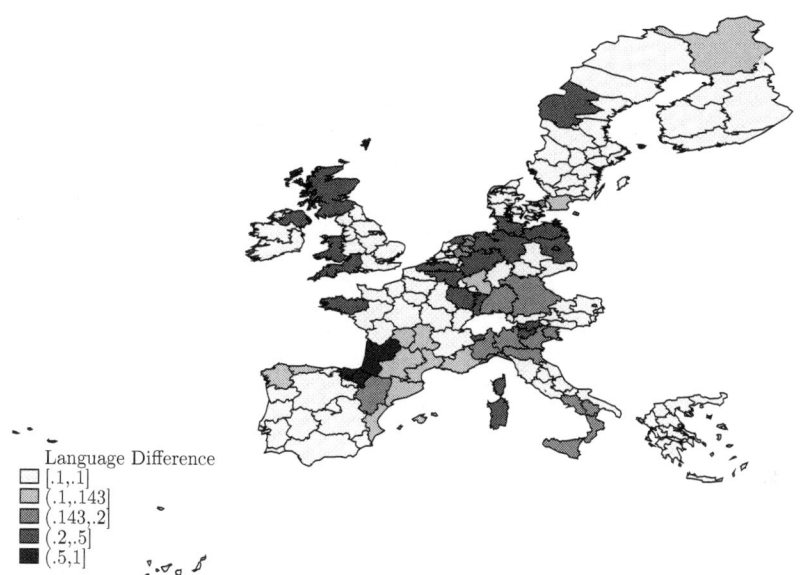

Figure 3.1: Language Difference in Western Europe

factor that can create grievances for a region: political-economic preferences.[10] Predictions vary about whether relatively poor or rich regions should seek autonomy; however, based on the idea that divergent preferences lead groups to seek autonomy,[11] I expect that regions with greater economic differences from the rest of the country will be more supportive of regionalist parties.[12]

---

[10] Ideally, I would be able to measure differences in political ideology between each region and the rest of the country; however, measuring this concept would be difficult at best. For instance, survey data would be imperfect because there are not adequate numbers of respondents in all regions within a country to create a proper measure. Further, sufficient survey data does not exist across the cross-sectional time series; hence, I utilize the economic difference variable and various region-level controls as proxies.

[11] de Miguel, for instance, argues that countries with larger inter-regional inequality are more likely to have "territorialized party systems" (2011, 33). The redistributive pressure generated by that inter-regional inequality serves to "motivate[s] voters in regions that expect to lose out on the redistribution game to vote for regional parties" (de Miguel 2011, 14).

[12] This variable is simply measured as the difference between the per capita income of a region and the country. Thus, economic difference increases as a region is either

In addition to economic difference, relative economic well-being may influence support for regionalist movements (see Bolton and Roland 1997). In the case of advanced groups in advanced countries, such as the Basques in Spain or the Northern League in Italy, their grievance tends to be that they are subsidizing poorer regions or that the center's economic policies are holding their growth down (Horowitz 1981, 184). Along these lines, the Scottish National Party attempts to garner favor among voters by demonstrating that Scotland is subsidizing the rest of the United Kingdom (Begg and Stewart 1971, 148). Though theoretical debates remain over whether rich or poor regions will be more assertive (cf. Hechter 1975), extant empirical studies suggest that richer regions are expected to be the more assertive regions (de Winter and Türsan 1998; van Houten 2000; Gordin 2001; Fearon and van Houten 2002; Sorens 2005; Meguid 2008).[13] Thus, I expect that richer regions will be more supportive of autonomy—and therefore regionalist parties—than poorer regions.[14]

Unfortunately, while economic difference and relative wealth are potentially interesting additional push variables because preference heterogeneity from income differentials could also encourage regional mobilization (Bolton and Roland 1997, 1059), cross-regional income distribution data are not available consistently before 1980 (van Houten 2000, 10). So this hypothesis cannot be fully tested alongside the EU hypothesis for the entire time period. As I discuss in the results section, though, I consider these variables in the robustness tests included in Appendix C and show that their inclusion does not affect the main results.

3.1.2 Strategic Interactions

Overemphasis on the demand side tends to ignore the strategic interaction inherent in domestic party competition. Significantly, sev-

---

richer or poorer than the national average. See footnote 2 in Appendix C for a detailed explanation of the measurement.

[13]In contrast, using formal theory and in-depth case studies, Beramendi considers the conditions under which poor regions will actually pursue autonomy even in the face of potential subsidy sacrifices (2012, 11).

[14]Relative per capita GDP of the region is included in robustness tests. See footnote 2 in Appendix C for a detailed explanation of the measurement. In contrast to the economic difference variable, this continuous variable measures whether a region is poorer or richer than the country's average.

eral authors argue new demand is necessary but may not be sufficient (Kitschelt 1995; Hug 2001; Tavits 2006; Meguid 2005, 2008). Successful new party entry also depends on the opportunity, or "pull." The opportunity structure includes the political institutions, such as electoral laws, but it also includes the strategies of mainstream parties (Meguid 2008; Selb and Pituctin 2010), which most studies of new parties fail to consider (Hug 2001, 37). Recent work redirects attention back to the mainstream parties. For example, Bonnie Meguid argues, "the electoral successes and failures of green, radical right, and ethnoterritorial parties are not merely the reflection of the institutional and sociological environment.... [T]heir electoral lows and highs are influenced by the strategies of the most powerful set of political actors—the electorally and governmentally dominant mainstream parties" (2008, 273–274). In other words, the decision of new parties to enter political competition hinges directly on the strategies of the mainstream parties. At least two strategic party opportunity structure hypotheses warrant discussion.

First, using a spatial model, Kitschelt (1995) contends that when the mainstream parties converge, there is space for new parties to enter the political marketplace. In his analysis of the New Radical Right, Kitschelt argues that whether a successful New Radical Right party emerges depends on the opportunity structure of party competition (1995, 14). When mainstream parties converge, space is opened up for right-wing entrepreneurs to exploit. It is only when this space is open that political entrepreneurs can attempt to seize the opportunity with a winning strategy of their own (Kitschelt 1995, 14).

Using the Comparative Manifesto Project data (Budge et al. 2001; Volkens et al. 2006),[15] the cumulative left/right ideological score for the largest party is simply subtracted from that of the second largest party [Party Divergence]. If the ideological distance between the two main parties decreases, implying convergence in the spatial model, then

---

[15]Admittedly, the Comparative Manifesto Project (CMP) has numerous critics. For these purposes, the most relevant criticism is that the CMP measures salience rather than position. But it does correlate with expert measures of party positions. Using confirmatory factor analysis on the CMP, the Chapel Hill Expert Survey, and the Benoit-Laver expert survey, Hooghe et al. (2010, 696–697) find that a single factor explains nearly 75 percent of the variance on attitudes toward the EU. On left/right positions, Keman (2007, 82) finds correlations higher than 0.6 between various expert survey measures and CMP-based measures. And one distinct advantage to the data, of course, is that the CMP is available for the full time-series cross section.

regionalist political parties will be more likely to enter competition.[16]

Second, both Meguid (2005, 2008) and Hug (2001) argue that mainstream parties can subvert potential new parties by incorporating their new issue into their platform. By accommodating new issues, the mainstream parties decrease the push for new parties, thereby limiting their electoral support.[17] Theoretically, Hug contends that mainstream parties can adopt the demands of the potential parties and reduce the likelihood of new entry (Hug 2001, 53); however, he does not directly empirically test whether the mainstream party strategies affect new party entry (Hug 2001, 118). With a variety of statistical tests, Meguid demonstrates that mainstream party strategies do affect the electoral strength of niche parties (2008). In the case of regionalist parties, if the mainstream political parties incorporate a more positive position on decentralization, as coded in the Comparative Manifesto Project, then voters will express less support for regionalist political parties.[18] To capture whether a major party accommodates the regionalist party's issue, the decentralization score for either the largest or second largest party, whichever has the higher decentralization position, is included [Party Accommodation].[19]

---

[16] Clearly, this measure is simply a proxy for the theoretical concept, but the ideological distance between the largest parties should offer some insight into the space available for niche parties.

[17] Meguid (2005, 2008) considers multiple mainstream party strategies, including accommodative, dismissive, and adversarial, but I focus on accommodative strategies in this chapter.

[18] This strategic move on the part of mainstream parties can be either pre-emptive or reactive. Mainstream parties can either accommodate the issue, thereby subverting potential regionalist political parties, or they can react to regionalist political party success and undercut an existing movement by accommodating their main issue. Either way, the logic suggests the move would decrease the likelihood of regionalist political party incidence.

[19] Potentially, the national party's official position may not reflect the position of the regional branch of the party, a point made by Meguid (2008). For example, in their study of Scotland, Bavaria, and Sardinia, Hepburn and Elias (2011, 7) demonstrates that "regional branches of statewide parties have taken on a stronger territorial identity and rhetoric, in some cases declaring themselves to constitute *the* party representing the nation/region in opposition to national parties." Thus, in many cases, the national party's position may be more complex than captured by the Comparative Manifesto Project (i.e., the regional branch of the national party may pursue a more accommodative strategy than the national party can); however, in the cross-sectional time-series analysis, the CMP data offers the most systematic and consistent coding of party positions. When evaluating the effects of the strategic variables on regionalist party success, I will return to this issue.

3.1.3 POLITICAL INSTITUTIONS

In early studies of regionalist political party success, political decentralization is relatively neglected. But states, similar to mainstream parties, are not innocent bystanders in this process and their evolving relationship with their regional units will affect the movements. Indeed, Rudolph and Thompson (1985) find that states are remarkably successful in placating sub-national movements with public sector policies and rather less so when they use repressive tactics. Political options to placate sub-national demands range from output concessions, or public policy changes to resolve some of the grievances of the groups, to changing the constitution to a more power-sharing model, to devolution (Keating 1988, 173).

Michael Hechter argues that when a central government is responsive to the demands of regionalist groups vis-à-vis devolution, it reduces the incentive to support regionalist parties (2000, 122), an argument very much in line with Meguid's accommodative strategy theory. In other words, the central government might try to undercut a burgeoning sub-state nationalist movement by providing a degree of decentralization. But the effect of decentralization is non-linear in his logic. Some degree of decentralization may subvert regionalist party supporters, but contrary to the goals of central elites, devolution could succeed in "whetting [regionalist party leaders'] appetites for even greater powers and privileges" (Hechter 2000, 140). For instance, devolution might provide them experience and resources at lower levels of government that increases their likelihood of success at higher levels (Brancati 2004, 2). Thus, beyond a threshold, political decentralization may actually increase electoral support for regionalist political parties.

Brancati (2008) argues for a simpler relationship between decentralization and "regional parties," with decentralization encouraging these parties to form and voters to support them. In part, politically decentralized governments provide opportunities for regional elites to govern, something less feasible at the national level (Brancati 2004, 139). Governing at the regional level gives regionalist party elites resources (e.g., offices, staff, name recognition) that make competing in national elections far less costly, vis-à-vis national elections in centralized systems. Further, regionalist party elites may not be satiated by decentralization, but may be encouraged to pursue more radical reforms, such as independence (Treisman 2007, 240). Both of these arguments imply a positive relationship between regionalist party success and decentralization.

In contrast, Connor (2001, 124) contends that devolution may in fact be "quite enough" to satiate ethno-national aspirations because regionalist groups are "more obsessed by the dream of *freedom from* domination by outsiders than by *freedom to* conduct relations with states." Thus, it may be that devolution undercuts regionalist success at the national level precisely because it meets the demands at the regional level. This logic implies a negative relationship.

Based on the theoretical predictions of the literature (especially Hechter 2000), I expect to find a non-linear relationship between centralization and support for regionalist parties; however, the statistical analysis will reveal if either of the simpler linear hypothesis is correct.

To control for the decentralization hypotheses, I include both political decentralization and a squared decentralization term [Regional Authority Index]. For the theoretical purposes of this chapter, the Regional Authority Index (RAI) created by Hooghe, Marks, and Schakel (2010) has several advantages over the most common alternatives, such as fiscal decentralization and a simple dummy variable measuring centralized or not.[20] First, the authors develop a measure focusing on the region as the unit of analysis; in other words, unlike other measures, it acknowledges that some countries have asymmetric federalism, with some regions having more devolved authority than others. Second, the index measures variation over time, taking into account institutional reform. Finally, it captures political decentralization, as measured by institutional depth, policy scope, fiscal autonomy, and representation. Importantly, the authors demonstrate that the RAI has convergent validity with seven other commonly used decentralization indices (Hooghe, Marks, and Schakel 2010, Ch. 3).

Finally, several authors attempt to find a relationship between electoral rules and support for regionalist parties. Though the general literature on electoral systems predicts that proportional representation should increase the support for small parties, such as regional ones, several authors find that when it has an effect on regionalist parties, PR actually dampens support for regionalist parties (de Winter 1998, 219; Gordin 2001, 164; Pereira, Villodres, and Nieto 2003, 11). Gener-

---

[20] As Hooghe, Marks, and Schakel (2010, 50–51) note, fiscal indicators fail to capture whether regional governments actually have control over what they do with the money.

ally, plurality systems are expected to discourage small parties in part because voters strategically decide between major parties rather than waste their votes (Pereira, Villodres, and Nieto 2003, 6). But the geographic concentration of regional minorities may explain this somewhat counter-intuitive finding, particularly in Europe. Rather than a simple PR dummy variable which would largely act as a country dummy for the United Kingdom, I use district magnitude as a measure of electoral system [District Magnitude].[21] District magnitude ranges from 1, in the case of the single-member district system of the United Kingdom, to 150 in the national PR system of the Netherlands. Higher district magnitude should be associated with more success for niche parties, or as Lago and Martínez (2011) put it, the lower the district magnitude, the lower the number of parties.

From this brief discussion, several determinants of party success emerge. In the following section, I consider the EU as a factor to explain the decision of regionalist political parties to enter political competition and their success upon entry.

3.1.4 THE EU AND SUB-STATE NATIONALISM

The European Union makes smaller states more viable by diminishing the advantages of larger state size (Bolton and Roland 1997; Alesina and Spolaore 2003). For sub-state nationalist political entrepreneurs, this increased viability increases the credibility of their party and demands for greater autonomy, thereby making the elites more likely to contest elections and citizens more likely to support them.

Further, research shows that European integration makes the regionalist parties' self-government goals more realistic and, therefore, more attractive to voters (de Winter 1998, 221; Dardanelli 2001, 25). European integration makes regionalist parties more attractive both by improving the perceptions of the economic implications of independence as well as the bargaining leverage of regionalist parties (Fearon and van Houten 2002, 22; Garrett and Rodden 2003, 94). Unfortunately, previous studies do not often test for an effect of European integration on support for regionalist parties. Lancaster and Lewis-Beck (1989, 39) test an indirect effect by regressing support for the European Union

---

[21] Average district magnitude is calculated by dividing the number of seats in the lower house by the number of constituencies. The data was drawn from LeDuc, Niemi, and Norris (1996, Table 1.2).

on evaluation of national party economic policy. They find that EU supporters tend to be less supportive of national party policy, which contributes to a vote for a regionalist party. But the theoretical argument of Chapter 2 contends that deeper integration will have a direct effect as well. This potential determinant is neglected in the quantitative models; this chapter fills that gap.

In order to test the EU hypothesis, I include a variety of operationalizations. First, I focus on Hooghe and Marks' National and Supranational Governance scale (2001, Appendix 1). This measure considers the level (i.e., national or EU) at which policies are made in 28 issue arenas, including economic, social and legal policy as well as international relations. Experts evaluated the policies based on these rules at various points in European Union history, including 1950, 1957, 1968, 1992, and 2000.[22] Each policy arena is assigned a score based on the following rules:

1: all decisions are made at the national level,
2: only some decisions are made at the EU level,
3: policy decisions are made at both levels,
4: most policy decisions are made at the EU level, and
5: all decisions are made at the EU level.

To aggregate the data in a useful way for this research, the scores are simply averaged for all 28 issue areas and rescaled from 0 to 1 [Supranational Governance Index].[23]

For robustness, I then created a simple EU index to capture different treaty stages in EU history.[24] While the index is simple and intuitive

---

[22] Based, as they are, on expert surveys, the measures are disputable, as Hooghe and Marks (2001, xi) readily admit; however, I use additional indicators to provide a robustness test for the key explanatory variable. Also, the EU index and the Supranational Governance Index are highly correlated, lending some confidence to the measures.

[23] The values for the rescaled and aggregated National and Supranational Governance scale are as follows: 1950 (or no EU): 0 (947 cases), 1957: 0.063 (178 cases), 1968: 0.17 (756 cases), 1992: 0.357 (349 cases), 2000: 0.464 (510 cases).

[24] For this index, the country-election year is assigned a score based on the following coding: is the country a member of the EU during the election year? If so, which treaty provision does the election year fall under? The scores follow:

0: the country is not a member of the EU (947 cases),
1: Treaty of Rome (signed 1957) (132 cases),
2: Merger Treaty (signed 1965) (534 cases),
3: Single European Act (signed 1986) (268 cases),

(and highly correlated with other integration measures), the characteristics of this index are less than ideal. This European integration index is not necessarily interval in nature.

While neither of these measures is ideal,[25] in addition to a dummy variable for EU membership (947 non-member cases and 1,793 member cases), these variables should provide a robust picture of the effect of EU membership on regionalist political parties. If the theory has validity in this implication, then the effect of integration on regionalist party success should be significant, positive, and consistent across the various indicators.

Hypothesis 3.1. With deeper European integration, regionalist parties will be more likely to compete in national elections.

Hypothesis 3.2. With deeper European integration, regionalist parties will be more successful in national elections.

Based on these variables, a simple analysis of the group means demonstrates there are obvious differences between those regions where regionalist political parties compete and those where they do not.[26] On average, regionalist parties compete when integration is deeper. Nevertheless, this bi-variate analysis is at best incomplete; thus, in the next section, I incorporate European integration alongside the preference,

---

4: Treaty of European Union (signed 1992) (224 cases),
5: Treaty of Amsterdam (signed 1997) (155 cases),
6: Treaty of Nice (signed 2001) (299 cases), and
7: Treaty of Lisbon (signed 2007) (181 cases).

[25] A potential problem for each index is that neither considers that some countries may be more integrated at the same time-point than other EU members. In other words, some countries opt out of certain treaty components and some countries simply do not enact all the legislation introduced by the EU. But this issue is not as problematic as it might be because regionalist political entrepreneurs are not necessarily looking at the specific integration patterns of their home country, but rather general patterns of integration. For example, there is no reason why Scotland would have to (or would have the option to) opt out of the Euro if they joined as an independent country.

[26] The Supranational Governance Index averages 0.17 when no regionalist parties compete and 0.25 when regionalist parties do compete, suggesting that regionalist parties compete more when more issues are handled at the EU level. The differences between these group means are statistically significant at the 0.001 level.

institutional, and strategic hypotheses to explain the conditions under which regionalist political parties compete and what explains their electoral success in those regions.

3.2 Where Do Regionalist Parties Compete?

This section introduces the dataset and methods used to test the theoretical propositions regarding regionalist political party entry. After reviewing the structure of the data and the dependent variable, I introduce the model specifications and analyze the incidence of regionalist political parties in national political competition. The next section proceeds to investigate the electoral success of these same parties.

3.2.1 Measurement and the Dependent Variable

For this dataset, I collected electoral data for each region in the EU-14 from 1950 to 2010.[27] Following the Assembly of European Regions (1996), the region is simply the "territorial body of public law established at the level immediately below that of the state and endowed with political self-government." The region was then matched with its corresponding EU designated NUTS code.[28] This process is critical in determining the appropriate universe of regions in the fourteen countries because the "zeros," or non-events, in this case are as important to explaining regionalist political party entry as those cases where parties do exist.

Table 1.1 lists the regionalist parties in Western Europe that competed in national elections between 1950 and 2010 that are included in this analysis. Parties with a regionalist agenda are included, not necessarily parties that only compete in particular regions or only parties

---

[27] For EU-14 countries, I compiled electoral data for each region starting in 1950 or the earliest election after democratization (e.g., 1977 for Spain). The district-level electoral data found in Caramani (2000) until 1997 and in national electoral commissions from 1997 to 2010 are aggregated by the appropriate regional NUTS code.

[28] The Nomenclature of Territorial Units for Statistics (NUTS) is the EU classification system for sub-dividing each member state (European Union 2010). As the NUTS number increases, the size of the sub-division decreases. For example, NUTS1 levels include regions with 3 to 7 million people, while NUTS3 groups, which are sub-divisions of NUTS1 and NUTS2, include 150,000 to 800,000 citizens. The region level is NUTS2 for all countries, except Belgium (NUTS1), Germany (NUTS1), UK (NUTS1), and Sweden (NUTS3).

that are explicitly pro-independence. Further, parties are only included in the dataset if the party gains either 5 percent of the national vote or at least 5 percent in any single constituency (Caramani 2000).[29] This coding yielded the first stage dependent variable, which is simply a dichotomous variable across regions in all fourteen countries measuring 1 if a regionalist political party competed in the national election held that year, and 0 otherwise. The unit of observation is region-election year.

For this analysis, the observation is the region-level result of a national election, or rather, whether a regionalist political party competes in a given national election in a particular region or not. Table 3.1 illustrates the distribution of the dependent variable across countries. The total number of cases is simply the number of regions multiplied by the number of elections in each country.[30]

As Table 3.1 shows, since 1950, regionalist political parties have only competed in national elections in eight countries in Western Europe, including Belgium, Denmark, Finland, France, Germany, Italy, Spain and the United Kingdom.

For those countries that have competitive regionalist political parties, Figure 3.2 shows the percentage of total observations, or number of national parliamentary elections measured at the region, in which these parties compete. This figure also represents the dependent variable for the incidence stage as each observation in which a regionalist political party competes is counted as a one in the dependent variable.

---

[29] Note that this definition necessarily excludes some regionalist parties that either compete only in regional or municipal elections or fall below the electoral threshold, such as the Basque nationalist party Abertzaleen Batasuna in France.

[30] There are a few exceptions to this simple multiplication. In Denmark, there have been 23 elections since 1950. Until 1971, there were no elections for the Roskilde region (14 total regions). In 2006, Denmark eliminated the counties, consolidating into five regions corresponding to the NUTS2 classification. Thus, 14 counties with 22 elections, one county with 14 elections, and five regions with one election sums to a total of 327 observations. In Finland, the six provinces (läänit) were abolished in 2010, replaced by five large areas. In France, the four overseas departments (NUTS2 regions) were excluded, leaving the 22 regions at the NUTS2 level. In Germany, no elections were held in Saarland until 1957 (15 total observations) and six German regions are only included since 1990 (six total observations per region). For Italy, the EU divides South Tyrol and Trento into two separate NUTS2 regions, but I combine them following Italy's own administrative division into 20 regions. In Netherlands, no elections were held in Flevoland until 1986 (eight observations for that region).

Table 3.1: Observations with Regionalist Political Parties

Country	Region (# of regions)	# of Elections	Total Observations (# with regionalist parties)
Austria	Bundesländer (9)	18	162 (0)
Belgium	Gewesten (3)	19	57 (50)
Denmark	Regioner (5)	23	327 (8)
Finland	Läänit (6)	16	96 (51)
France	Régions (22)	15	330 (4)
Germany	Länder (16)	16	195 (3)
Greece	Perifereies (13)	13	169 (0)
Ireland	Regions (2)	17	34 (0)
Italy	Regioni (20)	15	300 (133)
Netherlands	Provincies (12)	18	206 (0)
Portugal	Comissões de Coordenação Regional & Regiões Autónomas (7)	13	91 (0)
Spain	Comunidades autónomas (17)	10	170 (66)
Sweden	Län (21)	19	399 (0)
United Kingdom	Regions (12)	17	204 (59)
EU-14 total	165	229	2,740 (374)

All other countries and regions without a regionalist party are counted as zeroes.

For Belgium, nearly all region-election years are counted as having regionalist political parties because the party system is nearly entirely regionalized.[31] As shown in Table 1.1, in Germany, regionalist parties compete in national elections only in the 1950s in Bavaria and

---

[31] Considering the distinctiveness of the Belgian and Northern Ireland case, these outliers may bias the statistical results. To ensure robustness, I conduct sensitivity analysis by simply leaving out each country and running the models again. These robustness tests are discussed in Appendix C.

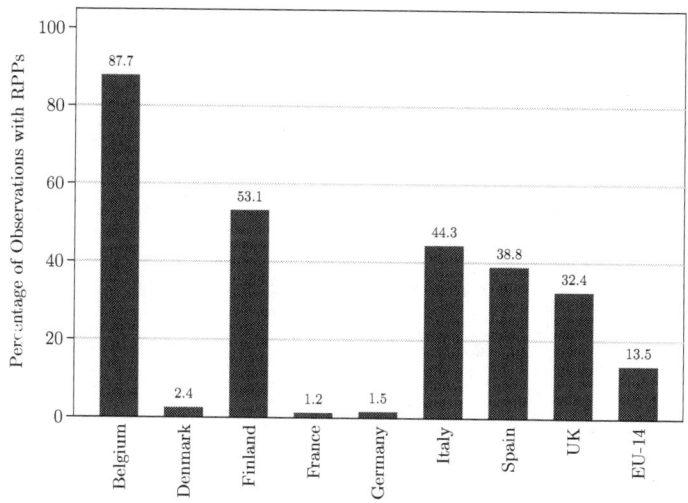

Figure 3.2: Observations with Regionalist Parties, by Country

Schleswig-Holstein,[32] while in the United Kingdom, regionalist parties compete in Scotland, Wales, and Northern Ireland in nearly every election since 1950, with Mebyon Kernow contesting Cornish elections since the 1970s. For both Italy and Spain, regionalist political parties compete in certain regions—such as Basque Country, Catalonia, and South Tyrol—in every election, but parties begin to compete in other parts of the country as time progresses.

Table 3.1, Figure 3.2, and Figure 1.6 demonstrate that variation occurs across space. Among the countries where regionalist political parties do compete, there is distribution over time as well. Figure 3.3 provides a histogram showing the percentage of regions in which regionalist political parties compete across decades.

Generally, regionalist political parties compete in more regions as time progresses, with regionalist parties competing in 9.4 percent of ob-

---

[32] As a reminder, I refer only to regionalist parties that compete and receive votes in national elections. Particularly small niche parties, or parties that receive fewer than 5 percent of the national vote *or* 5 percent of the vote within at least one constituency, are excluded simply due to measurement.

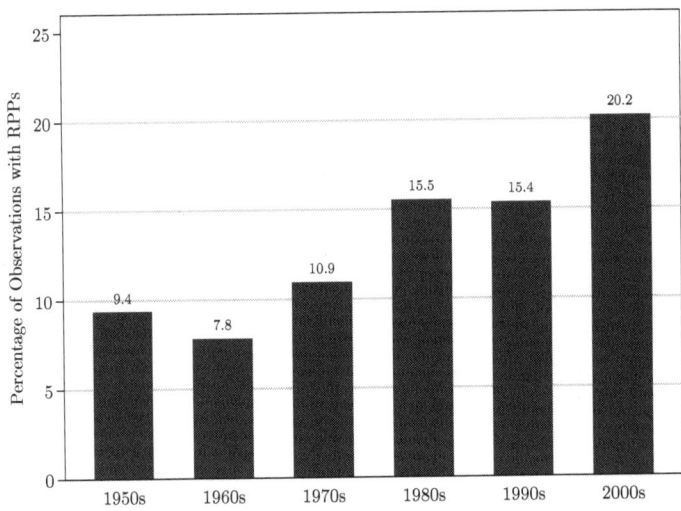

Figure 3.3: Observations with Regionalist Parties, by Decade

servations in the 1950s, 15.4 percent of the observations in the 1990s, and over 20 percent by the 2000s. But the trend is not linear, with the least amount of regionalist party activity in the 1960s (7.8 percent). Figure 1.6 provides further visual evidence that regionalist party incidence is not simply trending with time. Along with Table 3.1, these numbers demonstrate that variation over time and space exists, and that generally regionalist political parties compete in more regions in more recent decades, though the trend levels off in the 1990s before another dramatic increase in the 2000s. It is this variation in time and space the next section seeks to explain.

3.3 Does European Integration Affect Regionalist Party Incidence?

To evaluate the effect of the EU, I use the entire time series described in Section 3.2.1. The dependent variable, whether regionalist parties compete in national parliamentary elections in a region in a particular election year, is available since 1950 as are several key explanatory variables, such as language difference, and the mainstream party's attitudes toward decentralization and general ideology.[33]

While all the countries in the sample are current EU members, there is variation in depth of integration across time. Since some countries join later than others, 34.6 percent of the entire sample is actually at the "no EU" level. The time series allows variation on the key explanatory variable, level of European integration, while maintaining the cross-sectional focus on EU-14 countries. This focus maximizes the level of unit homogeneity within the sample as much as possible. By including only the EU-15 countries, excluding Luxembourg, the dataset controls for numerous international variables.

3.3.1 Model Specification

This section examines under what conditions regionalist political parties are more likely to compete in national-level elections. In this cross-sectional time series, the dependent variable is a simple dummy variable, where a "1" means that at least one regionalist political party competed for a national Parliamentary seat in that region.[34] Traditionally, analysts simply used standard logit or probit to deal with binary cross-section time-series data (Beck, Katz, and Tucker 1998) (BKT henceforth). Unfortunately, the bias from duration dependence is potentially significant. Standard logit and probit can underestimate variability by 50 percent or more (Beck, Katz, and Tucker 1998, 1263).

Recognizing that binary time-series cross-section data are actually grouped duration or event history data, Beck, Katz, and Tucker (1998, 1261) propose a fairly simple way to correct the temporal dependence problems, simply adding either a series of dummy variables or splines to a standard logit or probit analysis. In these data, temporal dependence seems obvious: whether a regionalist political party competes in a particular election depends on the electoral history of that party.

---

[33] As mentioned above, political economic variables at the regional or local level, such as economic difference are only available in a standardized form since around 1980, which obviously means less variation in the EU explanatory variables. To adequately test the EU hypothesis, then, I include the full time series and necessarily exclude some political economic variables. In the Appendix, I test the results for robustness by including the EU variables.

[34] Regionalist political parties competed in 374 cases. In 74 percent (276 cases) of these observations, only one party competed in the election. In 20 percent (76), two regionalist political parties competed, and in less than six percent of cases, either three or four parties competed.

Once a party enters competition at one election, it is easier to compete in future elections. A standard likelihood ratio test confirms the existence of temporal dependence in these data (Beck, Katz, and Tucker 1998, 1269).

Since adding numerous temporal dummies is not necessarily ideal due to the loss of degrees of freedom, Beck, Katz, and Tucker (1998, 1721) prefer to use natural cubic splines to correct for duration dependence.[35] This particular dataset presents an additional temporal complication. While most event history analysis has only one "failure" per unit, political parties can compete in multiple elections, and in fact should be expected to do so more frequently if they have an electoral history. The model in Table 3.2 follows the advice of Beck, Katz, and Tucker (1998, 1272) and includes a control variable which counts the number of previous events. This variable does not change the substantive results of the models.

To correct for the lack of independence within units, the model in Table 3.2 utilizes robust (Huber/White) standard errors, clustered at the regional level.[36] In addition, the second column of Table 3.2 presents a fixed effects logit to control for unobserved heterogeneity

---

[35] Tucker's software, BTSCS, creates the temporal splines from the data (Tucker 1999). The use of splines and temporal dummies is explained and justified in detail in Beck, Katz, and Tucker (1998). The model was also run with temporal dummies instead of splines with no difference in the significance or sign in the coefficients.

[36] This option in Stata changes the assumptions of probit so that independence is assumed across units—in this case, regions—but not necessarily within units. To ensure the results are not simply artifacts of this model choice, robustness tests included alternative model specifications, including a conditional fixed effects logit (with and without a lagged dependent variable) and a random effects probit. These alternative specifications included different ways to control for a time trend, as well, including temporal dummies, number of previous events, and a lagged dependent variable. Each deals with and introduces statistical problems of its own, yet together yield robust results for the key explanatory variables, particularly the EU coefficient. The discussion in this section focuses on the BKT model because it is the most theoretically appropriate for this particular dataset. This decision is supported by the fit and model comparison statistics (e.g., R^2, BIC, AIC). Further, other specifications controlled for Economic Difference, Relative GDP per capita, turnout, effective number of electoral parties, and the number of previous events. These control variables did not affect the significance or signs of the EU variable. Finally, I conducted sensitivity analysis by excluding each key country (e.g., UK, Belgium, etc.) one by one to see whether these countries were driving the result. The EU result is robust even in these stringent conditions. The full models are available in Appendix C.

Table 3.2: Logistic Regression of Regionalist Party Incidence

	Robust SE	Fixed Effects
Supranational Governance Index	5.28***	4.19**
	(0.55)	(1.29)
Language Difference	3.69**	
	(1.17)	
Party Accommodation	0.08*	0.02
	(0.03)	(0.07)
Party Divergence	−0.00	0.01
	(0.00)	(0.01)
District Magnitude	−0.01*	
	(0.01)	
Regional Authority Index	0.01	−0.08
	(0.10)	(0.22)
Regional Authority Index^2	−0.00	0.00
	(0.00)	(0.01)
Elections since Last Incidence	−2.13***	−1.03***
	(0.29)	(0.27)
Spline 1	−0.21***	−0.11*
	(0.04)	(0.05)
Spline 2	0.05**	0.01
	(0.02)	(0.02)
Spline 3	−0.00	0.01
	(0.01)	(0.01)
Constant	−1.31	
	(0.70)	
Pseudo R^2	0.54	0.19
N	2627	572

Note: The Robust SE model entries are unstandardized regression coefficients clustered by region, in parentheses. The Fixed Effects model reports the standard errors in parentheses. * $p \leq 0.05$, ** $p \leq 0.01$, *** $p \leq 0.001$

across regions. By incorporating a fixed effects model, I can focus on the European Union variable less fearful of omitted regional variables, such as relative wealth.[37] As Sorens (2004, 735) argues, fixed effects control for "all the essentially time-invariant explanations of variation in secessionist vote share across regions (language, population, electoral system, and so on)." But the presence of fixed effects limits the ability to explore all the explanatory variables, since language difference varies across region but not over time. Also, the fixed effects significantly diminish the degrees of freedoms in the model, and they ignore information from those regions that either always or never have competitive regional political parties. So, in the interpretation, I focus on the first model but the fixed effects model is displayed to show that the key result is robust.

When European integration is deeper, the likelihood that a regionalist political party competes in a national election is statistically significantly higher. Further, these results are not sensitive to alternative measures of European integration. I evaluated the basic model from Table 3.2 with three different measures of the European integration variable: the Supranational Governance Index, the EU index, and a simple EU membership dummy. Table 3.3 provides only the EU coefficients from these regressions (based on Table 3.2 with only the EU variable changing). In each case, European integration has a consistently significant effect in the predicted direction.[38] The consistent robustness across measures provides a degree of confidence in the results, in particular that the result is not an artifact of the Supranational Governance Index.

Using the results from Table 3.2, Figure 3.4 demonstrates this effect. Notice that Supranational Governance Index has a theoretical limit of 1.0 but the empirical maximum is only 0.464. I limit the interpretation to the empirical maximum.[39]

Figure 3.4 demonstrates that as European integration progressed

---

[37] In Appendix C, Table C.1, I include the economic variables, which dramatically reduced the number of observations (from 2,740 to 1,186) due to the lack of regional economic data prior to 1977. Nevertheless, the coefficient on the Supranational Governance Index remains positive and statistically significant even in the period from 1977 to 2010.

[38] Complete results for these alternative specifications are available upon request of the author.

[39] I created Figure 3.4 using the **predxcon** command in Stata. Language Difference varies while all other variables are held constant at their mean. I used *Clarify* to calculate the predicted probabilities in the text (King, Tomz, and Wittenberg 2000; Tomz, Wittenberg, and King 2003).

Table 3.3: Robustness Tests, by Different EU Specifications

	EU Measure	Coefficient
1	Supranational Governance Index	5.28***
2	EU Dummy	1.82***
3	EU Index	0.42***

Note: Robustness tests based on same model specification as Table 3.2, using different measures for the EU variable.
* $p \leq 0.05$, ** $p \leq 0.01$, *** $p \leq 0.001$

from pre–Treaty of Rome to Maastricht and beyond, the likelihood of regionalist political parties competing in electoral politics increased. Holding other variables, such as Language Difference (i.e., setting Language Difference to a region with average levels of cultural difference), at their means, the likelihood of a regionalist political party competing in national elections is relatively small under any circumstances, but varying European Integration from the minimum (0) to the maximum (0.464) increases the probability from 1.1 percent to 11.1 percent.

By increasing language difference to 0.5, which is the classification for Bretagne in France or Trentino Alto Adige in Italy, the probability of a regionalist party competing increases with European integration from a marginal 3.8 percent at no European integration to 30.4 percent at the highest level of integration. Further, the effect is consistent across very different statistical model specifications, with various other control variables—including Economic Difference, Relative GDP per capita, turnout, and effective number of electoral parties—and even if key countries are excluded from the analysis, as shown in Appendix C. Thus, Figure 3.4 and robustness tests provide strong evidence in support of the main EU hypothesis.

Beyond the EU variable, Table 3.2 demonstrates that the language difference variable is a robustly significant predictor of regionalist political party entry in electoral competition. Across Europe, regardless of the controls included or the model specifications attempted, the effect is significant and positive. The models demonstrate that as the language difference between the region and the capital region increases, the probability of a regionalist political party competing increases. The

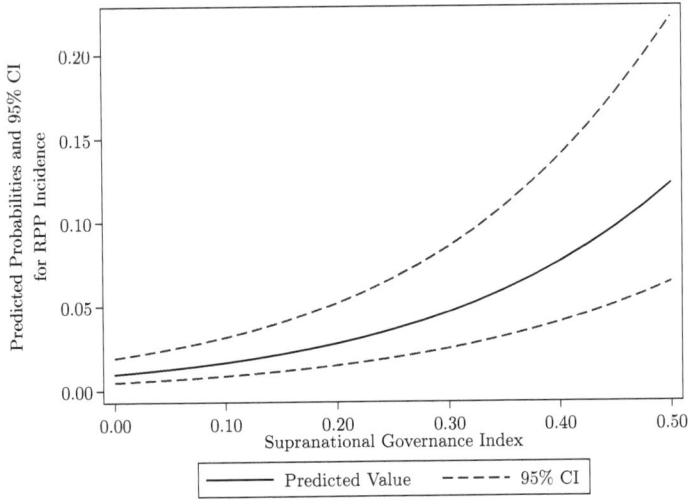

Figure 3.4: Predicted Probability of Regionalist Party Incidence, by European Integration

mean of language difference is actually quite low on the scale—0.17 on a 0.1 to 1 scale—and implies a difference akin to a dialect of the national language rather than a different language or culture. Examples include Calabria or Sicily in Italy or Aragon in Spain. For these culturally similar regions, the likelihood of a regionalist political party competing in national elections is just 2.6 percent. But at the highest value on the scale, where regions such as Pais Vasco are scored, the chances of a regionalist political party competing are nearly 38.1 percent. These results buttress previous studies that found the significance of a cultural or language difference variable to be an extremely powerful predictor of regional mobilization in Europe (van Houten 2000; Fearon and van Houten 2002).

For the strategic party hypotheses, the results are less consistent with the theories. Party Accommodation is significant but it has the incorrect sign. In other words, if either of the two largest parties takes a pro-decentralization position, it actually increases the likelihood that regionalist parties compete. While this finding contradicts the simple hypothesis outlined above, it is not inconsistent with the more sophisticated theory established by Meguid (2008). Unfortunately, it is not possible to fully test her full theory in this time series. In her discussion of the mainstream parties' responses to the Scottish National Party, for instance, it is not simply one party's strategic behavior but both parties' actions that matter (i.e., whether both parties are dismissive, adversarial or accommodative); further, local branches of national parties may have different policies than the national branch.[40] Given the differing results with different time series, it may also be the case that the effectiveness of the accommodative strategy changes over time, with other strategies becoming more effective.

While mainstream party attitudes toward decentralization has a modest effect on whether regionalist political parties compete, actual decentralization does not, at least as measured by the Regional Authority Index.[41] Given the theoretical relevance of decentralization, the insignificant finding for decentralization warrants more exploration in future work.

Meanwhile, the results do not support the Party Divergence hypothesis. I hypothesized that if the top two parties diverge in their left/right positions, then they would eliminate room for minor parties to enter the competition; however, the insignificant effect suggests that the strategic interaction is more complicated than can be captured by this simple variable.

In this model, District Magnitude has a significant negative coefficient, suggesting that small, regionalist parties do better in electoral

---

[40] In addition, mainstream parties may use actual decentralization to subvert regionalist party supporters.

[41] For robustness, I also use the Regional Governance Index, compiled by Hooghe and Marks (2001, 192). This index measures the formal regional governance structures in European countries on four criteria across four time periods: constitutional federalism, special territorial autonomy, the role of regions in central government, and whether regional assemblies use direct or indirect elections. This measure is highly correlated with the Regional Authority Index, but it is only measured at the country, not the regional level. Using the Regional Governance Index, I find a significant curvilinear result with increasing probability of incidence at lower levels of decentralization and decreasing probabilities at higher levels (an upside-down U shape). Rather than the Hechter logic, a simpler logic for decentralization fits this result. At low levels of devolution, decentralization does not satiate the appetite of proponents of regional autonomy but in fact may increase opportunities for regionalist political entrepreneurs to gather support; however, beyond a certain level, decentralization decreases the likelihood that regionalist parties will compete in national elections. Nevertheless, I find the RAI more theoretically appropriate for this test, given its more nuanced measurement.

systems with less proportional electoral rules. Generally, electoral system variables have a significant effect, with proportional representation increasing the number of parties; however, the negative finding for district magnitude is not as surprising as it might be, given the territorial concentration of minority nationalist groups within member states (de Winter 1998; Meguid 2008). These data provide evidence that the constraining effect of plurality electoral rules (and low district magnitude) are much diminished in the case of regionalist parties.

Finally, both models in Table 3.2 include multiple time-series controls, following BKT's advice. Not surprisingly, the variable that measures the number of elections since last incidence is significant and negative. Quite simply, the longer since the last time a regionalist party competed in an election in the region, the less likely a regionalist party will compete in the election.

3.4 What Explains Regionalist Party Success?

The previous section demonstrated how different variables affected the incidence of regionalist parties. Whether political elites decide to contest national elections is an important observable implication of the theory; however, it is only half of the story. This section proceeds to analyze the electoral success of these same regions and parties. Building on the prior sections, this section focuses on the vote share in national parliamentary elections of regionalist parties aggregated at the region-election year level.[42] In other words, in those regions where regionalist parties competed, how successful are they?

This analysis provides an opportunity to explore the various factors contributing to regionalist party success, in addition to testing whether European integration increases electoral support. This cross-national time-series analysis adds considerably to the literature on regionalist political parties, extending both the single case (country or region) quantitative studies as well as the qualitative research.

---

[42]The unit of observation in this analysis is region-election. If multiple regionalist parties compete in the same region in the same election, those votes are combined. Using this measurement, I can both build on the incidence analysis in previous chapters and focus on whether European integration affects aggregate regionalist party success.

3.4.1 Measurement and the Dependent Variable

As in the previous section, the first step in evaluating the determinants of regionalist party success is to identify relevant political parties. Again, these are parties—such as Herri Batasuna or Plaid Cymru—that have a regionalist agenda, not necessarily parties that only compete in particular regions of a country.[43] Extending the previous incidence model, this section analyzes only those regions where there is an active regionalist political party, thereby effectively excluding the cases where the regionalist party vote share is zero.[44] To be clear, the dependent variable is the regionalist party's share of the region-level vote in national or Parliamentary, not regional or local, elections (e.g., a regionalist party's vote share in the Westminster elections of 2005 aggregated at the level of Scotland or Wales; not the regionalist party's vote share in the Scottish Parliamentary election).

For regionalist party success, many of the same variables from the incidence model have the same predicted effects. Party Accommodation by the mainstream parties should reduce support for regionalist parties. Similarly, as mainstream parties diverge in ideological space, they are more likely to crowd out niche parties.

These data also provide another testing ground for the decentralization hypothesis. But in addition to these now familiar variables,[45] I also include the effective number of parties, which offers another opportunity to control for this crowding effect,[46] as more parties in the system will likely reduce vote share for niche parties.

---

[43] Table 1.1 lists these parties and their respective regions, countries and elections.

[44] The nature of these two dependent variables potentially point to a Heckman selection model. In Appendix C, I consider that alternative specification and find substantively similar results.

[45] Note that District Magnitude is excluded in this model. Since the sample is only eight countries, I simply include country dummies to control for electoral system, among other system-specific factors.

[46] The formula for effective number of parties [ENP] is as follows:

$$1/\sum_{i=1}^{n}(v_i)^2 \qquad (3.1)$$

or the inverse of the sum of the squared vote share of the parties in the region in that election. This index has been widely used in comparative politics, for both ethnic fragmentation and effective number of political parties, since being popularized by Laakso and Taagepera (1979).

3.4.2 Does European Integration Affect Regionalist Party Success?

Similar to the incidence question, I expect deeper European integration will be associated with greater electoral support for regionalist parties. By testing both observable implications, this section will clarify the relationship between the EU and regionalist parties.

3.4.3 Model Specification

This section examines under what conditions regionalist parties receive higher vote shares in national-level elections. In this cross-sectional time series, the dependent variable is vote share. The Ordinary Least Squares results, as well as the summary statistics, are reported in Table 3.4. As shown in Table 3.4, this regression incorporates controls for time and country-level effects.[47] In addition, Table 3.4 presents a fixed effects model for robustness.

Table 3.4 yields further evidence to support the contention that regional citizens are more supportive of regionalist parties when their preferences diverge from the rest of the country. Ceteris paribus, shifting Language Difference from one standard deviation below the mean to one standard deviation above the mean increases expected vote share by almost 11.5 percent (from 3.8 to 15.2). Supporting previous studies, Table 3.4 demonstrates that the more culturally distinct a region, the greater the support for regionalist parties.

Effective Number of Parties dampens electoral support for regionalist parties, as predicted. More theoretically interestingly, though, decentralization is significant over the full period, but there is no evidence for a curvilinear effect. At higher levels of decentralization, decentralization encourages support for regionalist parties, providing support for previous work, such as Brancati (2008) who argues persuasively that decentralization should encourage regionalist mobilization and does not even model for a curvilinear effect.

Neither Party Accommodation nor Party Divergence has a statistically significant effect on vote shares. Given the insignificant result, it

---

[47]As with Table 3.2, I subject these results to robustness tests using a range of alternative specifications and control variables, including a Heckman selection model, in Appendix C.

Table 3.4: OLS Regression of Regionalist Party Electoral Success

	Robust SE		Fixed Effects	
	b	(S.E.)	b	(S.E.)
Supranational Governance Index	24.43†	(12.86)	24.48**	(7.94)
Language Difference	36.09***	(5.15)		
Party Accommodation	0.10	(0.33)	0.14	(0.21)
Party Divergence	−0.01	(0.04)	0.02	(0.02)
Effective # of Parties	−1.38*	(0.59)	0.11	(0.51)
Regional Authority Index	−0.56	(0.76)	−0.47	(0.42)
Regional Authority Index^2	0.12***	(0.04)	0.02	(0.02)
Fifties	−0.96	(2.94)	−2.64	(2.03)
Sixties	0.54	(2.65)	−1.68	(1.91)
Seventies	5.35*	(2.35)	2.17	(1.39)
Nineties	−4.44	(3.41)	−0.85	(2.07)
Oughts	−16.82**	(5.38)	−6.82*	(3.20)
Belgium	−33.16***	(3.67)		
Denmark	−3.34	(2.52)		
France	−31.50***	(7.52)		
Germany	−48.90***	(5.73)		
Italy	−15.41***	(3.39)		
Spain	−18.68***	(3.62)		
UK	−17.85***	(2.85)		
Constant	13.19**	(4.61)	13.38***	(3.44)
R^2	0.69		0.17	
N	345		345	

Note: The Robust SE model entries are unstandardized regression coefficients clustered by region, in parentheses. Finland is the reference country. The Fixed Effects model reports the standard errors in parentheses. 1980s is the reference decade. † $p \leq 0.10$, * $p \leq 0.05$, ** $p \leq 0.01$, *** $p \leq 0.001$

seems likely that, as Meguid (2008) argues, the mainstream parties have more strategies available than simply accommodating new competitors by co-opting their issue. The insignificant result may also simply be attributed to a simplistic proxy for party strategies. If different mainstream parties target parties differently across regions, then the crude proxy is unlikely to pick up that nuance.

Regarding the main hypothesis, the statistical results demonstrate that European integration has a positive and significant effect on regionalist party electoral success. Supranational Governance Index has a p-value of 0.058, barely missing the usual 5 percent threshold of statistical significance. Notably, it has an even stronger effect (substantively and statistically) in a fixed effects model, which is also presented in Table 3.4. In addition, the magnitude of the effect is large. In fact, shifting the EU variable from one standard deviation below its mean to one standard deviation above its mean increases the vote share for regionalist parties by 8.5 percent, an effect that is quite substantively significant since the average vote share for regionalist parties is only 16.4 percent.

To further evaluate the magnitude of changes in European integration, I calculated the expected value of the dependent variable, holding all other variables at their mean values. These expected values represent a more informative way to present the statistical results than simply reporting the coefficients and the standard errors (King, Tomz, and Wittenberg 2000). If one holds all variables constant and only changes the level of integration, support for regionalist parties increases fairly dramatically. Figure 3.5 demonstrates this effect.[48]

Significantly, the fixed effects model, controlling for all regions in this dataset, provides a similar result for the effect of integration. In fact, the key result is even stronger. Likewise, a random effects model yields similar results for the Supranational Governance Index. These alternative specifications to deal with the time-series issues in the data suggest that the effects of integration are indeed significant and not simply artifacts of a time trend.[49]

---

[48] I created Figure 3.5 using the **predxcon** command in Stata.

[49] In addition to the fixed effects and random effects model, robustness tests included alternative control variables and sensitivity analysis dropping each country one by one (see Appendix C). Only in one sensitivity model in Table C.8 (when Belgium is excluded) does the effect fall below typical statistical significance. Overall, the effect is robust, especially in the fixed and random effects models. Further, in combined models, when the incidence and success stages are included together (see Table C.9), the effect of European integration remains significant and positive,

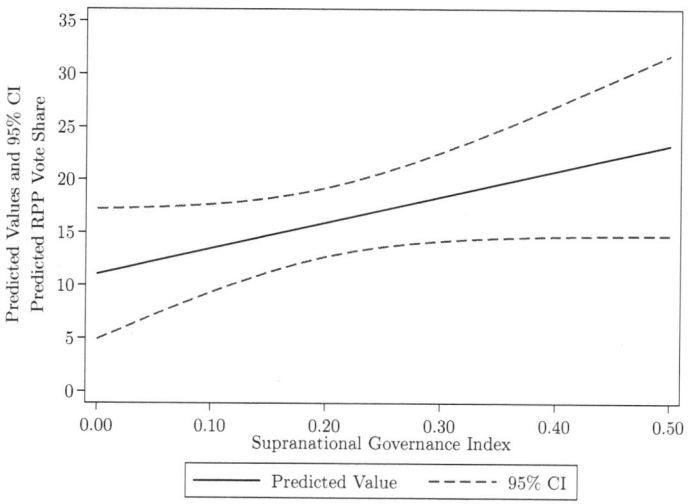

Figure 3.5: Expected Vote Share, by European Integration

3.5 Discussion

As Fearon and Laitin (2000), among others, have found, language difference is nearly a necessary if not sufficient condition for regional mobilization in Europe. Contrary to Hearl, Budge, and Pearson (1996, 177) who find that the presence of a regional language affects regionalist party vote share but not entry, these findings demonstrate that cultural difference greatly influences whether regionalist parties compete in national elections. This chapter confirms and extends earlier work on new or niche parties, in general, and regionalist political parties specifically.

Significantly, the wide range of statistical specifications provides consistent and robust results for a previously neglected factor in quantitative studies, namely European integration. As integration proceeds from a free trade area to a monetary union, deeper integration is associated with more incidence and electoral success for the regionalist parties.

The two sets of regressions demonstrate the descriptive inference:

---

providing more confidence in the key result.

European integration affects regionalist party success at the incidence and election stages. To move beyond the descriptive inference, or justify my argument that the Viability Theory is the driving force behind this relationship, both elites and citizens must recognize and acknowledge the strategic effect of European integration on the sub-state national autonomy movements.

The next two chapters therefore evaluate precisely these additional steps in the causal story. In Chapter 4, I analyze regionalist party attitudes toward European Union to determine which causal mechanism is at work. The statistical analysis above yields an additional observable implication. If the Viability Theory explains this descriptive inference, then regionalist political parties should recognize the advantage of European integration and become more supportive over time. Alternatively, if regionalist party views on integration do not change or even worsen, then the theory lacks support. In Chapter 5, I consider the role of voters. With these two analyses, I will evaluate whether the Viability Theory lies at the heart of the relationship between European integration and regionalist party success demonstrated in this chapter.

CHAPTER 4

Euroskeptic and Europhile Regionalists

IN A EUROPE characterized by multi-level governance, regionalist political parties can either frame the European Union as an ally against the central state or as yet another foreign power threatening local autonomy. In one line of reasoning, European integration decreases the necessity of traditional large states, making smaller, more homogeneous states more viable. Hence, the EU may be an unwitting ally of sub-national groups against central governments, thereby encouraging regionalist parties to be Europhiles. On the other hand, regionalist political entrepreneurs may exploit fear—either fear of yet another foreign authority encroaching on local sovereignty or simple xenophobia—to convince voters to leave mainstream parties and support alternative parties. By this logic, regionalist political entrepreneurs would be highly Euroskeptical to attract these voters.

In Chapter 3, I demonstrated that deeper integration does in fact increase both the probability of regionalist political parties competing in national parliamentary elections and their vote shares once they enter competition. In this chapter, I seek to understand whether regionalist parties perform better as a result of deeper integration because they frame the EU as an ally or as an enemy.

Typically, fringe, or non-mainstream, parties are theoretically and empirically seen as Euroskeptical (Taggart 1998; Taggart and Szczerbiak 2004; Aspinwall 2002; Marks 2004). But in these articles, little attention is given to the regionalist party family, which may serve as an exception to the extremism or non-mainstream Euroskeptic findings.

First, I outline the two competing hypotheses regarding regionalist attitudes toward European integration. Second, using expert survey data on party positions from 1984 to 2006, I directly test these two competing hypotheses. In this section, I replicate a prominent earlier study (Marks, Wilson, and Ray 2002) and extend the end point of the time series from 1996 to 2006. Finally, I evaluate the evolution of the official positions of the Scottish National Party on European integration.

To preview the analysis, I find that regionalist political parties are not Euroskeptical; rather, they are generally supportive of the European project. This finding is in line with research on voting in the European Parliament, where regionalist party Members of the European Parliament (MEPs) vote in a pro-EU manner (Jensen and Spoon 2010, 190). Further, with the Scottish case, where the Scottish National Party explicitly uses the European Union to frame independence as a more viable constitutional option to garner support for their movement, I find that the Viability Theory lies at the heart of regionalist Euro-enthusiasm; however, while "hard" Euroskepticism among regionalist parties remains rare, there is evidence that "soft" Euroskepticism among regionalists is rising in the post-Euro era.[1] Strategically, this soft Euroskepticism may allow regionalist parties to acknowledge popular Euroskepticism about particular policies while still emphasizing the increased viability of the regions associated with deeper European integration.

4.1 Competing Hypotheses

Despite the recent attention to multi-level governance in Western Europe, scholars have neglected the interactions between the sub-national and supranational levels. In fact, this neglect implies a null hypothesis for this study, simply that regionalist parties have no consistent position on European integration, ceteris paribus.

But two competing hypotheses predict diametrically opposed attitudes toward European integration. First, as Chapter 2 argues, the European Union makes smaller states more viable by diminishing the advantages of larger state size, and this is especially true in regions where regionalist parties compete. In the past, "[t]he types of argu-

---

[1] As Taggart and Szczerbiak (2004) argue, not all Euroskepticism is the same. In their classification and throughout this chapter, "hard" Euroskepticism implies "outright rejection of the entire project" while "soft" Euroskeptics oppose particular concrete aspects of European integration (Taggart and Szczerbiak 2004, 7–8).

ments used against minority nationalist and regionalist demands have often centered around the impracticalities of upsetting administrative and political traditions constructed around central institutions" (Lynch 1996, 12). Thus, for regionalist political entrepreneurs, European integration increases the credibility of demands for greater autonomy, ranging from independence to devolution to cultural rights, and, therefore, their parties' credibility. In return, this factor provides incentives for regionalist political parties to be pro–European Union or Europhiles.

Astute regionalist political entrepreneurs utilize these trends to argue more convincingly that the region is less dependent on the rest of the country by "fram[ing] their demands in European terms" (Keating 1995, 7). In Scotland in the 1970s, for instance, the Scottish National Party (SNP) could not convince factory workers that seceding from the United Kingdom would not result in even more unemployment if access to the British market was blocked (Esman 1977c, 266–267). In the 1980s, though, former MP Jim Sillars convinced the SNP to support a pro–European Union position as a "mechanism to avoid economic dislocation in the event of secession from the UK" (Lynch 1996, 39). Importantly, public opinion surveys demonstrate that this message has been received and understood. In a 2007 YouGov survey, only 14 percent believed an independent Scotland would lead to border controls with England; thus, opponents of independence trying to use scare tactics about border controls are no longer credible (Keating 2009, 60–61).

Similarly, Scottish MP Gordon Wilson described the Scottish National Party's support for the European Union as "a first class way of pushing the advantages of political independence without any threat of economic dislocation. Within the common trading umbrella the move to independence can take place smoothly and easily" (Lynch 1996, 38). Activists effectively use the EU to negate the arguments against autonomy based on fears of economic upheaval (Gallagher 1991).

Building on Chapters 2 and 3, I argue that the balance between large and small states has shifted in favor of smaller less heterogeneous states. Therefore, regionalist political parties will support the European Union as an ally against the central state, yielding *Hypothesis 4.1*.

> *Hypothesis 4.1.* Regionalist political parties should be supportive of European integration.

From a different perspective, Gary Marks and co-authors also hypothesize that regionalist parties will be Europhiles (Marks and Wilson 2000; Marks, Wilson, and Ray 2002). They derive hypotheses about party family positions on European integration from the classic cleavages that structure party competition in Western Europe: class, rural-urban, religious, and centre-periphery (Lipset and Rokkan 1967). Contesting the center-periphery cleavage, regionalist political parties should be more supportive of European integration precisely because the EU threatens national sovereignty (Marks and Wilson 2000). Furthermore, the EU may be a friendlier environment for sub-national groups because the European Union is multi-cultural with no single dominant or pan-European identity (Lynch 1996, 15), where the group will be one of many minorities in Europe rather than a permanent minority in their home country (Marks and Wilson 2000, 438–439). These considerations lead regionalist political parties to be more pro-EU, ceteris paribus. Based on these arguments alongside the viability logic, I expect regionalist political parties to support the European Union.

But an alternative hypothesis exists. It may not be that regionalist groups embrace the EU as a means of making smaller independent countries more viable. Rather, in some areas, regionalist parties may try to capture growing public Euroskepticism and opposition to globalization (van Houten 2003, 113–118). In addition to yet another distant government informing regions what to do, increased labor mobility from outside Western Europe threatens the cultural homogeneity of regions. In other words, integration creates new representation demands, such as a fear of economic competition or immigration, which regionalist parties rise to meet. Similar to the political entrepreneurs of the radical right parties (Kitschelt 1995), regionalist political parties may use this opposition as a mechanism to draw support to their movement.

In addition, as a fringe party, political elites within regionalist parties might oppose European integration for strategic reasons. While mainstream parties have little incentive to "rock the boat" on European integration, extreme or fringe parties desire to restructure the dimensions of contestation to try to gain electoral votes (Taggart 1998, 382; Hooghe, Marks and Wilson 2004, 123). Thus, because fringe parties know mainstream or government parties are all pro–European Union, regionalist parties may oppose European integration simply to establish themselves in voters' minds as different from the establishment. Strategic reasoning, fear of cultural assimilation or economic competition, and animosity toward immigrants each could factor into supporting fringe parties. As a result, regionalist political parties could try to mobilize electoral support from these voters by framing the EU in negative terms. In contrast with the first hypothesis, therefore, this logic yields *Hypothesis 4.2*.

> *Hypothesis 4.2.* Regionalist political parties will be strongly Euroskeptical.

While both theories seem feasible, there is some evidence that the Viability Theory and *Hypothesis 4.1* are correct. As mentioned above, the Scottish National Party adopted a policy of independence in Europe in the 1980s, precisely because the EU allowed for political autonomy without fear of economic dislocation (Lynch 1996, 38). Similarly, in 1989, the Plaid Cymru supported a policy of independence in the EU while encouraging the EU to evolve into a true Europe of the regions (Lynch 1996, 76). Across Europe, Kurzer (1997, 43) finds that regionalist politicians are generally enthusiastic about a federal Europe. Further, regionalist political parties apparently do not fear the loss of regionalist identity to a supranational European identity (Lynch 1996, 198–199).

But these studies do not conduct systematic cross-sectional empirical tests of these two hypotheses. Also, they cannot establish whether regionalist parties are more or less supportive than other party families, but rather just whether they are enthusiastic or not. With expert survey data and regression analysis, I establish a ranking of party families regarding positions on European integration. In doing so, I show that the regionalist family is highly supportive of European integration, especially compared to all other non-mainstream party families, and are much closer in attitudes to the mainstream party families.

Nevertheless, it is important to understand whether variation in support for European integration within the regionalist party family occurs and whether this variation is temporal or issue-based. As the EU evolves from simply the "negative integration" of opening markets to the potential "positive integration" of social and welfare policy (Scharpf 1996, 15), party families may change their level of support for the European project. For instance, social democratic parties have become more supportive of European integration as the agenda has turned from simply market integration to "regulated capitalism," while right-wing parties have gone in the opposite direction (Hooghe, Marks, and Wilson 2004, 129). It could be that some regional groups supported a form of "independence in Europe" as long as the integration was mainly economic in nature, yielding economic benefits without threats to political sovereignty, but when economic integration completed and the attention turned to political matters, the groups perceived a greater threat. Or, as Elias (2008, 2009) argues with case studies of Wales, Galicia and Corsica, while regionalists still support the EU as an idea, they are increasingly frustrated at the concrete reality, especially the lack of a clear role for sub-state actors. In this chapter, I begin to explore whether this finding holds for regionalist parties across Western Europe.

Having demonstrated in Chapter 3 that there is in fact a relationship between depth of integration and support for regionalist political parties, I now begin to adjudicate between these two hypotheses. With data on elite positions on political and economic integration available over time, I test these propositions and find that regionalist political parties are generally Euro-enthusiastic across issue area, region and time; however, this general finding does not imply that all regionalists are Europhiles throughout the entire time period. Understanding the variation within the party family is another goal of this section.

4.2 Data and Methods

To evaluate these hypotheses, I utilize expert evaluations of party positions on the European Union as the dependent variable. The Chapel Hill Expert Surveys (CHES) request country experts to evaluate each party in their country on several key questions, including each party's position on European integration. Leonard Ray's original survey included the following years: 1984, 1988, 1992, and 1996 (Ray 1999). The UNC Chapel Hill Center for European Studies replicated the surveys in 1999, 2002, and 2006 (Steenbergen and Marks 2007; Hooghe et al. 2010).[2] The values for this variable range along a 7-point scale from strongly opposed to European integration to strongly in favor. Following Marks, Wilson, and Ray (2002), I rescale the variable from 0 to 1 for ease of interpretation.[3]

---

[2]For more technical information on the dataset as well as access to the data, codebooks, and questionnaire, see chesdata.eu. I conducted the data analysis with Stata11.

[3]For the graphs that follow, note that I also rescaled salience, which was originally scaled 1 to 4, from 0 to 1.

Several factors contribute to the decision to use these particular data. Most significantly, the surveys cover a wide range of years and political parties, including 23 regionalist political parties across five West European countries.[4] Table 4.1 lists the parties from the CHES and their peak and average vote shares in the national elections prior to the survey years.[5]

Neither the Comparative Manifesto Project (Budge et al. 2001) nor inferred party positions from Eurobarometer individual-level surveys provides nearly this coverage of regionalist political parties because of their small national vote shares. Whereas the expert survey attempts to include any party in the most recent election, the manifesto project only includes electorally significant parties. While regionalist political parties are often significant electoral contenders at the regional level, even for national offices, their aggregate national vote totals are generally too low to warrant inclusion in the dataset. Thus, not even relatively significant regionalist political parties, such as the Plaid Cymru in the United Kingdom, are included (Budge et al. 2001).[6]

---

[4] In 2001, the Flemish People's Union (VU) split, with the New Flemish Alliance (N-VA) emerging with a substantial plurality of support from the predecessor party. While the descriptive tables and graphs group these two parties together, the analysis is not dependent on this grouping. The Initiative for Catalonia party was included in the 1999 survey, but is marked as 0 percent national vote share because it ran in the 1996 elections as a partner of Izquierda Unida, or the United Left. The Belgian ID21 party is also included in the 1999 survey because it competed in the 1999 European Parliament election (in coalition with VU), but it did not earn any votes in the national election prior to the 1999 survey, so it is listed with a 0 percent vote share. Both of these parties drop out of the analysis in the following section because only parties with vote share greater than 0 percent are included.

[5] There are a few discrepancies between my coding and the CHES coding of regionalist political parties. The Chapel Hill Expert Survey team codes the VB as a new radical right party, but consistent with earlier work, I recoded them as a regionalist party. In Northern Ireland, the SDLP is coded socialist in the dataset, but I include them as a regionalist party. Finally, CHES includes Sinn Féin in Ireland as a regionalist party, but while I include Sinn Féin in Northern Ireland as a regionalist party, I exclude Sinn Féin in Ireland. For discussion of the coding of regionalist political parties, see Chapter 1.

[6] In an extraordinary ongoing effort, the Manifesto Research Group continues to expand the coverage of parties included in the dataset (Volkens et al. 2010) and generously offers the data to researchers on their website. Recently, certain regionalist parties, such as the Scottish National Party (1992–2001) and Convergence and Union (1979–2008) have been included. But many others, such as the Plaid Cymru in the UK, have yet to be incorporated. As coverage expands, manifesto data will offer regionalist party scholars another dataset to evaluate general ideological positions and support for the EU.

Table 4.1: Peak and Average National Vote Shares of Regionalist Parties (1984–2006)

Party	Peak National Vote Share	Average National Vote Share	Elections Contested
Belgium			
Francophone Democratic Front (FDF)	10.30	4.12	5
ID21 (ID21)	0.00	0.00	1
Flemish Interest (VB)	11.60	6.97	7
People's Union (VU)/ New Flemish Alliance (N-VA)	9.90	6.11	6
Finland			
Swedish People's Party (SFP)	5.80	5.14	7
Italy			
Northern League (LN)	10.10	5.60	7
Sardinian Action Party (PsDA)	0.70	0.70	1
South Tyrolean People's Party (SVP)	1.70	1.10	2
Spain			
Andalusian Party (PA)	1.00	0.56	5
Aragonese Council (CHA)	0.40	0.40	1
Aragonese Regionalist Party (PAR)	0.40	0.12	5
Basque Nationalist Party (PNV)	1.90	1.47	7
Basque Solidarity (EA)	0.46	0.19	6
Canarian Coalition (CC)	1.10	0.96	3
Catalan Republican Left (ERC)	2.50	0.85	6
Convergence and Union (CiU)	5.00	4.37	7
Galician Nationalist Bloc (BNG)	1.30	0.63	7
Herri Batasuna (HB)	1.20	0.95	5
Initiative for Catalonia (IC)	0.00	0.00	1
Valencian Union (UV)	0.40	0.21	5
United Kingdom			
Plaid Cymru (Cymru)	0.70	0.51	7
Scottish National Party (SNP)	2.00	1.64	7
Social Democratic and Labour Party (SDLP)	0.60	0.50	4

Table 4.1 demonstrates that the majority of regionalist political parties are merely fringe parties at the national level. By not competing throughout the entire country, even larger regionalist political parties have relatively small national vote shares, which explains their exclusion from most datasets such as the Comparative Manifesto Project (Budge et al. 2001).

Furthermore, while the Comparative Manifesto Project provides an invaluable resource for the study of party manifestos over time, there are problems using these data to infer EU positions (Ray 1999). In particular, parties have incentive to strategically neglect an issue in their manifesto either due to low salience or internal dissent. In other words, parties can adopt a "dismissive strategy" for a variety of reasons (Meguid 2008). This strategic behavior would affect the manifestos and, therefore, the coding.

Unfortunately, using public opinion data to infer party positions has similar problems. From a practical standpoint, the Eurobarometer and other multi-national surveys simply do not yield sufficient survey respondents in each region to allow for a longitudinal study of regionalist political parties and their supporters. Thus, as with manifesto data, the logistical problems complicate, or even preclude, the ability to infer regionalist political parties' views using Eurobarometer survey data.

Finally, when compared to other available datasets for the years collected, the expert surveys prove to be reliable and valid measures for political party positions on European integration (Ray 1999; Marks et al. 2007; Steenbergen and Marks 2007; Hooghe et al. 2010). Hooghe et al. (2010) compare the EU positions of 72 parties in the CHES 2002 survey, the 2003 Benoit-Laver expert survey, and the Comparative Manifesto Project. Confirmatory factor analysis "reveals that a single factor explains almost three-quarters of the variance of positioning on European integration" (Hooghe et al. 2010, 696). In other words, the factor analysis reveals a common structure across these different datasets. This combination of practical availability, statistical reliability and validity makes the expert survey the best available dataset for this research.

4.3 The Regionalists and the EU

To evaluate the first two hypotheses, or whether regionalist political parties are Europhiles or Euroskeptics, I initially compare the regionalist party family to other party families in Western Europe in Figure 4.1. Note that Figure 4.1 provides an unweighted aggregation of regionalist parties.[7]

Figure 4.1 demonstrates that regionalist political parties are consistently more pro–European Union than other small party families, such as the Greens, Radical Left, or Radical Right, and nearly as favorable to European integration as mainstream party families, such as the Christian Democrats, the Liberals and the Socialists at least until the late 1990s. Starting in 1999 and continuing through 2006, the regionalists become noticeably less pro-EU in the view of the experts, along with the Conservative party family. This trend coincides with a widening and deepening of the EU, which shifted the stances of some regionalist parties from a "permissive Europhile position to a more—and probably more realistic—Eurotepid position" (Lynch and de Winter 2008, 604). Meanwhile, during the same period, the Greens become more favorable to the EU while the Radical Left and Right parties remain the most Euroskeptical by far.

This graph merely shows the bi-variate relationship, though, and does not control for other potential explanatory factors. Nevertheless, Figure 4.1 provides preliminary support for *Hypothesis 4.1*, which predicts that regionalist political parties will be supportive of European integration; however, it is important to note that relatively strong support prior to 1999 does diminish in the post-1999 era. But does the relatively strong support persist across parties, or is there substantial intra-family variation? In other words, is the family decrease due to a few party's evolving positions, or is it a more general trend?

---

[7] Over time, there is some variation in the regionalist parties that are included in the CHES data. The list below captures this variation.

    1984: 16 parties
    1988: 17 parties
    1992: 17 parties
    1996: 17 parties
    1999: 20 parties
    2002: 12 parties
    2006: 14 parties

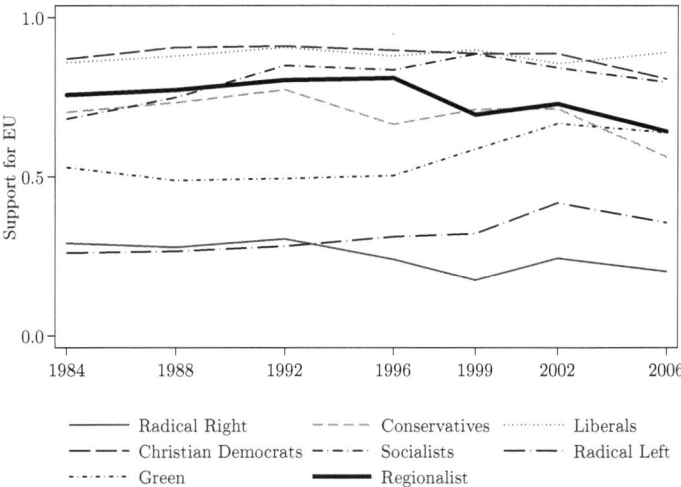

Figure 4.1: Support for European Union, by Party Family

Figure 4.2 breaks down these aggregate data by individual regionalist party (averaged across all years), with the average position for all political parties from all families included as the baseline. The figure shows that nearly all of the regionalist political parties are more supportive of the European Union than the average party in the EU.

Only a few exceptions exist: Herri Batasuna in the Basque region of Spain and the Vlaams Blok, or Vlaams Belang, in Belgium.[8] Each of these parties is ideologically extreme. According to the CHES data, Herri Batasuna is one of the most extreme left-wing regionalist political parties in Europe and is actually the most left-wing party in Spain. On the other end of the spectrum, the Vlaams Blok is the most right-wing regionalist political party and is in fact only slightly less extreme than the National Front in France. Thus, another predictor of party attitudes toward European integration may explain the outliers: ideology.

---

[8] Because this graph averages the party's positions over time, a currently Euroskeptical party, like Lega Nord, appears moderate. As I discuss in more detail below, Lega Nord is an example of a party that changes its positions significantly over time, evolving from a supporter to the most Euroskeptical party in the dataset.

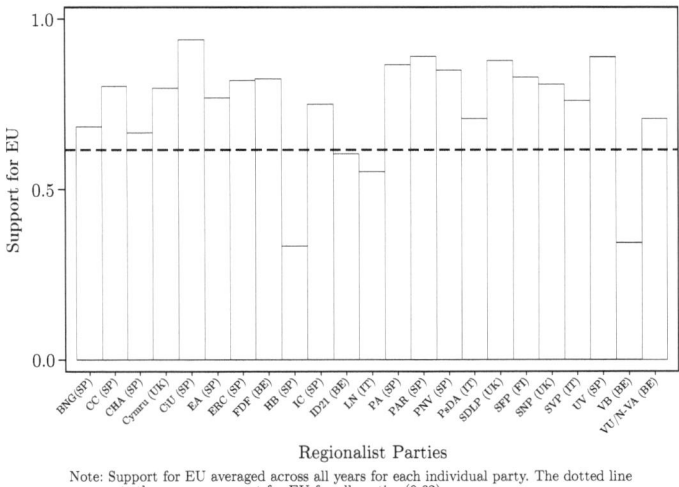

Note: Support for EU averaged across all years for each individual party. The dotted line represents the average support for EU for all parties (0.62).

Figure 4.2: Average Support for European Union, by Party

The literature on party position provides a clear expectation for the effect of general left/right ideology on party support for the European Union: an inverted U-curve, which places extreme left- and right-wing parties in opposition to European integration while centrist parties support it (Marks 2004, 238). Aspinwall (2002) argues that ideologically centrist parties support the EU as a "fait accompli" and perceive it as a positive development in European history. Empirically, mainstream parties, or parties in the government, are relatively absent from lists of soft or hard Euroskeptic parties in Western Europe (Taggart 1998; Taggart and Szczerbiak 2004). As one might expect, the reasons for opposition on the left and right are much different. Extreme left-wing parties oppose the EU either on the basis of "old politics" anti-market socialism or "new politics" anti-centralist activism, while right-wing parties oppose any attempts to diminish the state's autonomy, in cultural or economic terms (Aspinwall 2002, 86–87). Thus, ideology matters but it is mainly the extremism of ideology that determines the position of the party on European integration, yielding a curvilinear relationship.

Figure 4.3 simply shows an unweighted scatterplot of the regionalist

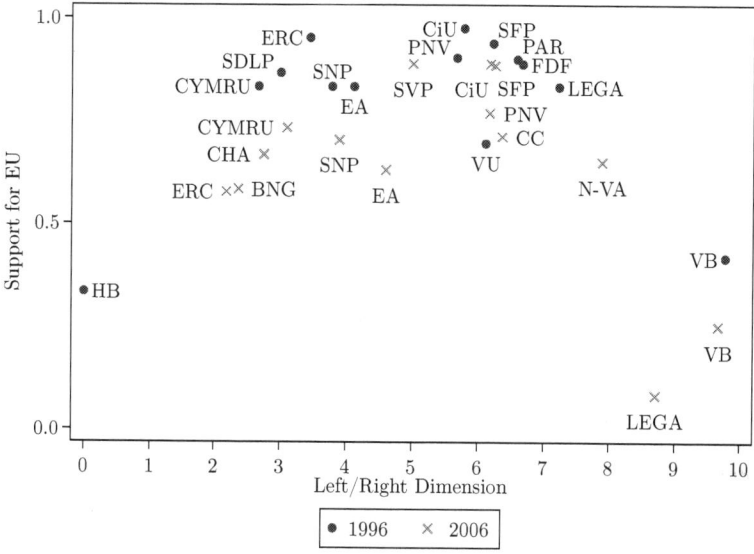

Figure 4.3: Regionalist Support for the EU, across Left/Right

parties with ideology on the x-axis and support for European integration on the y-axis, with the party positions in 1996 and 2006 noted for comparison.[9]

Let me reiterate that there are only a few regionalist political parties from which to draw inferences. With a small number of observations, outliers can be more influential. With this qualification in mind, the graph indicates that the inverted U-curve holds for regionalist political parties, at least at the aggregate level. The most extreme left-wing parties, Herri Batasuna and Sinn Féin, and the most right-wing parties, Vlaams Belang and Lega Nord, are relatively Euroskeptical while the centrist parties have higher levels of support for European integration. Notice, also, the dramatic change for Lega Nord, which goes from Euro-enthusiastic in the 1996 survey to among the most Euroskeptical parties in 2006. Certainly, this drop contributes to the noticeable drop in

---

[9]The Flemish People's Union (VU) party split in 2001, with the New Flemish Alliance (N-VA) replacing it in the CHES dataset. Thus, the figure includes VU in 1996 and the N-VA in 2006.

support in the regionalist family line in Figure 4.1. Further, this finding of a curvilinear relationship reinforces much of the literature on party positions on the EU.

While traditional left/right ideology structures contestation on the European Union with an inverted U-curve, the relationship between the EU and the "new politics" dimension is more straightforward, both theoretically and empirically. Whether this dimension is labeled GAL/TAN (green-alternative-libertarian/traditional-authoritarian-nationalist) or "left-libertarian/right-authoritarianism," this second dimension has a significant effect on party positions on European integration.[10] TAN parties, both extreme right and mainstream conservative parties, are much less supportive of European integration (Hooghe, Marks, and Wilson 2004, 133); they oppose European integration because it weakens the traditional authority of the state.

Thus, theoretically, GAL/TAN should also explain variation within the regionalist political party family. Figure 4.4 presents another unweighted scatterplot with GAL/TAN on the x-axis.[11]

As expected, there is a negative linear relationship between support for European integration and GAL/TAN among regionalists, though the scatterplot shows that the relationship is not particularly strong or robust against the exclusion of outliers. The correlation is −0.47 and, reinforcing the results for the entire European national party system, the extreme TAN parties drive the relationship. In fact, without Vlaams Blok and Lega Nord, the correlation is insignificant (−0.01). Unfortunately, with the small number of parties, it is somewhat difficult to discriminate between the effects of left/right ideology and the effects of GAL/TAN, especially since the correlation between left/right and GAL/TAN for regionalist political parties is 0.76. The biggest visual difference is that extreme left-wing parties tend to be Euroskeptical, while extreme GAL parties are as supportive of European integration as the centrist (on GAL/TAN) regionalist parties.

---

[10] For political parties in Western Europe, left/right ideology and GAL/TAN are correlated at the 0.78 level. For regionalist parties, the correlation is even higher (0.92). Thus, the distinction between the two dimensions may not be quite as clear-cut as outlined. But the findings for ideology, extremism, and GAL/TAN are robust if both variables are included (Marks et al. 2006).

[11] The scatterplot does not feature the party positions in 1996 because the survey did not yet collect these data.

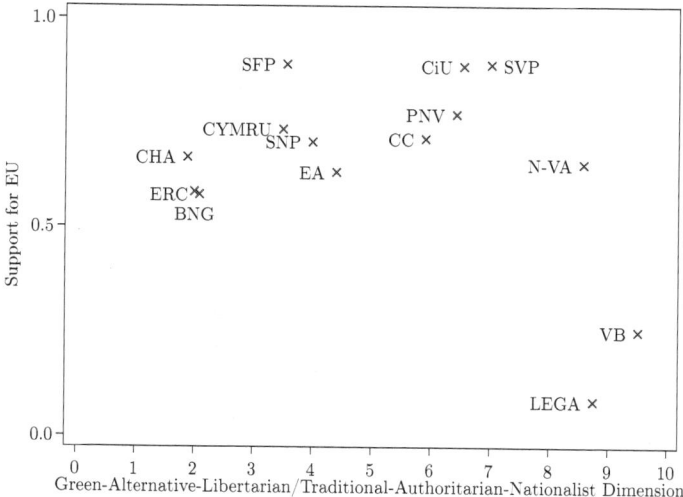

Figure 4.4: Regionalist Support for the EU, across GAL/TAN

Because Figure 4.3 and Figure 4.4 rely on aggregated data at the party family level, the descriptive statistics and figures do not answer whether variation among regionalist political party positions occurs across issue areas or across time. Using CHES expert evaluations, in Figure 4.5, I focus on six of the electorally larger regionalist political parties, at least in their own region, and show trends for position on European integration and salience of the issue.

For the Convergence and Union (CiU), Francophone Democratic Front (FDF) (through 1999), and the Flemish People's Union or New Flemish Alliance (VU/N-VA), little variation in party position or salience occurs across time. The Swedish People's Party (SFP) became more supportive of European integration between 1988 and 1992. Since Finland was not yet a member of the European Union in that period, it is not altogether surprising the party's position was in flux. Experts perceive the Scottish National Party as being less supportive in the new millennium; however, this decrease must be weighed against the extreme levels of support in 1999. More recent numbers actually seem more in line with the historical position of the SNP, with 1999 as an

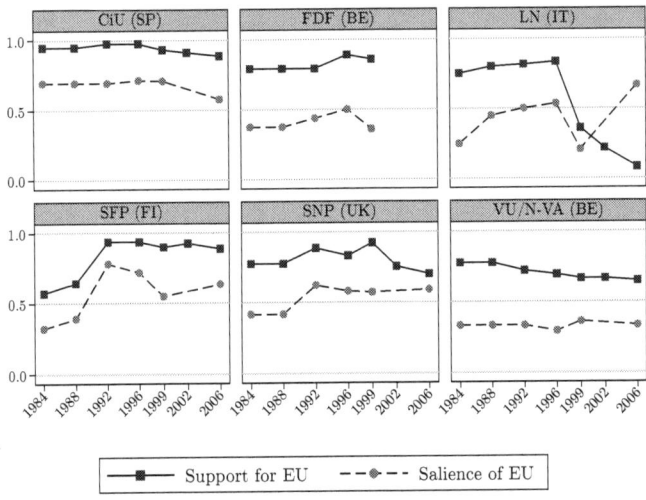

Figure 4.5: Trends in EU Support and Salience, by Party

outlier.

But Lega Nord (LN) did experience a significant and persistent decrease in support between 1996 and 1999. Internally, this shift from relatively pro-EU to increasingly Euroskeptic attitudes toward the EU occurred with some degree of internal dissent.[12] Averaged across all other years, CHES experts evaluated Lega Nord as somewhere between complete unity and minor internal dissent over the EU issue (1.82), and well within the average level of dissent for all parties (mean of 1.7, standard deviation of 0.46); however, in 1999, dissent surged to 2.4 (between minor dissent and significant dissent). By 2006, internal dissent over the EU fell to below pre-1999 levels (1.65), while support for the EU plummeted to 0.08, the lowest of any regionalist party in the CHES data.

As Figure 4.5 shows, when Lega Nord first became Euroskeptical,

---

[12] In addition to position and salience, CHES asks experts to evaluate the internal dissent over support for the EU, with scores ranging from complete unity (1), minor dissent (2), significant dissent (3), party evenly split (4), and the leadership opposed by a majority of the party (5). In 2006, the scale is 0–10, so I rescaled it to match the earlier surveys.

the issue was simply not as salient for Lega Nord as for other regionalist political parties, perhaps because the leadership feared highlighting an issue that the party was internally divided over. By 2006, as dissent fell and opinion within Lega Nord had consolidated behind the leadership, Lega Nord's position became more negative and dramatically more salient, suggesting that experts perceived Lega Nord as not just being Euroskeptic but highlighting that issue. At a 2014 rally in Lombardy, for instance, Lega Nord MEP Matteo Salvini wore a shirt with "Basta Euro" or "Enough of the Euro"; however, as McDonnell (2014) suggests, it is still not a primary issue for the party as it is for other fringe parties like UKIP in the United Kingdom. Barring this exception, the attitudes toward European integration among some of the major regionalist political parties seem remarkably consistent over time, at least as evaluated by the experts of the Chapel Hill Expert Survey.

In addition to time, it may be that variation in position for regionalist political parties occurs across issue areas. For instance, Marks, Wilson, and Ray (2002, 587) contend that regionalist political parties will be strongly in favor of economic integration but only moderately supportive of political integration based on cleavage theory. To analyze the consistency in pro–European Union attitudes across issue areas, I consider the party positions on three aspects of European integration—a general EU question, powers of the European Parliament, and the internal market—in Figure 4.6. In the most recent surveys, CHES experts evaluate party positions on multiple EU issues, including the powers of the European Parliament, internal market, and several policies, including employment, agricultural, cohesion, environmental, asylum, and foreign. None of the questions directly corresponds to either economic or political integration per se, but the internal market question seems closest to "negative integration" and the EP question may proxy for extending political integration.[13]

---

[13]The wording of the questions is as follows:

General EU "First, how would you describe the general position on European integration that the party's leadership has taken over the course of 2002?"

European Parliament "First, take the position of the party leadership on the powers of the European Parliament. Some parties want more powers for the European Parliament. Other parties are opposed to expanding further the powers of the European Parliament. Where does the leadership of the

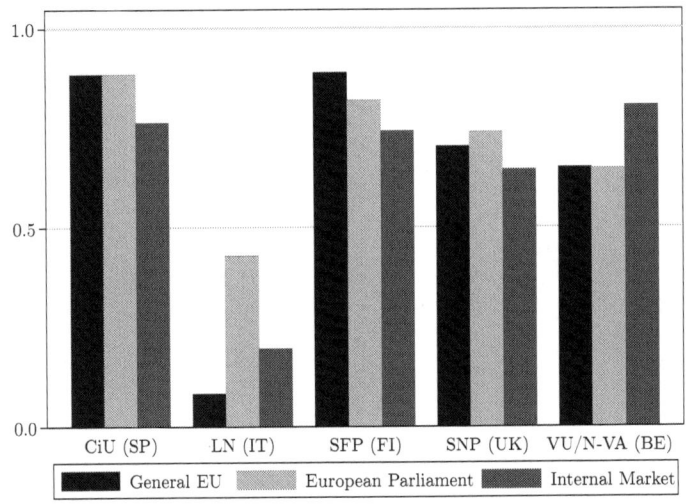

Figure 4.6: Support for European Union in 2006, by Party and Issue

Not surprisingly, for all parties in Western Europe, these three aspects of integration are highly correlated.[14] For example, for all parties, the correlation coefficient between the European Parliament and internal market questions is 0.58. Among regionalist parties, though,

> following parties stand?"
>
> **Internal Market** "Next consider the internal market. Some parties wish to strengthen EU powers to eliminate market barriers (i.e., free movement of goods, services, capital, and labor). Other parties oppose strengthening EU powers in this area. Where does the leadership of the following parties stand?"

Answers for these questions range from:

> 1 = strongly opposes
> 2 = opposes
> 3 = somewhat opposed
> 4 = neutral
> 5 = somewhat in favor
> 6 = favors
> 7 = strongly favors

As noted above, the responses are rescaled to range from 0 to 1.

[14] General support for the EU has a correlation of 0.8 or higher with support for European Parliament and the Internal Market if all parties or just regionalist parties are considered.

these correlations are even higher, with a correlation coefficient of 0.65 between EP and internal market positions. This high correlation suggests that, for these parties at least, support for political and economic integration go hand in hand. These simple statistics suggest that regionalist political parties are generally as consistent in their support for European integration across issue area as they are across time and space.[15]

Among major regionalist political parties,[16] the Catalan Convergence and Union supports political integration more than market integration. Except for the Belgian VU/N-VA, the parties have more diffuse support (general EU) and specific support for the European Parliament than for market integration. The differences (and the sample size) are relatively small, though, so it would be imprudent to conclude regionalist political parties are less supportive of market integration than political integration. The data suggest that regionalist political parties are generally consistent in their support for European integration across issue area as they are across time and space.

This descriptive data analysis yields several conclusions. First, I find additional support for the viability argument in *Hypothesis 4.1*. With the notable exceptions of Lega Nord and Herri Batasuna, I do not find evidence to support the main alternative hypothesis (*Hypothesis 4.2*) that regionalist political parties seek to increase electoral support by mobilizing anti-EU sentiments. Second, I find further support for the U-curve relationship between left/right ideology and the EU found in the literature and show that these factors appear to explain variation within the regionalist political party family. Finally, I find little evidence to show that support for integration among regionalist political parties significantly varies across time, region or issue area. Exceptions, such as Lega Nord, are explained by other critical factors, such as left/right ideological extremism.

However, while these simple graphs and statistics provide a useful starting point, in the next section, we reconsider the regionalists' attitudes toward the EU using regression analysis.

---

[15] Within the regionalist party family, the standard deviation for general support is 0.20 while the standard deviations for support for Internal Market and the European Parliament are 0.14.

[16] The internal market evaluations are only available for 2006 when FDF was not in the survey. So that party is excluded from the figure.

4.4 Analysis

To more systematically test the two hypotheses, I replicate an Ordinary Least Squares (OLS) regression analysis on the attitudes of European party families toward European integration in Table 4.2 (Marks, Wilson, and Ray 2002). The model is fairly straightforward, with dummy variables included to explain variation among the party families, countries, and years. The other explanatory variables are Median Supporter position, Left/Right Extremism, Electoral Support, and Government Participation. Following Marks, Wilson, and Ray (2002), Median Supporter position is interpolated from Eurobarometer data as the median position of self-identified party supporters. Higher Median Supporter position should be positively related to party position, either because parties cue or follow their voters (Carrubba 2001). In the model, Marks, Wilson, and Ray (2002, 588) operationalize mainstream parties in three different ways, in terms of left/right ideological position, vote shares, and government inclusion. Left/right extremism is measured as the squared distance between the particular party's left/right position and the average position for all parties in the same country-year and is expected to be negatively related to support for European integration (i.e., the further from the center of the ideological space, on either the left or the right, the less support for the EU.). Electoral Support is simply the party's vote share in the national election prior to the survey year while Government Participation is a dummy variable for whether the party has ever been in a government coalition since 1965.[17] Both of these variables are predicted to be positively related to support for integration (Marks, Wilson, and Ray 2002). These predictions follow the theoretical and empirical literature on party positioning on European integration.

---

[17] Certainly, the government participation variable is a blunt instrument, with parties in government 3/50 years counted the same as parties in government 40/50 years. But in terms of the marginalized parties theory put forward by Marks, Wilson, and Ray (2002), the crucial factor is whether parties are even plausible potential coalition partners. Since the theoretical interest of this chapter is party family, though, I will simply replicate their analysis.

Table 4.2: OLS Analysis of Party EU Positions, 1984–1996

Independent Variables	Model 1 1984–1996 b	(S.E.)	Model 2 b	(S.E.)
Party Family				
Extreme Right	−0.08	(0.05)	−0.01	(0.05)
Conservative	0.15***	(0.05)	0.33***	(0.05)
Liberal	0.36***	(0.04)	0.50***	(0.04)
Christian Democratic	0.36***	(0.05)	0.47***	(0.05)
Social Democratic	0.29***	(0.04)	0.40***	(0.04)
Green	0.05	(0.05)	0.19***	(0.05)
Regionalist	0.29***	(0.05)	0.38***	(0.05)
Protestant	0.07	(0.05)	0.10	(0.05)
Agrarian	0.19**	(0.06)	0.34***	(0.07)
National Location				
Austria	−0.07	(0.06)	−0.04	(0.08)
Belgium	−0.07*	(0.03)	0.07	(0.04)
Germany	−0.15***	(0.04)	−0.01	(0.05)
Greece	−0.01	(0.07)	0.14	(0.09)
France	−0.21***	(0.04)	−0.08	(0.04)
Finland	−0.10	(0.05)	−0.08	(0.06)
Ireland	−0.25***	(0.04)	−0.12*	(0.05)
Italy	−0.17***	(0.04)	0.06	(0.04)
Netherlands	−0.22***	(0.04)	−0.06	(0.04)
Portugal	−0.28***	(0.07)	−0.14	(0.09)
Spain	−0.12*	(0.05)	0.07	(0.06)
Sweden	0.01	(0.05)	0.05	(0.06)
UK	−0.12**	(0.04)	−0.06	(0.05)
Left/Right Extremism	−0.60***	(0.15)	−0.92***	(0.17)
Median Supporter	0.78***	(0.07)	—	
Electoral Support	0.004***	(0.001)	0.003*	(0.001)
Govt Participation	−0.05	(0.03)	−0.02	(0.03)
1984	−0.05*	(0.02)	−0.02	(0.03)
1988	−0.04	(0.02)	0.00	(0.03)
1992	−0.05	(0.02)	−0.00	(0.03)
Constant	0.09***	(0.05)	0.42***	(0.05)
Adjusted R^2	0.80		0.70	
N	261		277	

Note: Reference values for categorical variables are: Communist/Extreme Left, Denmark, non-government party, and 1996. * $p \leq 0.05$, ** $p \leq 0.01$, *** $p \leq 0.001$

In Table 4.2, Model 1 simply replicates the Marks, Wilson, and Ray (2002) model.[18] Notably, the series of party dummies are the strongest predictors, even more than the country dummies. The rest of the variables behave as predicted, except for Government Participation, which is insignificant. Considering the high correlation between vote share and government participation, in addition to the wide array of dummy variables, this result is not surprising despite the theoretical expectations.

This model explains much of the variation in party positioning on European integration, as reflected by the high adjusted R^2; however, for the purposes of this chapter, it has a missing data problem that adversely affects regionalist parties. Median Supporter, interpolated from Eurobarometer data, hits the small niche parties hardest in terms of missing data for precisely the same reasons inferring party positions from Eurobarometer data is problematic for small parties. The individual-level survey simply does not poll enough regional respondents that favor these small parties to yield usable data. For example, this variable drops 32 percent of the cases in the 1984–1996 sample (174/545 parties), with 18 percent of these being regionalist parties, 14 percent Green parties, and 6.4 percent Radical Right. Overall, 45 percent of the regionalist parties drop from the regression model due to missing data in the Median Supporter variable.

So, to increase the number of regionalist parties in the sample, I drop this variable in Model 2 in Table 4.2. The explanatory power of the model decreases, as measured by adjusted R^2, but it is still quite high (0.70). Among the party family variables, only one change in significance occurs. The Green party dummy variable becomes significant with the exclusion of Median Supporter. As expected by Marks, Wilson, and Ray (2002, 587), the model shows that the Greens are slightly more favorable to European integration than the reference category,

---

[18] Carole Wilson graciously provided her data and code to replicate their results. The only minor difference between the replicated results, as shown in Model 1, and the original model is the sign of the Government Participation variable and the constant. I flipped the reference category in the dummy variable coding for government participation, so that 1 is government participation and 0 is non-government party, for ease of interpretation. In the original, the coefficient represents non-government parties with government parties as the reference category. Since it is statistically insignificant in their model, the point is minor, but, considering the match of the rest of the replication, worth mentioning. Also, I recoded the Irish Sinn Féin to not be included as a regionalist party.

the Extreme Left or Communists. Besides the Green variable, several country and year variables become insignificant, though generally of the same sign as in Model 1, but these variables have only minor effects on the dependent variable vis-à-vis the party family variables anyway. Importantly for this chapter, the regionalist party family variable remains positive and statistically significant with more cases.

In Table 4.3 Model 3, I extend the time series using more recent expert surveys (Steenbergen and Marks 2007; Hooghe et al. 2010).[19] In general, the results of this model look very similar to those from the earlier period. Recalling that the reference category is the Extreme Left, the significant negative coefficient on the Radical Right family variable suggests that either the Extreme Left have moderated their position or the Radical Right has become more extreme. Or as Figure 4.1 graphically shows, both may have occurred. Another difference is that the Government Participation variable is now significant in the predicted positive direction. This result bolsters the theoretical arguments regarding mainstream parties being more supportive of European integration than fringe or outsider parties (Taggart 1998; Marks, Wilson, and Ray 2002).

Although the regression results confirm the relative stability of the coefficients with the addition of new cases in the time series, they are difficult to interpret considering the number of variables in the model and the need to compare to the reference categories. Further, the dummy variable coefficients do not incorporate the national (country or year) or electoral (Electoral Support, Government Participation, Left/Right Extremism) context in which each party resides. Thus, to compare the effects of the party dummy variables, and to rank order them simultaneously, I predicted party positions on European integration based on Table 4.3. Averaged by party family and across years, I present these predicted values in Figure 4.7.

---

[19] Beyond these two extensions, I considered other robustness tests of the Marks, Wilson, and Ray (2002) model. Ordinary Least Squares (OLS) assumes independence across units, but this is unlikely to be the case considering the importance of national context. Hence, I ran the model with robust standard errors, clustered at the country level. Also, analysis of the dependent variable in a histogram shows that it may be censored at the endpoints. To correct for this problem, I ran Model 3 again with Tobit. The results were robust across these alternative specifications so I presented the simpler OLS results for comparability with the replicated model.

Table 4.3: OLS Analysis of Party EU Positions, 1984–2006

Independent Variables	Model 3 (1984–2006) b	(S.E.)
Party Family		
Extreme Right	−0.07	(0.04)
Conservative	0.27***	(0.03)
Liberal	0.48***	(0.03)
Christian Democratic	0.44***	(0.04)
Social Democratic	0.34***	(0.03)
Green	0.28***	(0.03)
Regionalist	0.32***	(0.03)
Protestant	0.11*	(0.04)
Agrarian	0.17***	(0.05)
National Location		
Austria	0.03	(0.04)
Belgium	0.02	(0.04)
Germany	0.03	(0.04)
Greece	0.09	(0.05)
France	−0.07	(0.04)
Finland	−0.09*	(0.04)
Ireland	−0.08	(0.04)
Italy	0.07	(0.04)
Netherlands	−0.05	(0.04)
Portugal	−0.02	(0.05)
Spain	0.17**	(0.04)
Sweden	−0.07	(0.04)
UK	0.01	(0.04)
Left/Right Extremism	−0.01***	(0.00)
Electoral Support	0.001	(0.001)
Govt Participation	0.14***	(0.02)
1984	−0.07*	(0.03)
1988	−0.04	(0.03)
1992	−0.00	(0.03)
1999	−0.01	(0.03)
2002	0.01	(0.03)
2006	0.01	(0.03)
Constant	0.31***	(0.04)
Adjusted R^2	0.58	
N	670	

Note: Reference values are Communist/Extreme Left, Denmark, non-government, and 1996. * $p \leq 0.05$, ** $p \leq 0.01$, *** $p \leq 0.001$

Euroskeptic and Europhile Regionalists 111

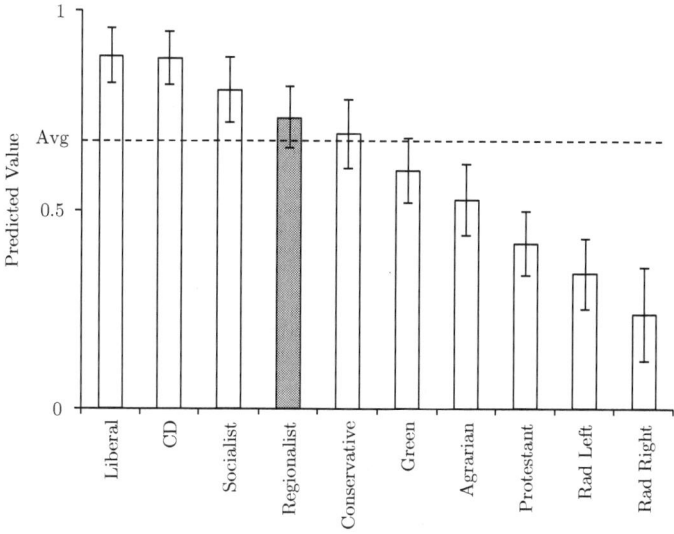

Figure 4.7: Predicted Support for EU, by Party Family

This figure clearly demonstrates that, ceteris paribus, regionalist political parties are highly supportive of the European Union and hold similar attitudes as the mainstream parties, though less supportive than the Liberals and Christian Democrats. In fact, regionalist parties are more pro-European than the mainstream Conservative parties, though the standard deviations suggest caution in over-interpreting that finding. Based on Table 4.3, none of the other fringe parties are above the EU mean. The whisker, which reflects the standard deviation around the mean, shows that the regionalists are as coherent as many other families, and significantly more coherent than the radical right, another niche party family. Certainly, Euroskeptic outliers exist, such as Herri Batasuna in the Basque region of Spain. But Herri Batasuna is the most extreme left-wing regionalist party in Europe and the most left-wing party in Spain. Thus, Left/Right Extremism, one of the included predictors, explains this outlier.

Because the previous analysis relies on aggregated data at the party family level and pooled time-series data, respectively, these results do not conclusively answer whether variation among regionalist political party positions occurs over time or across issue areas. To analyze the robustness of the regionalist party family dummy variable over time, I split the sample by survey year and ran separate regressions for each year, based on Model 3 without the year dummy variables.[20] In each regression, the regionalist variable is significant and positive from 1984 through 2006, except for 2002. In this case, as suggested in Figure 4.1, regionalist and the reference category, Extreme Left parties, are closer together than in previous years, yielding a positive but statistically insignificant coefficient. But the predicted values still rank the regionalists as more supportive of the EU in 2002 than the Extreme Left parties.

More significantly, though, the rankings based on predicted values remain remarkably consistent. In each case, the regionalist family is the fourth most pro-EU party group, after Liberals, Social Democrats and Christian Democrats. Also, in each year, regionalists are above the EU average for all parties. Relative to other fringe parties, this consistently strong support demonstrates that the regionalist party family remains remarkably consistent in their Europhile positions over time.

This data analysis yields a simple conclusion. I find that the regionalist party family is in fact still pro-EU, supporting *Hypothesis 4.1*, though the support for the EU among regionalists is less uniform than in previous analysis (Jolly 2007). I do not find evidence to support the main alternative hypothesis according to which regionalist political parties seek to increase electoral support by mobilizing anti-EU sentiments (*Hypothesis 4.2*).

Although this analysis establishes the generally pro-EU nature of regionalist parties, it does not clarify the causal mechanism underlying this relationship. In the next section of the chapter, I explore this further with a detailed case study of Scottish National Party rhetoric.

---

[20]These models and predicted value tables are available upon request or are replicable from the expert survey data, simply by using Model 3 and splitting the sample by year.

4.5 THE SNP AND THE "INDEPENDENCE IN EUROPE" POLICY

To complement the cross-sectional analysis above, I consider the official positions of the Scottish Nation Party on European integration. The SNP provides fruitful ground for this research because it is not only one of the more electorally successful regionalist political parties, but also one of the few that actively promotes independence. Within Western Europe, Scotland also stands apart as having one of the longest traditions of a regionalist autonomy movement. Analysis of this single case may not confirm or disconfirm the main hypotheses, but it allows me to conduct a more nuanced evaluation of the SNP position toward the EU and to flesh out the general findings discussed above.

In the following pages, I analyze all election manifestos of the Scottish National Party from 1974 through 2010 (Scottish National Party 1974a, b, c, 1976, 1979, 1983, 1987, 1990, 1992, 1997, 1999, 2001, 2003, 2005a, b, 2010), along with much earlier documents (Scottish National Party 1947, 1949) as reference. These manifestos represent the evolving official positions of the Scottish National Party, as projected to the public during election years.

Consistent from the *Policy of the Scottish National Party* of 1947 to the most recent election manifestos, the Scottish National Party's main identifiable goal is independence from the United Kingdom.[21] In the *Policy of the SNP* (1947) and the *Constitution and Rules of the SNP* (1949), the aim is explicitly stated: "Self-Government for Scotland—that is, the restoration of Scottish National Sovereignty by the establishment of a democratic Scottish government, freely elected by the Scottish people...." At this early stage, and in the aftermath of World War II, the realization that independent countries cannot escape international ties and commitments is apparent (Scottish National Party 1947, 4). But, realizing that isolationism was not a viable strategy even at this early stage, the SNP's international concerns centered on the British Isles for most issue areas rather than Europe.

Between the 1940s and the 1970s, the SNP's position on a "European Union" shifted from a positive view to a negative one (Lynch 1996,

---

[21]The most recent SNP manifestos are available at the SNP website (www.snp.org). SNP headquarters generously provided copies of the manifestos from 1979 to 1992. Earlier official documents were obtained directly from the National Library of Scotland.

27–30).²² In the 1960s and 1970s, the negative linkage can be traced to a lack of representation and fear of economic dislocation (see, for example, Scottish National Party (1976)). They feared that a common market would hurt Scotland and argued that Scotland needed independence prior to joining in order to negotiate the best possible deal for Scotland (Lynch 1996, 31).

In the 1974 pamphlet *SNP&You*, the SNP complained particularly that the EU was "highly bureaucratic, centralist, and undemocratic—remote from the control of ordinary people" (Scottish National Party 1974c, 6). In fact, they derisively labeled the Common Market as yet another foreign "centralist empire" for whom Scotland's interests are sacrificed (Scottish National Party 1974a, 5). In this period, the SNP position could be characterized as hard Euroskeptic, which provides some suggestive support for *Hypothesis 4.2*. Hepburn (2010) argues that the SNP Euroskepticism in the early period of European integration could be found among other regionalist parties as well, include the SVP in Italy, and the BNG and PA in Spain.

As an alternative, the SNP proposed an association of British states and an agreement with the European Union along the lines of Norway's that "encourag[ed] trade but maintain[ed] genuine sovereignty" (Scottish National Party 1974c, 6). Lack of representation in the European Union, of both Scotland as a nation and its citizens, is clearly at the heart of SNP opposition to the common market (Scottish National Party 1974b, 7). In terms of regional viability argument, throughout 1974 (Scottish National Party 1974a, b, c), the SNP attempted to convince voters that Scotland was self-sufficient, thanks in no small part to the discovery of oil, and would be better equipped to promote economic growth as an independent country than as a region of the UK.

In the 1976 manifesto, *Scotland's Future*, which laid out the SNP case for self-government, the SNP acknowledged that isolationism was not a viable strategy and that nations must yield a certain amount of sovereignty to promote peace and stability (Scottish National Party 1976, 3). Nevertheless, they continued to oppose British membership in the European Union despite the new status quo of membership. The SNP's arguments focused on the "centralist thinking inherent in the

---

²²Over time, the nomenclature of the European Union as used by the Scottish National Party changes from the European Economic Community or the Common Market to the European Community to the European Union. For ease of reading, I use European Union throughout.

Treaty of Rome," a lack of representation of Scotland, and on the belief that the Common Market was not necessarily beneficial for Scottish citizens (Scottish National Party 1976, 11).

This rhetoric is very consistent with the expectations of *Hypothesis 4.2*. But, since Labour was pro–European Union and electorally dominant in Scotland, it also corresponds to the strategic theories regarding fringe parties, which suggest that fringe parties will take extreme positions to differentiate themselves from their more popular competitors. Further, at this early stage of European integration, the issue was simply not particularly salient for the SNP (Lynch 1996, 21).

By 1979, the SNP was softening its anti–European Union stance. Complaints about the European Union were more specific in the 1979 election manifesto, suggesting a shift from hard to soft Euroskepticism. Consistent with later manifestos, the SNP complained that the European Union has tried to "virtually take over Scotland's fishing grounds" (Scottish National Party 1979, 5). The SNP also complained about unfair subsidized agricultural competition from other European Union member countries (Scottish National Party 1979, 8). Nevertheless, the party endorsed negotiations with the European Union to resolve these complaints and guarantee Scottish control of energy resources and fishing limits (Scottish National Party 1979, 28). Only if such negotiations failed would the SNP oppose membership in a referendum campaign.

Despite more intra-party dissent over European integration in the early 1980s than in the 1970s (Lynch 1996), they maintained the stance in the 1983 manifesto that upon independence they would immediately call a referendum on membership and urge a "no" vote (Scottish National Party 1983). Their main complaints concerned the Common Fisheries Policy and other agricultural matters. In the 1983 manifesto, they complained that United Kingdom had "sold Scottish fishermen short" on the Common Fisheries Policy. Again, a lack of representation for Scotland in the EU contributed to their disaffection.

During the 1980s, several factors conspired to increase support for the EU, both in the SNP and among other regionalist parties (cf. Hepburn 2010, 216). As Hepburn (2010, 190–191) points out, the EU underwent many changes in the late 1980s, with the Single European Act, the reform of European structural funds, and a new vision of a social Europe. In particular, regionalists enthusiastically endorsed the new rules favoring the protection of minority languages and cultures

(Hepburn 2010, 190–191).

Highlighting these structural trends, the 1987 party manifesto shows a remarkably different stance on European integration (Scottish National Party 1987). While the SNP continued to warn against centralist tendencies in Brussels, they recommended membership in the European Union. Perhaps because of the major change in policy, the SNP listed several reasons why they supported membership in the European Union for an independent Scotland. Noting the influence and availability of regionalist and social funds, they demanded a direct voice within the EU, which would be achieved by independence within the European Union. Beyond securing funds and support, the SNP guaranteed protection for the fishery industry as well as other Scottish interests, such as agriculture and industry (Scottish National Party 1987; Sillars 1986, 187). Finally, a seat at the table would allow Scotland to contribute more to European affairs (Scottish National Party 1987).

In addition to these reasons, party elites saw the issue as a way to distance themselves from the Tories (cf. Hoppe 2007, 21), a sharp contrast to the strategic logic of anti–European Union rhetoric in the 1970s (Lynch 1996, 38–39). Utilizing the viability logic, Jim Sillars, a former SNP MP, argued that only by endorsing a strategy of "Independence in Europe" could the SNP credibly argue that independence from the UK was a viable option (Sillars 1986, 186). This policy would guarantee mobility of labor and trade between Scotland and England after independence, thus negating a key argument of independence opponents. These factors contributed to the SNP's newfound support for European integration.

The SNP's policy of "Independence in Europe" was in full swing by the local elections of 1990, with the 1990 manifesto making it clear that the EU is at the heart of the SNP independence strategy: "Scotland's future lies as an independent member of the European Community. ... [W]e can and must achieve the premier league status of an independent and equal partner in the European family of nations" (Scottish National Party 1990). More recent manifestos continue the push for "Independence in Europe," including a defense of the plausibility of this policy, in which they claimed that legal opinion supports their assumption that an independent Scotland would continue to be part of the EU, as a successor state (Scottish National Party 1992, 1997).

But it is in the 1997 manifesto where the viability argument becomes most evident (Scottish National Party 1997). Noting the success of small European countries and of small countries in general ("25 out of the 35 most prosperous nations are small nations!"), along with a presumed favorable distribution of North Sea oil revenue after independence, the SNP highlights that an independent Scotland would be the eighth richest nation in the world.

In contrast to the optimism sparked by changes in the 1980s, though, the EU at the turn of the century presented a less rosy picture. Hepburn (2010, 200) notes that several factors, including the perceived failure of the Committee of the Regions, the continued centralization of powers, and the failure of the regions to gain more strength in the constitutional draft forced many regionalist parties to reevaluate their position toward the EU. In related work, Tatham and Bauer (2011) survey regional administrators to explore how they view the EU. Building on recent work by Hepburn (2008) and Elias (2008, 2009), Tatham and Bauer (2011) challenge the idea of a general pro-EU feeling among regionalists, with separatists showing more Euroskepticism than other regionalists; in particular, they argue that some regions feel that Brussels itself is starting to encroach upon regional prerogatives.[23]

The rhetoric of the SNP also reflects this shift. In the 2001 manifesto, the SNP continues to support membership in the EU, but also rejects the possibility of a super-state headquartered in Brussels (Scottish National Party 2001). In this manifesto especially, the European Union receives much more attention than it had in previous manifestos. While the "SNP stands for Scotland in Europe" and they admitted real advantages in membership, the SNP outlined areas in which they would not support further policy shifts to the European level, including natural resources and taxation.

This shift was noticed by the experts of the Chapel Hill Expert Survey, which reflects downward shifts in the 2000s among all regionalist parties (Figure 4.1) and particularly for the Scottish National Party (Figure 4.5); however, in direct contrast to the earliest time periods, the SNP of the 2000s is by no means a hard Euroskeptic. They have very specific complaints, regarding items such as natural resources and the constitution. Within the SNP, internal dissent increased over what kind of Europe the SNP favored, whether centralized or federal or con-

---

[23] In the SNP case, there is evidence of this line of thinking in Jim Sillars' open letter to the SNP leadership (2011).

federal (Hepburn 2010, 76–77, Hoppe 2007, 21). Later in the 2000s, the SNP's stance toward the EU hardened, with greater emphasis on defending fishing interests against the EU and the European fisheries policy (Hepburn 2010, 91).

Significantly, though, in the 2000s, they pay great attention to their potential representation effectiveness within the EU as an independent Scotland compared to a region of the UK, in terms of Commissioners, members of the European parliament, and the Council of Ministers (Scottish National Party 2001, 2003). This lack of representation at the EU level became more significant in the run-up to the EU constitution. In fact, the SNP opposed the constitution in part because it lacked effective representation on one of its key issues, Common Fisheries Policy (Scottish National Party 2005a). But, despite this clear shift in attitudes, they still favored membership in the early 2000s; more importantly for this chapter, they continued to view the EU as a necessary part of the independence process.

In the 2010 general election, the Scottish National Party won 20 percent of the Scottish vote, its best result in several elections, and the SNP followed that up by winning a majority of seats in the 2011 Scottish parliamentary elections (Carrell 2011). In both elections, the SNP ran a campaign focused on independence. In particular, the SNP campaigned heavily for a referendum on independence, which was held in September 2014, but failed to receive the support of a majority of Scots. The SNP manifesto sets a clear tone of optimism about an independent Scotland, its disaffection with the UK, and its viability within the EU. The manifesto argues for fiscal autonomy largely on the basis of the efficiency of smaller, more homogeneous, political units.

> The more responsibilities our parliament has, the more we can achieve and the more effectively we can respond to local concerns and community campaigns.... Others believe the Parliament can best serve Scotland by taking on substantial new responsibilities including over our economy and public finances. This would enable Scotland to respond more effectively to economic pressures, and speed our nation's recovery. And, of course, with independence, Scotland would be able to achieve even more. (Scottish National Party 2010, 17)

Further, the SNP makes clear that it is London who is the enemy, not the EU: "People recognise the areas where Scotland today is held back by decisions taken in London ..." (Scottish National Party 2010, 17). It is also abundantly clear, though, that the SNP politicians understand they need to persuade voters of the economic viability of an independent Scotland and that disruption would be minimal. For this purpose, they use the EU: "It is about creating a new partnership of equals—a social union to replace the current political union. Scotland and England will share the same Queen, the same currency and as members of the EU there will be open borders, shared rights, free trade and extensive co-operation" (Scottish National Party 2010, 22).

Of course, the SNP are not unfettered Europhiles; they are instrumental in their support. In this manifesto, they continue to lodge complaints against the Common Fisheries Policy and their underrepresentation at the EU level, especially on issues like fisheries policy (Scottish National Party 2010, 27). In contrast with the Euro-enthusiasm of manifestos in the 1980s and 1990s, the SNP's discussion of the EU in the 2010 manifesto is muted, a signal that they know they are walking a fine line between growing Euroskepticism in the UK voting population and a need to persuade voters that Scotland is viable.

Over time, the official SNP position on European integration evolved from opposition to support. Throughout the era of support, the SNP continued to point out areas of disagreement with the EU. This finding is consistent with the recent work of Elias (2009), who argues that many regionalists are more supportive of the EU as an abstract idea than as a concrete reality, or Hoppe (2007), who sees many regionalists as only instrumental Europeans, not Europhiles. But rather than return to opposition to the EU, they focused on the ability of an independent Scotland to challenge those policies only as a full-fledged independent member of the European Union. Consistent with the viability logic, they argue that small states can succeed and even thrive in an interdependent Europe, providing support for *Hypothesis 4.1*.

4.6 Discussion

In Chapter 3, I demonstrated that deeper European integration increased electoral support for regionalist political parties; unfortunately, in that analysis, I could not discriminate between the two causal mechanisms: fear or viability. In this chapter, I disentangle whether this effect can be attributed to Euroskepticism or Euro-enthusiasm.

For earlier time periods, it was clearer the regionalist parties were consistently Europhiles across regions, time, and issue area (Jolly 2007). As the EU deepened in the 2000s, though, the evaluation must be more nuanced. As Lynch and de Winter (2008) argue, whereas the EU certainly enhanced the political opportunity structure of regionalists prior to 2000, the widening and deepening of the EU since then has changed the dynamic.

In recent years, there is increasing evidence that some regionalists are less enthusiastic about particular aspects of integration, as Elias (2008, 2009) argues. Several major regionalist parties, such as Lega Nord and Herri Batasuna, are at the very least "soft Euroskeptics."[24] Other parties, such as the SNP, express more soft Euroskepticism in the 2000s than they did during the 1980s and 1990s. Many other groups suffer from internal disagreements over Europe. For example, moderate Basque nationalists support the EU while more radical nationalists view Brussels as a threat to the Basque nation (Keating 2001*b*, 33). In general, though, Lynch (1998, 198) finds that the regionalist parties that form the European Free Alliance, a party in the European Parliament, support the principles of European integration, while remaining suspicious of particular aspects of integration. Similarly, Jensen and Spoon (2010) find that regionalist MEPs tend to vote in a pro-EU manner during European Parliament votes.

The regionalist party family is not a monolithic bloc, but simply a collection of parties grouped together because they share a main goal of increased autonomy for their regions. Strategically, the regionalists should utilize the EU differently depending on the context, or as Hepburn and Elias (2011, 877) argue in the cases of Corsica and Sardinia, these parties change their positions on the EU in direct response to opportunities to enhance their territorial autonomy. In Belgium, for instance, Laible (2001) focuses on the Vlaams Bloc and demonstrates that, while they are not blindly Euro-enthusiastic, they recognize the importance of the structure of the EU if Flanders were to become in-

---

[24]Liang (2007) argues that even Lega Nord's position should be considered soft Euroskepticism: not anti-Europe per se, but certainly not supportive of the direction the EU is going. Hoppe (2007, 22) seems to agree with this assessment, categorizing Lega Nord as instrumental Europeans; similarly, McDonnell (2014) points out that Lega Nord's 2014 EP manifesto discusses reform of the European Commission and Parliament rather than exit.

dependent. This logic supports the Viability Theory developed in this book.

In conclusion, regionalist parties are supportive of the European project, unlike other niche parties in Western Europe. They are generally pro–European Union across time and issue area, though they are by no means blindly or uniformly pro-Europe. The existence of this Europhile niche party family contradicts the expectations of the mainstream versus fringe party theories on support for European integration. These conclusions are consistent with the theoretical predictions of this chapter and earlier work on cleavage theory (Marks, Wilson, and Ray 2002), as well as the qualitative work on regionalist political parties (Lynch 1996; Kurzer 1997).

But why is this party family different from other fringe parties? In the case of Scotland, regionalist elites clearly favor European integration because it creates a more favorable political opportunity structure for their sub-national autonomy movements. This finding bolsters earlier work on Scottish citizens that finds Europhiles as well as instrumental Europeans among the population (Haesly 2001). In his Q-sort experiment, Haesly finds some Scots to be Europhiles, or to have a European self-identity, while others were merely instrumental Europeans. As with the Scottish National Party, support among instrumental European Scots derives from the perception that European integration delivers economic benefits or potentially even provides an opportunity for Scotland to be an independent nation (Haesly 2001). Both the statistical results and the analysis of Scottish National Party rhetoric confirm that regionalist parties may also be fairly characterized as instrumental Europeans, if not Europhiles.

A supranational organization and sub-national autonomy movements may seem strange bedfellows, but instrumentally their interests align. Regionalist elites will continue to utilize European integration to increase the legitimacy and validity of their movements while, in a context of constitutional crisis at the European Union level, Eurofederalists will no doubt appreciate support from an unlikely source; however, the evidence in this chapter suggests that the regionalist support should not be taken for granted. So long as the EU represents a source of increased viability for the movements, regionalists are likely to support the project. But if structural changes in the EU occur that make Brussels more of a threat to regionalists, then support will no doubt decay.[25]

In the next chapter, I shift the attention from elites to citizens, evaluating whether the relationship between deeper European integration and increased electoral success of regionalist political parties can be attributed to the logic of the Viability Theory.

---

[25] While official SNP policy supports membership in the EU if Scotland becomes independent, debate exists. As Jim Sillars (2011), one of the original architects of the SNP policy of "Independence in Europe," argues in an open letter to the SNP leader Alex Salmond, if the EU is no longer a useful strategic tool for regionalist parties because it represents a bigger centralizing threat than central states, then parties like the SNP should simply "ditch the EU." Instead, Sillars urges Scotland to consider membership in the European Free Trade Agreement (EFTA) as an alternative. Significantly for the theory developed in this book, even critics of the EU within regionalist parties understand that autarkic independence is not a viable option. Rather, small states, like Scotland, look to broader regional organizations to persuade voters that their region is viable.

CHAPTER 5

Public Support for the EU and Decentralization

BETWEEN 1979 AND 1997, Scottish public support for European integration increased by 25 percent (Miller and Brand 1981; Jowell, Heath, and Curtice 1998), while support for European integration among all Europeans dropped nearly 14 percent (Schmitt and Scholz 2005). At the same time, Scottish public support for independence also increased dramatically, from 6.9 percent in 1979 to 34.3 percent in 1997. In addition, as early as 1997, a majority of Scottish citizens thought Scotland would be completely independent within 20 years (Brown, McCrone, and Patterson 1999, 147), while 2007 opinion polls showed that more than half of Scottish respondents favored Scottish independence (Keating 2009, 45).[1] The 2011 SNP victory in the Scottish Parliamentary elections suggests a referendum on independence is quickly approaching (Carrell 2011). While the European Union (EU) deepens, the United Kingdom itself seems ever more likely to fragment, or, at the very least, devolve further.

Are these two trends linked? Regionalists, resentful of centralization and threats of homogenization, could either perceive a deeper European Union as yet another threat to their culture or as an ally in their broader bargaining game with the state. If regionalists view the EU as a threat, then they should be skeptical of European integration, especially regarding political integration. I argue that regionalists more often view the EU as an ally, in large part by diminishing the advan-

---

[1]Opinion polls on independence fluctuate considerably. For instance, Keating (2009) mentions that half the respondents favored independence in the ICM poll from January 2007, yet only 34 percent supported independence in the Scottish Social Attitudes Survey of 2005.

tages of incorporation in a large, multi-national state. By this logic, regionalists should not only be supportive of the EU project, but they should also find autonomy itself, whether devolution or independence, a more viable and plausible prospect within a deeper European Union. Connecting the final link, as more voters find independence or devolution viable thanks to European integration, regionalist parties should reap the electoral rewards.

Extending from Gabel's initial work on public support for European integration (Gabel 1998a, b) to ever more intricate models (Steenbergen and Jones 2002; Ray 2004; Brinegar and Jolly 2005; Gabel and Scheve 2007a, b), scholars find that economic interest drives public opinion on European integration. Recently, though, scholars have focused more attention on identity to explain support for the EU (Carey 2002; McLaren 2002; Hooghe and Marks 2004, 2005, 2009). This literature tends to focus on conceptions of national or state identity, with little emphasis on sub-state, or regional, identity;[2] thus, this chapter's focus on sub-state identities supplements this literature.

Due to data limitations on regional identity questions in surveys, I both directly and indirectly evaluate whether regionalists are pro-European. In addition to using respondents' intention to vote for regionalist party as an explanatory variable for EU support, I take advantage of a sophisticated literature that evaluates whether elite cues drive public opinion on European integration (Hooghe and Marks 2005; Steenbergen, Edwards, and de Vries 2007; Gabel and Scheve 2007a, b; De Vries and Edwards 2009). After dealing with the obvious endogeneity issues between public and elite attitudes, these studies demonstrate that parties and elites do cue their supporters with either elite Euroskepticism or support. In Chapter 4, I demonstrated that, on average, the regionalist party family is pro-European and, further, regionalist parties use the EU rhetorically to strengthen their case for independence or greater autonomy. Hence, I leverage these earlier findings to evaluate the effectiveness of these cues on attitudes toward the European Union.

In many ways, this research fits neatly in Hooghe and Marks' Postfunctionalist Theory of Integration (2009). Hooghe and Marks (2009) argue that European integration is increasingly politicized and that po-

---

[2] Two recent exceptions to this generalization are Brigevich (2011) and Chacha (2013), which I discuss below.

litical party and public attitudes toward the European Union are crucial for Europeanization. Among others, they argue that this contestation over Europe is shaped by identity, in particular whether individuals hold inclusive or exclusive conceptions of national identity (Hooghe and Marks 2005, 2009). Brigevich (2011) and Chacha (2013) extend these arguments by focusing on inclusive and exclusive regional identities.[3] Brigevich (2011) isolates these two types of identity in France, using localized public opinion survey data. In many ways, her inclusive conceptualization of regional identity matches the theoretical arguments laid out in this book, while the exclusive version corresponds to some of the Euroskeptical regionalists, such as Lega Nord and Vlaams Belang, parties that blur the line between regionalist and new Radical Right. She argues, "With the growing heterogeneity and multiplicity of identities in an ever-enlarging EU, exclusive regionalists are even less likely to see their preferences addressed or realized at the European level than exclusive nationalists" (Brigevich 2011, 10). Unfortunately, the detailed analysis she undertakes in French regions is difficult to replicate in the full cross-sectional time series in my analysis, because the survey data simply do not exist. In terms of nuance, the inclusive-exclusive conception of identity is a useful framework, but empirically, if anything, aggregating all regionalists together should make this test a conservative one, working against finding a positive, significant result.

By showing that regionalist partisans (and parties) are, on average, pro-EU, this chapter bolsters these earlier findings, suggesting that the EU may find allies precisely among those groups that are commonly seen as opponents of centralization; however, the Viability Theory makes little reference to long-term attachment to the European Union. Rather, I expect the public, along with elites, to express support for the EU for instrumental and strategic reasons. Regardless, a crucial observable implication of the theory laid out in Chapter 2 is that the regionalist public should be pro-EU.

Next, I focus on the Scottish case to test the second observable implication of the theory: regionalists should find regional autonomy, even independence, more viable in a deeper European Union than in autarky. The devolution referenda in Scotland in two distinct time pe-

---

[3]Similar to Hooghe and Marks (2009) and others, Chacha (2013) finds that inclusive identity, in his case inclusive regional identity, is associated with greater support for European integration. Unlike exclusive national identity, though, exclusive regional identity is not associated with Euroskepticism.

riods provide a unique opportunity to compare attitudes and actions regarding devolution and independence. In the first referendum, a slight majority voted for devolution but the margin was not enough to overcome the electoral threshold set by Westminster by the "Cunningham Amendment." In 1997, though, the result was overwhelmingly pro-devolution. In the ethnic politics literature, cultural heterogeneity is the leading explanation of regionalist or autonomy movement support. But in the Scottish case, that factor is held constant over time.[4] Supranational integration, however, is not. With public opinion surveys from each referendum available, I show that the devolution referendum succeeded in 1997 precisely because Scots find an independent Scotland a more viable prospect. Following the logic of the Viability Theory and the elite cueing literature, I argue that deeper European integration is responsible for revised Scottish attitudes toward independence and, therefore, a positive outcome in the 1997 devolution referendum.

The chapter proceeds as follows. First, I introduce the theories that explain why regionalist party supporters should support European integration, and why European integration should increase perceptions of viability among the population. Second, I analyze public support for European integration using the Mannheim Eurobarometer Trend File (Schmitt and Scholz 2005). In the final section, using data from the 1979 Scottish Election Study and the 1997 Scottish Referendum Study (Miller and Brand 1981; Jowell, Heath, and Curtice 1998), I demonstrate that voters support devolution at higher rates, in terms of voting behavior, and they also have much more favorable attitudes toward independence from the United Kingdom, albeit within the European Union, in the survey data. This finding suggests that the increased belief in the viability of an independent Scotland within a deeper European Union encourages support for autonomy in Scotland.

With this chapter, I triangulate on the main research question with the analysis of EU support and the detailed quantitative case study of these referenda. As Chapter 2 notes, the research question does not lend itself to direct and straightforward empirical testing. Rather, I tease out numerous observable implications in a variety of research domains to maximize the observable implications and the observations available for testing. Individually, each part may be insufficient to

---

[4]In the 2001 census, 87 percent of the Scottish population was born in Scotland and 96.2 percent were born in the UK. The 2001 census data is available at www.scrol.gov.uk.

confirm the Viability Theory is at work in the European case. But collectively, I present these chapters as evidence that deeper European integration did in fact encourage regionalist mobilization, in part because European integration makes smaller more homogeneous countries more viable independent entities.

5.1 Citizens and the Viability Theory

The Viability Theory hinges on rational behavior by two sets of actors, regionalist political elites and citizens. Regionalist political elites must perceive the changing political opportunity structure and support European integration, in part as an ally against the central state. Regionalist party support for the EU is not naive or inflexible, but rather tactical or even cyclical (Hepburn 2007, 2008). The Scottish National Party, for instance, held negative attitudes toward the EU in the 1970s, only shifting in the 1980s (Jolly 2007; Hepburn 2008).[5] Nevertheless, the CHES data show the standard deviation of the family's attitude toward Europe is smaller than nearly all other party families, implying a relatively coherent party family, at least on this issue.[6]

More than just pro-European attitudes, though, the regionalist parties tend to use rhetoric that supports the causal mechanism proposed in this chapter. In tracing the official party positions of the Scottish National Party, in particular, Chapter 4 illustrates that European integration becomes an integral component in their strategy and rhetoric for independence. Similarly, the Plaid Cymru in Wales remained hostile to the EU until party elites realized the EU could "serve as a wedge between Wales and the controlling authorities in London," which in turn increased the viability of Plaid Cymru's autonomist goals (Van Morgan 2006, 277).

In addition to elites, citizens must perceive that European integration changes the political opportunity structure in favor of sub-state regions. If so, then public opinion among regionalist supporters should

---

[5] As discussed in Hepburn (2007, 2008), regionalist attitudes toward the EU may be cyclical, and may in fact currently be in a less pro-Europe part of the cycle. However, given that the Mannheim Eurobarometer data ends in 2002, this shift does not affect the analysis in this chapter.

[6] Compared to the relative coherence regarding the EU, the excellent volume edited by de Winter, Gómez-Reino, and Lynch (2006) makes the diversity of the regionalist party family on many other issues and goals abundantly clear.

also be in favor of European integration. In addition to the size of states argument, Hooghe and Marks' Postfunctionalist Theory also predicts that individuals with non-exclusive national identities (i.e., national and regional identities) will be more supportive of European integration (Hooghe and Marks 2004, 2005, 2009). Generally, then, I expect that respondents with regionalist identity will be pro-EU.

Unfortunately, while the Eurobarometer is a valuable resource, it does present some problems for this analysis. The Eurobarometer includes a very small number of regionalist supporters in 2000 ($N = 388/32,145$ or 1.21 percent). In addition, there are few questions regarding sub-state identification available, which restricts a more direct test of the theory in the cross-sectional time series. As an alternative observable implication, therefore, I focus on party cues. By testing for an effect of party cues on support for European integration, I can indirectly test a critical link in the theory, namely that citizens are likely to catch the pro-EU signals of regionalist elites.

5.2 Support for European Integration

With evidence from the Mannheim Eurobarometer Trend File (Schmitt and Scholz 2005), which tracks public opinion in the EU from 1970 to 2002, and the 1996 and 2002 Chapel Hill Expert Survey (CHES) (Ray 1999; Steenbergen and Marks 2007), I focus on two questions: whether regionalists are pro-EU and whether respondents' public attitudes match their party elites' cues.

As Gabel (1998a, 333) points out, public attitudes are an ever-increasing constraint on the European integration project; thus, it is not surprising to find a large and growing literature on the subject (Gabel 1998b; McLaren 2002; Marks and Steenbergen 2004; Brinegar and Jolly 2005). This prior literature provides a starting point for the current analysis of public attitudes toward European integration. Building on the work of Gabel (1998a), I extend the baseline model by adding whether respondents are regionalist party supporters.[7] Based on the viability theory and the Scottish evidence, I expect to find that regionalist party supporters, ceteris paribus, are more likely to support the European Union.

---

[7]Intention to vote for a regionalist party is simply a proxy for regionalist or sub-state nationalist sentiment. Though not perfect, it provides a cross-temporal and cross-sectional measure of identification with a regionalist organization.

In the first test of this hypothesis, I utilize Eurobarometer data from 2000, the most recent data in the Mannheim Eurobarometer Trend File for which respondents answer party affiliation and the classic EU support question: is the EU a good thing or a bad thing?[8] Similar to McLaren (2002), the other variables and controls simply replicate the Gabel (1998b) model and provide a starting point to analyze regionalist sentiment toward the EU.[9] Table 5.1 provides the results of this Ordinary Least Squares model.[10]

Briefly, what is apparent from Table 5.1 is the robustness of the original model. Nearly every variable matches the original results in sign and significance. Of particular importance are the occupational, skill, and income variables. In short, higher skilled, better positioned citizens are more likely to support European integration in 2000, just as they were from 1973–1992 in the original model (Gabel 1998b). With new data, this model provides further evidence in favor of the robustness of the economic interest explanation.

The two party variables warrant closer attention. First, the positive and significant party cue variable suggests that when parties are supportive of the EU, their supporters follow that cue. This variable

---

[8] See Brinegar and Jolly (2004) or Brinegar, Jolly, and Kitschelt (2004) for further discussion of this dependent variable. Perfect, it is not. However, it is largely correlated with other systematic measures of support for European integration (Gabel 1998a). Further, it is the only measure collected consistently through the time series.

[9] In addition to the regionalist party variable, three other exceptions to a perfect replication stand out. The materialism/postmaterialism questions used in the Gabel model are not collected consistently after 1992, the end date of his study. Therefore, I exclude these out of necessity, but even in the original model, they are fairly weak, in terms of statistical significance and magnitude. Second, the border variable used in Gabel's original study is not available. Finally, rather than the simple, support proletariat/bourgeois/governing party dummy variables, I use a party cue variable developed in Brinegar and Jolly (2005), which matches a respondent's vote intentions with their party's EU position, drawn from the Chapel Hill Expert Survey data (Ray 1999; Steenbergen, Edwards, and de Vries 2007). For this chapter, this revised variable better captures the theoretical justification for party cues.

[10] This particular dependent variable is frequently modeled as a continuous variable despite its discrete three-response nature (see, for instance, Gabel 1998b). In this analysis, I follow the convention to improve comparability and interpretability; however, I also ran the model as an Ordered Logit model, with very similar results. In fact, even the three insignificant variables (small business owner, farmer, and housewife) remain insignificant in the other model.

Table 5.1: OLS Regression of EU Support in 2000

Variable	b	(S.E.)
Political Interest & Party Variables		
Discuss politics never	−4.722***	(0.441)
Discuss politics frequently	1.979**	(0.587)
Party cue	17.908***	(1.242)
Regionalist Party	4.401**	(1.746)
Skill Variables		
Low education	−4.155***	(0.587)
High-mid education	2.817***	(0.650)
High education	5.664***	(0.557)
Income & Occupation Variables		
Low income	−2.631***	(0.560)
High-mid income	3.125***	(0.537)
High income	5.088***	(0.520)
Professional	5.974***	(1.210)
Executive	6.568***	(0.798)
Manual Laborer	−1.810**	(0.733)
Unemployed	−2.016*	(0.891)
Retired	1.635*	(0.742)
Small business owner	0.717	(0.897)
Farmer	−1.785	(1.621)
Student	7.281***	(0.755)
Housewife	1.185	(0.723)
Demographic Variables		
Female	−2.336***	(0.406)
Age	−0.078***	(0.017)
Country Dummies	included	
Constant	44.506***	(1.407)
N	32,145	
Adjusted R^2	0.1371	

Note: Table entries are unstandardized regression coefficients with standard errors in parentheses. * $p \leq 0.05$, ** $p \leq 0.01$, *** $p \leq 0.001$

matches a voter's party intention with the chosen party's position on the EU. In general, then, if the respondent's party supports the EU,

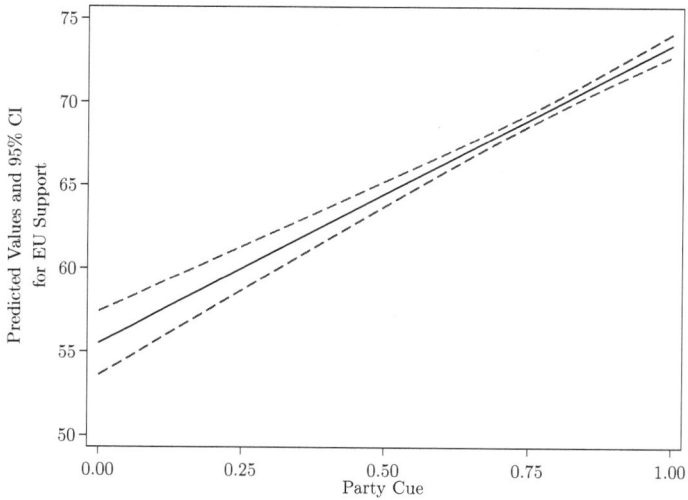

Figure 5.1: Expected Support for the EU

then the variable will have a positive value.[11]

To further evaluate the magnitude of changes in party cue, I calculated the expected value of the dependent variable, holding all other variables at their mean values. Figure 5.1 demonstrates this effect.

Since regionalist parties are pro-EU, and in fact, utilize the viability logic to bolster their own credibility while encouraging support of the European project, this variable indicates that regionalist party

---

[11]Scaled from 0 to 1, party cue scores range from 0.27 to 0.89. As shown in Chapter 4, the regionalist party family is pro-EU and close to the mainstream party families. Based on Chapel Hill expert evaluations of the EU positions, the party family scores are listed below:

Radical Right: 0.27
Communist: 0.31
Agrarian: 0.51
Green: 0.55
Conservative: 0.72
Regionalist: 0.75
Socialist: 0.81
Liberal: 0.88
Christian Democrat: 0.89

supporters are more likely to support the EU than any of the other niche party supporters, such as Radical Right or Green parties. Alternatively, if the regionalist parties become more Euroskeptical, then pro-EU forces will lose an important ally.

Also included is a simple dummy variable, measuring 1 if the respondent intends to vote for a regionalist party in the next election. This variable is also statistically significant and positive, again suggesting that regionalist party supporters hold more positive attitudes about the EU than their fellow citizens.[12] In the next section, I evaluate this conclusion more fully within the Scottish case.

Nevertheless, the number of self-identified regionalist supporters is small. Therefore, I turn to the larger time series available in the Mannheim Eurobarometer Trend File, starting in 1984 to match the CHES data. As the 2000 regression suggests, I expect party cue to be significant across time in the larger dataset. I reran the model from Table 5.1, separately for each year of the Mannheim Eurobarometer Trend File.[13] In doing so, I find that the party cue coefficient is statistically significant throughout the time series, and has a powerful effect on the dependent variable. Rather than showing a chart with the Party Cue coefficients from these regressions (based on Table 3.2 with only the year changing), Figure 5.2 represents the size of the coefficient for each year's model, with a 95 percent confidence interval. Again, the coefficient in the figure reflects just the Party Cue coefficient from separate regressions for each year, based on the model from Table 5.1.[14]

Figure 5.2 is striking for two reasons tangential to this chapter. First, despite the common perception that parties have lost much of their influence in Western Europe during this period, their attitudes toward the EU continue to have a powerful effect on their supporter's attitudes.[15] Second, there is a striking and noticeable decline in the

---

[12] Using the 2008 *Eurobarometer* 69.2, Chacha (2013) finds that individuals with regional attachments are more likely to support the European Union as well. Thus, the finding is robust to other operationalizations of the key independent variable.

[13] Each individual regression is available upon request of the author, as are the Stata do-files.

[14] This figure, inspired by Andrew Gelman's discussion of a secret weapon to detect trends in the effects of variables over time, allows us to consider the changing effect of the crucial variable over time without pooling the data and oversimplifying the model (Gelman 2005).

[15] As a discussant at the 2008 Midwest Political Science Association annual meeting pointed out, there are at least two plausible alternative explanations. First,

Public Support for the EU and Decentralization 133

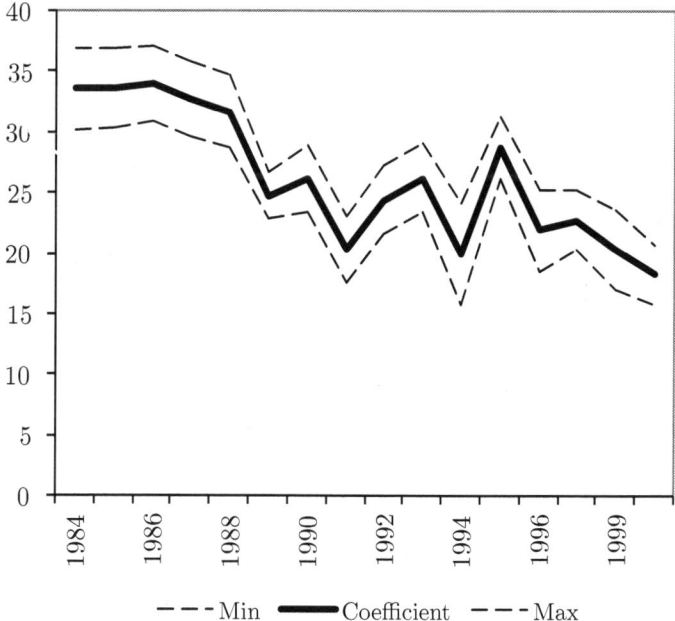

Figure 5.2: Party Cue Coefficient, over Time

effectiveness of party cues starting in the mid-1990s. Both observations warrant more research.

But for the purposes of this chapter, Figure 5.2 demonstrates that party cues have a significant and powerful effect throughout the period. Given the knowledge that regionalist parties are pro-EU, on average, this finding suggests that regionalist party supporters throughout Western Europe are likely to be pro-EU as well. As noted above, though, where exceptions exist, or if regionalist parties change tactics to Euroskepticism, this positive effect will vanish.

---

rather than parties cueing voters, parties could simply be pandering to the public by choosing policies they support (or oppose). Second, voter preferences on European integration could drive their partisan preferences. However, recent work, using statistical tools designed to test for this type of endogeneity, suggests that there is a significant effect of elite cues on partisan attitudes (Gabel and Scheve 2007a, b; Steenbergen, Edwards, and de Vries 2007; De Vries and Edwards 2009).

For the Viability Theory, this analysis provides suggestive evidence that regionalist party supporters, along with their elites, favor the EU; however, these results do not allow us to infer that the effect of the EU on the viability of regions is part of the causal story. To address this link, I turn to the Scottish case.

5.3 Scotland

In addition to attitudes toward the EU, the revised political opportunity structure should affect attitudes toward autonomy for regionalists. An observable implication of the Viability Theory logic is that citizens perceive greater viability of an independent small country within the European Union than outside, thereby making regionalist parties themselves more viable and electorally attractive. The devolution referenda in Scotland in two distinct time periods provide a quasi-experiment in which to explore this observable implication. In 1979, not only was European integration itself at a less developed stage, but the Scottish National Party did not yet see the EU as a potential partner in making its case for independence. In the first referendum, a slight majority voted for devolution but the margin was not enough to overcome the electoral threshold set by Westminster in the "Cunningham amendment," which stipulated that devolution must not only achieve a majority of support among voters but also meet at least a 40 percent threshold of the entire potential electorate (Harvie and Jones 2000, 115). In 1997, though, the result was overwhelmingly pro-devolution. By 1997, as shown in the tracing of the Scottish National Party (SNP) official party positions in Chapter 4, the Scottish National Party framed the EU as an integral component of its "Independence in Europe" policy. In part, Scottish National Party elites intended this strategy to demonstrate that Scotland would be a viable independent country apart from the United Kingdom. If the viability mechanism is at work, I should find evidence in multiple observable implications.

First, Scottish respondents should be more likely to support European integration. Scottish National Party elites frame the European Union as a mechanism to achieve independence without economic upheaval. In other words, European integration increases the viability of Scotland as an independent country. Thus, nationalists should perceive the European Union more positively in 1997 than in 1979. Using

Table 5.2: Scottish Perceptions of EU as a Good Thing

Year	Conservative	Labour	SNP	Liberal	All
1979	29.29%	15.97%	12.66%	25.33%	21.12%
1997	49.59%	43.75%	47.54%	50.98%	45.86%
Change	+20.30%	+27.78%	+34.88%	+25.65%	+24.74%

data from the 1979 and 1997 Scottish Referendum Surveys (Miller and Brand 1981; Jowell, Heath, and Curtice 1998), Table 5.2 provides some simple statistics regarding attitudes toward the EU.[16]

Across party types, Scottish citizens have far more favorable attitudes toward the EU in 1997 (45.86 percent) than 1979 (21.12 percent). While SNP supporters are not the most Euro-enthusiastic in these surveys, they also increased their support most dramatically. In contrast, support for European integration among all Europeans dropped nearly 12% during the same timeframe (Schmitt and Scholz 2005).[17] In particular, citizens who identify with the Scottish National Party are much more favorably disposed to European integration. Only 13 percent of Scottish National Party supporters thought the European Union was a "good thing" in 1979, but 48 percent did so in 1997.[18] This trend follows the rhetoric of the Scottish National Party, which shifted from being anti-integration to supporting the European Union specifically as

---

[16] For 1979, 729 respondents are included. The breakdown by party identification is 239 Conservatives, 288 Labour, 79 SNP, and 75 Liberal. For 1997, the total N is 676, with 123 Conservatives, 336 Labour, 122 SNP, and 51 Liberal Democrats.

[17] According to the Mannheim Eurobarometer Trend File, which compiles and standardizes the many individual Eurobarometer surveys, approximately 58 percent of Europeans surveyed thought the EU was a "good thing" in 1979 (58.9 percent in Eurobarometer 11 and 57.9 percent in Eurobarometer 12), while 50 percent or fewer respondents thought it was a "good thing" in 1997 (48.2 percent in Eurobarometer 47, 48.6 percent in Eurobarometer 47.1, 47.2 percent in Eurobarometer 47.2, and 50.8 percent in Eurobarometer 48) (Schmitt and Scholz 2005).

[18] In 1997, the survey asked the standard Eurobarometer question about European integration that is commonly used in analysis of support for European integration (Gabel 1998b; Brinegar, Jolly, and Kitschelt 2004; Brinegar and Jolly 2005): whether the respondent thinks the EU is a "good thing," a "bad thing," or neither. In 1979, the survey asked respondents to score the Common Market on a 10-point scale [v467]. Following Dardanelli (2005b), I standardized this variable to compare to the 1997 version by grouping 0–3 as bad for Scotland, 4–6 as neither good nor bad, and 7–10 as good for Scotland.

a lever against the United Kingdom, and suggests the citizens caught the cue sent by party elites.

Second, support for independence should be related to European integration. Dardanelli (2005b, 328) argues that attitudes toward the European Union actually determine perceived costs of secession. Certainly, Scottish National Party officials used the European Union to diminish fears of economic displacement associated with independence (Harvie and Jones 2000, 152; Pittock 2001, 127). In other words, deeper European integration implies lower costs of secession (i.e., increased viability of independence), thereby making both independence and devolution more attractive options.

In the following pages, I will demonstrate that this "Independence in Europe" option drives the increased support for independence. Many fewer respondents prefer independence outside of Europe to independence in Europe as their first or second option. The existence of the EU as an alternative political opportunity structure allows citizens to favor independence much more strongly, either as a first or second option. By convincing its supporters that the European Union was a "good thing," the Scottish National Party made independence a more reasonable option and increased support for devolution in the referendum in the process (Dardanelli 2001, 14).

Two related empirical implications present themselves. First, I expect to see more Scottish citizens view independence as a viable option in 1997 than in 1979, in large part thanks to the European integration project. Second, these perceptions of viability and increased support for devolution and independence should hold across economic classes, including those most concerned about potential economic upheaval due to independence, such as the middle class.

5.4 The Scottish Referenda on Devolution

Scotland presents a unique opportunity to test the main alternative causal mechanisms. First, Scotland is a region in Western Europe with a long and rich tradition of a regional autonomy movement. Second, the referenda on devolution at two different points in time provide an opportunity to analyze both attitudes toward autonomy and how those attitudes are translated into votes on devolution, as well as their change over time. Comparing the failed referendum in 1979 to the successful

1997 vote yields variation in both the dependent variable and the explanatory variable of interest (Dardanelli 2001, 2). Finally, the questions available in the 1979 and 1997 surveys allow exploration of the European Union's role in determining attitudes toward self-government.

In both 1979 and 1997, the Labour party introduced a referendum for Scottish citizens to decide whether to establish a Scottish Parliament. While a majority of voters supported devolution in both referenda, it failed in 1979 due to the "Cunningham amendment." In other words, abstention served as a de facto "No" vote.[19] As a result of the threshold, the referendum failed in 1979 and, after the Conservatives won that year's general election, the government promptly removed devolution from the agenda.

During the 1997 general election campaign, Labour, under Tony Blair, promised another referendum on devolution.[20] The 1997 version of the devolution referendum passed by large majorities in every district in Scotland (Taylor, Curtice, and Thomson 1999, xxvii). Considering that during both years Scottish citizens claimed to support devolution, the positive outcome of the devolution referendum in 1997 compared to the negative outcome in 1979 yields a puzzle. In the next section, I consider the alternative explanations for the different outcomes and then explain why the European Union is a significant factor.

---

[19]This poison pill, "a brilliant act of anti-democratic political manipulation" (Mitchell 1996, 47), influenced the outcome of the referendum as well as perceptions about the outcome. When newspapers referenced the vote, they gave the result as percentages of the electorate and not actual voters. So instead of a 52–48 percent outcome in favor of devolution, it appeared that only one-third of Scots supported devolution (Pittock 2001, 123). Indeed, even Scottish voters saw the result as indicative of a negative result (Mitchell 1996, 46–47).

[20]Labour supported a referendum rather than simply legislating devolution for multiple reasons. Uncertain of their eventual Parliamentary majority from the 1997 general election, they feared a difficult parliamentary battle over devolution as they faced in the 1970s. Also, a referendum could secure decentralization in the face of future Tory governments. Presumably, if devolution were granted after a referendum, then only a referendum could reverse the decision (Taylor, Curtice, and Thomson 1999, xxv–xxvi). Labour also used the referendum to avoid association with the potential higher taxes of a Scottish Parliament, the so-called Tartan tax. The two-part referendum asked voters to first choose whether to support a Scottish Parliament and then decide whether the Parliament should have tax-varying authority.

Table 5.3: Attitudes and Actual Voting Positions on Devolution in 1979 and 1997

	Voting Positions on Referenda					
Devolution	1979			1997		
Attitudes	Yes	No	(N)	Yes	No	(N)
Status Quo	11.1%	79.9%	(189)	4.0%	92.1%	(126)
Devolution	54.1%	39.3%	(394)	86.2%	9.0%	(289)
Independence	80.0%	12.0%	(50)	94.0%	3.5%	(232)
Don't Know	8.3%	14.6%	(96)	34.5%	17.2%	(29)
All	38.7%	44.7%	(729)	71.3%	22.9%	(676)

5.5 Similar Preferences, Different Outcomes?

Since at least 1947, a majority of Scots have consistently supported devolution in opinion polls.[21] In 1979, 61 percent of respondents, a clear majority, in the Scottish Election Survey supported self-government, with 54.1 percent in favor of devolution and 6.9 percent supporting independence (Miller and Brand 1981). Yet, despite this consistent support of devolution in theory, a plurality of respondents in that same poll either voted "No" or favored the "No" position, with 44.7 percent against the referendum and only 38.1 percent in favor. Table 5.3 demonstrates the gap between respondents who claimed to favor devolution yet opposed the referendum.[22]

Respondents at either end of the spectrum, either in favor of the status quo or in favor of independence, vote consistently either for or against the referendum in both surveys, though they do become

---

[21]In a 1947 survey, over three-quarters of Scots supported a Scottish parliament. In 1949, a Scottish Plebiscite Society poll in Kirriemuir in Angus found that 23 percent were in favor of an independent Parliament, 69 percent supported a Parliament to deal with Scottish affairs, and only 5 percent favored the status quo (Mitchell 1996, 149).

[22]See Appendix D for question wording. For Table 5.3, the two independence and two devolution options in the survey are combined. All questions and survey responses are drawn from the 1979 Scottish Election Study and the 1997 Scottish Devolution Study (Miller and Brand 1981; Jowell, Heath, and Curtice 1998). All analyses were done with Stata 11.

more entrenched in 1997. But a clear disconnect exists in 1979 with 39.3 percent of devolution supporters actually opposing the referendum. By 1997, this disconnect between attitudes and action virtually disappeared, yielding a near consensus on the devolution referendum questions (Surridge and McCrone 1999, 44). What explanations might account for this disconnect in 1979?

Paolo Dardanelli introduces several explanations prevalent in the literature (2005, 321–323). First, the actual content of the devolution package was more contentious in 1979, with the First-Past-The-Post electoral system perceived as heavily Labour-biased (Harvie and Jones 2000, 186). The observable implications of the Labour bias logic are that non-Labour party supporters would be expected to be against devolution while Labour party supporters would be supportive (Dardanelli 2005*b*, 322). But in fact, apart from Tory supporters, who were strongly anti-devolution in each referendum, Liberal Democrats were just slightly less supportive of devolution than Labour supporters while SNP supporters were much more favorable. Also, Labour supporters themselves were split, with a plurality—not a majority—in favor of devolution. The evidence casts doubt on this explanation.

Second, many scholars point to Scotland's increasingly strong sense of being a perpetual political minority in the United Kingdom as the reason devolution gained support from 1979 to 1997 (McCrone and Lewis 1999, 18). Basically, Scotland voted for Labour in every general election from 1979 to 1992, but the Conservatives won in the rest of the United Kingdom and therefore governed, leaving Scottish voters feeling disenfranchised and the Conservatives increasingly unpopular in Scotland (Mitchell et al. 1998, 178; Taylor, Curtice and Thomson 1999, xxiv). These anti-Tory sentiments could potentially fuel pro-devolution sentiment. If true, then Scots, especially non-Conservatives, should be less satisfied with the United Kingdom and devolution should be a higher priority for citizens. But Scottish nationalists are actually more satisfied in 1997 than 1979 and the issue of self-government is no more or less salient, suggesting this hypothesis is not sufficient either (Dardanelli 2005*b*, 323).

The third main explanation is the incoherence and ineffectiveness of the pro-devolution campaign. In 1979, the political parties, especially Labour, sent mixed signals to the electorate, with a faction of the Labour party opposing the referendum with a "Labour Vote NO" campaign (Denver 2002, 830). Also, little cross-party coordination existed among the "Yes" campaign, with as many divisions among the pro-devolution parties as between them and the anti-devolution campaign. A Labour party official disdainfully stated that Labour would not be "soiling our hands by joining any umbrella Yes group" (Mitchell et al. 1998, 167). In all, the "No" campaign in 1979 was more effective in terms of funding, coordination, and campaigning than the "Yes" campaign (Mitchell 1996, 163).

In 1997, on the other hand, the pro-devolution parties, Labour, Liberal Democrats, and the Scottish National Party, supported a double "Yes"—for a Scottish Parliament and for tax-varying authority—and coordinated their campaign as "Scotland FORward" (McCrone and Lewis 1999, 24). In doing so, they sent clearer messages to their party supporters as to their constitutional preferences. In the 1997 campaign, 90 percent of Labour party and 86 percent of Scottish National Party supporters knew their party favored devolution (Denver 2002, 830). The pro-devolution campaign also successfully convinced businesses that devolution was not a threat to their livelihood, undercutting a major supporter of the "No" campaign in 1979 (Mitchell et al. 1998, 175). This change, detailed in Dardanelli (2005a), is yet more evidence that business interests no longer feared an independent Scotland as they did in the late 1970s, in part due to the "Independence in Europe" option.

Finally, the "Think Twice" campaign against devolution, led by the Conservative party, lacked sufficient resources or supporters to oppose the devolution referendum (Mitchell et al. 1998, 174). Thus, the strength and coordination of the campaigns clearly shifted in favor of a "Yes" vote. Nonetheless, this explanation still has some difficulty explaining why so many Scots voted against devolution even though they favored the concept in surveys (Dardanelli 2005b, 323).

This gap between supporters of devolution in theory and practice in 1979 is stark. Table 5.3 demonstrates that only 54 percent of those who claim to support devolution actually favored the "Yes" position on the referendum in 1979, while 86 percent of devolution supporters voted "Yes" in 1997. Supporters of the status quo and independence were both strongly in the "No" or "Yes" camps, respectively, in each of the campaigns. So, the shift among devolution supporters in actual voting behavior explains much of the difference between the 33 percent

Table 5.4: Expected and Actual Voting Positions on Devolution in 1979 and 1997

	1979			1997		
	Yes	No	Don't Know	Yes	No	Don't Know
Actual	38.7%	44.7%	16.6%	71.3%	22.9%	5.8%
Expected	60.9%	25.9%	13.2%	77.1%	18.6%	4.3%
Difference	−22.2%	18.8%	3.4%	−5.8%	4.3%	1.5%

increase in support of the referendum between 1979 and 1997. In Table 5.4, I present the actual votes and the expected positions based on attitudes toward devolution.[23]

In both 1979 and 1997, fewer Scots supported the referendum than expected from their attitudes toward devolution. But the gap diminished significantly. In 1979, 60.9 percent claimed to support self-government but only 38.7 percent either voted for or favored the devolution referendum, meaning 22.2 percent fewer devolution supporters voted for the referendum than expected. In contrast, only 6 percent fewer Scots favored the "Yes" position in 1997 than expected from their attitudes. In addition, by 1997, attitudes toward devolution had crystallized to a degree that significantly fewer respondents did not have an attitude on devolution (16.6 percent compared to 5.8 percent). As discussed above, though, explaining this discrepancy between self-identified supporters of self-government and those who actually voted for the referendum is critical.

Dardanelli (2001, 2005a) argues that preference orderings are the key to understanding this gap between expected and actual behavior in the failed referendum vote of 1979. Whereas attitudes about devolution, independence and the status quo can be kept conceptually distinct in surveys, the preference ordering actually affected voting behavior (Dardanelli 2005b, 326). For instance, if a citizen preferred devolution to the status quo, then observers would expect that citizen

---

[23] Expected "Yes" and "No" based on attitudes toward devolution, with self-identified supporters of self-government, either devolution or independence, counted as Expected "Yes" and supporters of the status quo counted as Expected "No."

to vote for the referendum. But if that citizen preferred the status quo to independence, and expected independence to be a likely outcome of devolution, then the citizen would be more likely to oppose the referendum. In other words, if citizens perceive a high probability of devolution leading to independence, then the referendum vote appears to be a choice between the status quo and independence rather than status quo and devolution (Dardanelli 2001, 10). And voters in both referenda thought that independence was a likely outcome of devolution (Dardanelli 2005b, 326). This perception provided reason for citizens with this preference ordering to strategically oppose rather than sincerely support the referendum.

To determine the distribution of voter preferences, I reconstructed the preference orderings in Table 5.5 using a series of questions in the 1979 survey which asks respondents to rank each constitutional option from highly unfavorable to very much in favor.[24]

Table 5.5: Preference Ordering on Devolution in 1979

	2nd Preference				
1st Preference	Status Quo	Devolution	Independence	Don't Know	(N)
Status Quo	—	78.3%	0.0%	21.7%	(189)
Devolution	59.4%	—	25.1%	15.5%	(394)
Independence	4.0%	80.0%	—	16.0%	(50)
(N)	(236)	(188)	(99)	(206)	

---

[24] See Appendix D for question wording. To extract a preference ordering for 1979, I used the attitude toward devolution question above to determine first preference then turned to the follow-up questions [v323–v327] (Miller and Brand 1981), which asked the respondent to say whether they were very much in favor of (or against), somewhat in favor of (or somewhat against) each constitutional option. Knowing each respondent's first preference, I evaluated which constitutional option they favored second best and created an index variable for the various preference orderings. For example, if a respondent favored the status quo, I determined whether they ranked independence or devolution higher. If the respondent ranked devolution higher, then I coded them as Status Quo > Devolution > Independence. In the case of ties, I coded the respondent as don't know. Coding is available upon request.

Not surprisingly, Scottish voters who favored the status quo preferred devolution as their second best alternative. Similarly, nationalist Scots, or those who chose independence as their first preference, much preferred devolution to the status quo. These preference orderings yield little explanatory power, though, for respondents in both categories are strongly in their respective camps regardless of their second preference.

But as Dardanelli (2001, 9) contends, for devolution supporters, the second preference may be critical in determining behavior on the referendum. Devolution supporters who consider independence their second best preference should be supportive of the referendum because even if independence is a likely outcome of devolution, it is preferable to the status quo. But Table 5.5 shows that only 25 percent of the devolution supporters share this preference ordering. By contrast, devolution supporters who fear independence and favor the status quo over independence should be more skeptical of the referendum (Dardanelli 2005a, Ch. 4). In 1979, nearly 60 percent of Scottish devolution supporters consider the status quo to be their second-best option. Table 5.6 shows the actual referendum positions of devolution supporters split by their second preferences.[25]

Table 5.6 clearly demonstrates that those who favor devolution over independence over the status quo supported the referendum by a large majority while those devolution supporters who favored the status quo over independence were actually slightly opposed to the referendum. Those devolution supporters who favored the status quo over independence were actually slightly opposed to the referendum, with 50 percent voting against the referendum compared to 45 percent voting in favor. Combined with the consistent opposition of status quo supporters, the divided cohort of devolution supporters contributed to the gap between expected and actual support for the referendum.[26]

---

[25] In Table 5.6, respondents who said they voted for the referendum and those who said they did not vote but favored the "Yes" position are included. The ratios are similar if abstentions are excluded from the analysis, with the Devolution > Independence > Status Quo group voting for the referendum 85 percent of the time and the Devolution > Status Quo > Independence group split evenly between a negative and favorable vote.

[26] Because the Parliament instituted the threshold on the referendum vote in 1979, abstentions acted as de facto votes against devolution. 46 percent of abstentions did not know their attitude toward devolution. But 40 percent favored the status quo as their first (16 percent) or second best constitutional option (24 percent). Only 14

Table 5.6: Referendum Support in 1979, by Preference Ordering

	Yes	No
Devolution > Independence > Status Quo	75.8%	18.2%
Devolution > Status Quo > Independence	44.9%	49.6%
All Devolution Supporters	54.1%	39.3%

By 1997, preference orderings shifted to a degree that the majority of citizens either favored independence as their first or second most preferred constitutional option.[27] Whereas devolution supporters in 1979 preferred the status quo to independence, the majority of devolution supporters preferred independence to the status quo in 1997. Excluding the alternative devolution option, for those who favor a Scottish Parliament with tax-varying authority—which comprises 78 percent of the devolution cohort—independence is the preferred second option. For those who favor the weaker devolution option—22 percent of the devolution cohort—more prefer the status quo to independence, but there are significantly fewer respondents in this category. In the end, 86 percent of those who favor either type of devolution either voted for or favored the referendum.

To summarize, the success of the 1997 referendum can be linked to a diminished fear of independence. This significant shift is relevant to the Viability Theory argument. In 1979, a majority of respondents claimed to support devolution as their most preferred constitutional option, with a sizable group favoring the status quo and a very small minority favoring independence. By the time of the 1997 Scottish Devolution Study, this distribution of first preferences changed dramatically. Support for the status quo and devolution decreased 7 percent and 11 percent, respectively, while support for independence increased

---

percent favored independence as their first (4 percent) or second favorite option (10 percent). The abstentions, therefore, provide further support that those who feared independence or at least considered it their least preferred constitutional option did not support the referendum, yielding a cumulative negative vote on devolution in 1979.

[27] For 1997, the preference ordering was much more straightforward than in 1979 because the survey asked a follow-up question [21b] to the attitudes toward devolution question that asked respondents to list their second most preferred constitutional option (Jowell, Heath, and Curtice 1998).

Table 5.7: Constitutional Attitudes in 1979 & 1997

	1979	1997	Change
Status Quo	25.9%	18.6%	-7.3%
Self-Government	60.9%	77.1%	16.2%
Devolution	*54.1%*	*42.8%*	*-11.3%*
Independence	*6.9%*	*34.3%*	*27.5%*
in EU		*25.6%*	
from EU		*8.7%*	
Don't Know	13.2%	4.3%	-8.9%
(N)	(729)	(676)	

Note: The Self-Government category includes the Devolution and Independence questions. The italicized categories represent sub-categories (e.g., devolution and independence combine to form self-government and "independence" includes the two EU options).

28 percent. I present these data in Table 5.7.

Significantly, the increase in support for independence occurs across all party groups, according to the Referendum Study (Jowell, Heath, and Curtice 1998). Only 4 percent of Labour party supporters favored independence in 1979, while 36 percent did so in 1997. For Scottish National Party supporters, independence became the most preferred option, increasing from 35 percent to 72 percent. Even 6 percent more Conservatives supported independence in 1997 than in 1979. Because many respondents believe independence is a likely consequence of devolution, the increased support for independence as a first option significantly affected the outcome of the 1997 referendum. But this finding only raises another question: why is independence so much more popular in 1997 than 1979? I contend that European integration, and its strategic use by the Scottish National Party, plays an important role.

First, notice the disaggregated independence options in Table 5.7. Very little of the increased independence support arises from an autarkic, non-EU, version of independence. In 1979, the independence in EU option was not even available to survey respondents. By 1997,

Table 5.8: Referendum Positions in 1979 & 1997, by Class

	1979			1997		
	Yes	No	(N)	Yes	No	(N)
Class Identity						
Middle Class	29.6%	62.5%	(152)	55.8%	41.0%	(156)
Working Class	46.5%	44.1%	(458)	77.5%	17.3%	(457)
Other	20.2%	24.4%	(119)	65.1%	19.0%	(63)
All	38.7%	44.7%	(729)	71.3%	22.9%	(676)

Note: The "Yes" and "No" categories include respondents who either voted for or did not vote but favored that position in the referendum.

independence in EU, the policy espoused by the SNP, is actually more preferred than the status quo by itself.[28] This finding suggests that citizens recognize the significant change in the political opportunity structure that the EU created.

Further, the Viability Theory predicts that the distribution of supporters should change as well. If independence is a more viable option economically, then both the middle class and the working class will be more favorably disposed to independence. For example, traditionally in the Basque country, industrialists, fearing the economic disruption that may result from independence, have been less supportive of Basque nationalism (Linz 1973; da Silva 1975, 241). But capitalists or industrialists should be more supportive of autonomy if the European Union provides more economic security than independence without such a union. Thus, I expect a new "bourgeois regionalism" should emerge in response to the changing economic context (van Houten 2003, 10). Table 5.8 demonstrates that such a shift occurred in Scotland.[29]

---

[28] In the 1997 Scottish Election Survey (McCrone et al. 1997), support for independence was weaker than in the Referendum Study. In the Election Survey, 17.9 percent supported independence in the EU while 7.8 percent supported independence outside the EU, compared to 25.6 percent and 8.7 percent in the Referendum Study, respectively. But similar to the Referendum Study, the independence option was preferred by more respondents than the status quo (Jowell, Heath, and Curtice 1998; McCrone et al. 1997).

[29] Class identity is derived from questions 62a and 62b in 1979 and 29a and 29b in 1997. For each identity question, the respondent had an option to self-identify

A mere 30 percent of the middle class supported the referendum in 1979, while over 56 percent favored devolution in 1997. Similarly, the working class supported the referendum in 1997 in far greater numbers. Hence, this finding provides additional evidence for the theoretical argument regarding the Viability Theory.

As shown above, the independence debate underwent a fundamental change between 1979 and 1997. Scottish citizens correctly perceive the EU as a political institution capable of reducing the costs of independence. This perception frees the Scottish voters to favor independence much more strongly in surveys, and to support devolution in the 1997 referendum.

5.6 Discussion

Using the Mannheim Eurobarometer Trend File, I established that regionalists are pro-EU, ceteris paribus, and that respondents' attitudes are linked to their preferred party's position on the EU. These results bolster the findings of Olson (2011), who uses elite interviews and Eurobarometer data to investigate why regionalists tend to be pro-EU. Building on the exclusive/inclusive identity literature, she isolates regions that are culturally heterogeneous and politicized to see whether democratic representation at the EU level boosts support among these regions. She finds significant evidence that respondents in politicized, culturally different regions are more likely to support the EU, a result very much in line with my findings in Chapters 4 and 5. Both in the Scottish case and in Western Europe, generally, regionalist party supporters perceive the EU positively, matching the theoretical implications of the Viability Theory.

Using the 1979 Scottish Election Survey and the 1997 Scottish Referendum Study, I evaluated why the referendum failed in 1979 but passed in 1997 despite having a majority in favor of devolution in both years. Following Dardanelli (2005a), I contend that the fear of independence, coupled with a preference ordering where the second choice for devolution supporters was the status quo, explained the strategic voting behavior in 1979. Between 1979 and 1997, the European Union project fundamentally altered the political opportunity structure for

---

and then, if no choice was made, a follow-up question asked the respondent which option they would choose if forced (Miller and Brand 1981; Jowell, Heath, and Curtice 1998).

autonomy movements, making devolution and independence a more viable prospect for regionalists. In turn, increased support for independence, as both a first and second option for Scots, fueled the dramatic increase in sincere voting for devolution in 1997.

I also presented evidence to support the contention that European integration, especially the Scottish National Party's successful framing of the EU as a mechanism to reduce the costs of secession, contributed to this increase in support for independence. And significantly for the causal chain discussed throughout this book, support for independence is a significant and powerful predictor of identification with the SNP. Using the 1997 Scottish Referendum Study, a simple logit model regressing devolution attitudes on SNP party identification, with or without a variety of controls, confirms this relationship. Thus, by increasing the viability of independence and making independence and devolution a more popular attitude, the European integration project also improved the electoral prospects of regionalist parties such as the SNP. Though regionalists, who want greater autonomy in one form or another, and supranational integration supporters seem natural opponents, this research suggests they are, in fact, yet another example of the old adage: an enemy of my enemy is my friend.

In the context of this book, this chapter provides evidence that it is in fact the Viability Theory that provides the causal link between deeper integration and more sub-national mobilization. The findings of this chapter suggest that the viability logic is at work at the individual level, just as Chapter 4 demonstrated at the political party level of analysis.

Conclusion

AFTER THE JUNE 2010 ELECTIONS, Belgian political parties could not form a governing coalition for 541 days. At the center of the stalemate sat Bart de Wever, the leader of the biggest party in Belgium, the New Flemish Alliance (N-VA), who rejected any compromise with the Walloon parties. But de Wever does not seek some sort of ideal-type Westphalian independence. Rather, he seems to desire that Belgium slowly "dissolve into the EU" (*The Economist* 2011a).

Belgium is exceptional, certainly, but it is by no means the only country facing regionalist challenges. In September 2012, nearly 20 percent of the Catalan population (1.5 million people) marched in support of independence in Barcelona (*BBC News Europe* 2012). As in other regions such as the Basque region and northern Italy, Catalan elites focus their ire on fiscal and financial issues, made more dramatic by the Euro crisis (Tisdall 2012). In a 2012 opinion poll, 51 percent of Catalans claimed they would vote yes for independence (*The Economist* 2012). And yet, like de Wever, Catalan leaders are fully aware that their independence is integrally tied to the European Union: "That is why [Artur Mas i Gavarró, the Catalan nationalist leader of the regional government,] recoils from the *independentista* or secessionist tags. 'I am a sovereigntist,' he explains, adding that nobody is independent within the European Union" (*The Economist* 2012).

As seen in Chapter 1, regionalist parties compete in more regions within European Union member states than ever before. These parties are the key strategic actors concerned with translating the center-periphery cleavage into political conflict; furthermore, regionalist party elites recognize the European Union as creating more permissive conditions for the success of regionalist movements. By investigating the relationship between European integration and regionalist parties, this book provides a crucial *political* link missing from the optimal size of states literature, which, if taken to its extreme, would predict greater autonomy support in all regions.

With this book, I demonstrate that deeper political and economic integration at the European level has in fact encouraged regionalist mobilization in the form of regionalist political parties. Though political parties are just one form of regionalist mobilization for autonomy, I consider regionalist political parties to be major players in the bargaining game between the regions and the central government. If regionalist political parties are stronger, regionalist movements have more bargaining leverage vis-à-vis the state. Further, I contend that it is precisely the context of the European Union, which makes smaller, more homogeneous states more viable, which in turn explains why European integration strengthens regionalist movements.

In this chapter, I have three main goals. First, I summarize the main theoretical and empirical findings and consider their contributions. Next, I discuss the theoretical implications of these findings for Eastern Europe and other parts of the world. Finally, I consider how the recent economic crisis in Europe affects the Viability Theory and the empirical expectations moving forward.

Main Findings

In Chapter 2, I develop the causal mechanism that explains the relationship between supranational integration, on one hand, and subnational fragmentation, on the other. European integration creates a new political opportunity structure for sub-state regions, such that these small potential states no longer need the traditional states to be economically viable. In terms of the size of economic market, public goods, and regional insurance, European integration diminishes the advantages of large state size to the advantage of small potential states, such as Scotland or Catalonia, thereby increasing the incentives of regionalist groups to mobilize for autonomy.

This theory builds on the optimal size of states literature in economics by focusing on the political dynamics. Since the benefits of being a small state are either increasing or at least held constant while the benefits of being part of a large state are decreasing in the presence of the EU, understanding how political actors act in this changing political opportunity structure is crucial. For instance, the strategic behavior of political parties, especially their rhetorical use of the EU in their electoral pleas to voters, is a critical aspect of the causal link between European integration and the potential fragmentation of traditional states.

To test this theory, I pursued a multi-faceted research design. First, I explored the descriptive inference that European integration did in fact strengthen regionalist political parties. In Chapter 3, I test this inference against the main alternative, that European integration would have no effect at all (i.e., the null hypothesis). In the literature on regionalist political parties, the null hypothesis, or simply the theory that European integration has no effect on support for these parties, is frequently assumed rather than tested.

In Chapter 3, I demonstrate that European integration does in fact have a clear and significant effect on the electoral success of regionalist political parties. Prior to elections, European integration makes regionalist political parties more likely to compete in national parliamentary elections. Once the parties enter competition, European integration encourages voters to support these parties. Consistent with the theoretical predictions of the Viability Theory, I present consistent and robust evidence to support the descriptive inference that European integration strengthens regionalist political parties and, therefore, sub-national movements. This finding is robust after controlling for a variety of statistical specifications and other theoretically relevant explanatory variables, such as preference heterogeneity between the region and the rest of the state. With this analysis, I extend and validate earlier research on the significance of cultural factors in regionalist mobilization, contributing to the cumulative knowledge of regional movements in Western Europe largely based on qualitative research methods. Further, these robust findings on European integration, based on the cross-national time-series analysis of entry and success of regionalist political parties, suggest that scholars too often ignore the interaction between the supranational and sub-national levels of multi-level governance. The implicit assumption among many scholars that European integration has no effect is, therefore, unjustified and unwarranted.

But this finding cannot adequately discriminate between alternative theories that predict greater support for regionalist political parties. Second, therefore, I considered two implications of the Viability Theory, with which I evaluate the inference that it is precisely the increased viability attributable to European integration that explains this relationship between the European Union and regionalist parties. If the Viability Theory is the causal mechanism, then both elites and citizens must recognize and take advantage of the new political opportunity structure. By analyzing the attitudes of regionalist political parties toward European integration, I show that regionalist political parties are generally pro-Europe, not Euroskeptics. This finding is consistent across time, regions, and even issue area, controlling for ideological extremism. Hence, regionalist political parties frame the European Union in a positive way, consistent with the theoretical expectations.

Further, with the in-depth analysis of the official positions of the Scottish National Party, I show that, in this critical case, the regionalist political party explicitly places the European Union at the heart of its independence policy, using the European Union to reduce the fears of citizens that independence will inevitably lead to economic dislocation and lost income. Thus, with Chapter 4, I find significant support for the viability logic. This evidence proves that regionalist political parties view the European Union positively and, at least in the Scottish case, frame the EU as an ally in their struggle for autonomy with the central state.

Beyond elite rhetoric and behavior, I evaluated the causal mechanism at the individual level with a statistical case study of Scottish public opinion. With the analysis of the 1979 and 1997 devolution referenda in Scotland in Chapter 5, I find further evidence in favor of the viability logic. Scottish citizens favored devolution in 1997 much more than in 1979 in large part because independence was a more favorable constitutional option in 1997. The data suggest that the option of "Independence in Europe," as favored by the Scottish National Party, nearly entirely explains the increased support for independence among Scottish respondents, thereby explaining the increased support for the devolution referendum. In other words, Scots are more likely to view independence favorably, which increased the likelihood they would support the devolution referendum in 1997. Also, the distribution of supporters of independence in Scotland changed so that more middle class, or capitalist, respondents favored independence. This shift in opinion suggests that independence is a more viable constitutional option within the European Union. These findings show that the viability logic is at work at the individual level, which, along with the evidence from political parties, provides significant support for the Viability Theory.

By triangulating on the research question with multiple techniques and levels of analysis, I show that European integration does strengthen regionalist movements, as predicted by the Viability Theory.

CONTRIBUTIONS

This book contributes to several literatures in comparative politics, international relations and political economy. First, it is one of the first comparative, cross-national analysis of both the incidence and electoral support of regionalist political parties. Much of the previous literature studies one region or one country and is not necessarily focused on generalizable results for regionalist political parties in Europe. Even among the quantitative studies, most studies focus on either one country or even one region (Lancaster and Lewis-Beck 1989), and nearly all neglect the incidence question altogether (Gordin 2001; Tronconi 2006; Brancati 2008). With the inclusion of all regions in Western Europe rather than just those with active regionalist political parties, I extended the analysis to explain when, where, and why regionalist political parties compete in national elections as well as their relative success.

Though most regionalist parties are relatively niche players at the national level, their success matters for national politics. At the very least, they increase the fragmentation of the party system, complicating coalition-building and party competition more generally. With the revived relevance of the center-periphery cleavage, party competition is centrifugal, with policy distances increasing, not decreasing (de Winter 1998, 241–244). In the most extreme cases, such as Belgium or Spain, they can fracture the party system itself. As de Winter (1998, 240) argues, "We can no longer talk of the 'Belgian' or 'Spanish' party system, but only of their party systems." Understanding these parties, therefore, helps us better understand party competition and European politics.

Along with the findings on European integration, the auxiliary hypotheses and findings have implications for the burgeoning literature on new or niche parties (Kitschelt 1995; Hug 2001; Tavits 2006; Meguid

2005, 2008; Spoon 2011). Both the political opportunity structure, in terms of decentralization, and strategic behavior, in terms of mainstream party behavior, affect the decisions of regionalist political party elites to enter competition as well as their success upon entering. In the general case of new or niche parties, the lessons of regionalist political parties, as an example where both push and pull variables prove significant, shed light on the empirical puzzles that remain.

This research also contributes to the growing literature on party positioning on the EU by concentrating on an under-studied party family, the regionalist political party (Marks and Wilson 2000; Marks, Wilson, and Ray 2002; Hooghe, Marks, and Wilson 2004; Marks et al. 2006). Also, this research extends the multi-level governance literature by focusing attention on the interaction between the supranational and sub-national levels (Marks and Hooghe 2000; Hooghe and Marks 2001).

Determining the extent to which regional integration affects regionalism should be particularly valuable for the field of ethnic conflict. Some scholars who study the alleviation of ethnic conflict consider regional integration to be a potentially important tool to achieve this goal. Theorists argue that increasing the size and heterogeneity of a political jurisdiction inhibits the chances for any one group to dominate.[30] Some observers, therefore, infer that regional integration may reduce ethnic conflict. Evaluating the veracity of this claim could prove important as the European Union expands into Eastern Europe and if the world continues to move toward regional blocs (e.g., the Americas, Asia, and Africa). Thus, when considering the advantages of larger markets and freer trade, scholars and practitioners must also consider the impact on regionalist autonomy movements.

Generalizing beyond regionalist political parties, I provide yet another example of international organizations—specifically the European Union—influencing the domestic politics of its member states (Kelley 2004; Vachudova 2005; Spendzharova and Vachudova 2012). The causal mechanism in Western Europe is more strategic than direct, but the effects are clear, suggesting that scholars must reconsider the role of the European Union in their analysis of domestic politics in Europe. Finally, while much of the work in economics on the optimal size of states is formal in nature, this empirical analysis provides compelling

---

[30] Considered by James Madison in *Federalist #10*, this argument is also discussed by Horowitz (1985).

evidence that this implication of the optimal size of states logic, in the framework developed by Alesina and Spolaore (2003), is empirically valid in the most likely case of Europe and is worthy of future empirical research.

Theoretical Implications

With the finding that European integration increases regionalist party success at the national level, a new set of questions about regionalist party success emerge. First, how does European integration affect regionalist party entry and success at other electoral levels, especially regional and European elections? The SNP won a majority in the 2011 Scottish Parliamentary elections, leading to an independence referendum in 2014. Theoretically, regionalist party success and strategies at these levels should also be powerfully affected by European integration. Going further, the interaction between the three levels of elections seems like a fruitful area of research, both for testing the effects of European integration but also decentralization.

In addition to these other levels of governance, the Viability Theory has clear theoretical implications for regions outside Western Europe. In the aftermath of the fall of the Soviet Union, several of the countries that emerged were quite small, with several countries, such as Estonia and Slovenia, far smaller than Scotland's 5 million or Catalonia's 7 million people. As Alesina and Spolaore (2003) argue, it would have been far harder for these countries to opt for independence in an era of autarky. The network of international institutions, including trade regimes, and the prospect of European Union membership created a political opportunity structure where these small states could survive. European integration is also likely to influence the success of minority nationalist parties both during accession negotiations and after enlargement. In this case, the causal mechanism may be even more direct. Whereas the European Union affects the incentives of regionalist parties by creating more permissive conditions in the Western European, the EU has more active leverage tools at hand to pressure Eastern European states (cf. Vachudova 2005).

Beyond Europe, many other regions are experimenting with regional integration, from ASEAN to Mercosur to the African Union. Though these organizations are at lower levels of integration, the argument that globalization and regional integration increases the viability of small states offers some leverage on understanding regionalist and even separatist movements in other parts of the world. Sorens (2004) evaluates this argument, finding strong evidence that globalization increases support for secessionist parties. Similarly, in their study of secessionist movements across the world, Fazal and Griffiths (2014) offer some evidence that international institutions more broadly—specifically the international norm against conquest, international financial institutions, and regional organizations like the EU—have an effect on secession movements in other parts of the world as well. They argue "that the benefits of sovereignty in the post-1945 period have increased without a commensurate increase in the costs. These dynamics produce new equilibrium conditions where a greater percentage of potential secessionists will have an incentive to secede" (Fazal and Griffiths 2014, 96).

Based on the results of this book, I would expect that increased integration into the global economy would have similar effects on ethnic mobilization in other parts of the world. Using the Minorities at Risk dataset, Susan Olzak (2006) evaluates the effect of global integration on ethnic rebellion. In her book, she wants to evaluate the extent to which a country's participation in international organizations affects the salience and political power of ethnic identities. Olzak (2006, 130) finds that "the process of economic and political integration among the world's states has caused a rise in ethnic political mobilization." At least in recent years among the non-periphery countries, she provides statistical evidence that increased linkage to the international system, measured by memberships in intergovernmental organizations, actually increases the likelihood of ethnic rebellion (Olzak 2006, 128). Though the causal mechanism plays out differently at the global scale, with more emphasis on international human rights groups and the varying abilities of states to repress ethnic minorities in Olzak's narrative, this result is consistent with the theoretical implications of the Viability Theory.

EU IN CRISIS

In 20 years, the EU could look very similar to its current form, it could resemble a federal state (i.e., a United States of Europe), or it could collapse into its separate component parts. This uncertainty has implications for the long-term nature of multi-level governance in Europe.[31] When the European Union was mainly an experiment in market integration, rational actors within regionalist movements could (and did) argue that the European Union was an ally in the center-periphery political conflict; however, in the 2000s, ever more policies are handled at the European level, edging ever closer to a time when Brussels would be considered a centralizing threat to regionalist actors focused on defending their territorial autonomy. The potential future conflicts became apparent during the build-up to the constitutional treaty, when regionalist parties began to express more soft Euroskepticism, particularly on specific policy issues. In other words, if the European Union centralizes power, wielding more authority over states and regions, the regionalist parties will have to adjust their strategies and attitudes toward the EU.

The financial crisis of 2007–2008 and Eurozone crisis which began in early 2009, however, projects a very different future for the European Union. Rather than centralizing, the struggle within the Euro-zone over the bailouts for Greece and other countries creates an impression that the European Union is more fragile than at any time in its history.[32] Not only are Euro countries struggling during the financial crisis, but the EU itself seems either institutionally or politically unable

---

[31] The Euro crisis has arguably politicized the European Union in national elections like never before. In Greece, the 2012 elections centered on the EU's austerity measures, with the pro-bailout New Democracy barely defeating the anti-austerity Syriza party (30 – 27 percent). The two 2012 Greek elections—and riots—demonstrate the potential for turmoil when the European Union forces conditions on member states, in an attempt to assist troubled states in their adjustment efforts (Donadio 2012).

In less troubled parts of Europe, the EU also played a pivotal role in the election campaigns. Early polls suggested that the 2012 Dutch elections would strengthen the Euroskeptical parties in the Netherlands, the radical left Socialist party and the radical right Freedom Party. But pro-EU parties won 110 of 150 seats, with a likely governing "Purple" coalition of the pro-EU Liberal and Labour parties (Schumacher 2012). Thus, despite the potential for a Euroskeptical turn in the north and south of Europe, recent elections can be seen as a vote for Europe. In fact, the Swedish Foreign Minister Carl Bildt highlighted the Dutch result as a defeat for populist anti-Europeans (Bildt 2012).

[32] While much of the narrative around the Eurozone crisis focuses on the potential for Euro-collapse, there is a path from the crisis to even deeper integration. Because the Lisbon-treaty EU has proven itself inadequate to manage the crisis of its members, French President Nicolas Sarkozy argued at times for more, not less, economic governance. In fact, he claimed, "I am a federalist," an unusual sentiment for a French Gaullist, and encouraged the EU to consider a European Finance Minister to coordinate more integrated economic policy (*The Economist* 2011b).

to respond to the crisis quickly and efficiently. In contrast, the British government's quick and decisive bailouts created space for UK politicians to rhetorically strike against Scottish independence activists. As then prime Minister Gordon Brown argued, the United Kingdom was "stronger together": "We were able to act decisively with 37 billion pounds; that would not have been possible for a Scottish administration" (Sullivan 2008). Others scoffed at the SNP's glowing admiration of Iceland, given that Iceland suffered tremendously during the crisis. While the SNP continued to point to the EU as an ally for an independent Scotland during financial crisis, unionists such as the *Daily Mail* editorial writer argued otherwise: "One lesson of the financial crisis is already starkly clear: A Scotland independent of the Union would today be an economic basket case" (Sullivan 2008).

Thus, similar to Catalonia and northern Italy and Flanders, economic issues lie at the center of the Scottish independence debate (Tisdall 2012). As Curtice (2013) concludes in his analysis of the 2012 SSA, "expectations of the economic consequences of independence probably matter more than identity.... The independence debate is quite clearly more than just an issue of the heart." Modern Scottish nationalism first spiked in the 1970s with the discovery of oil and the potential for a natural resource boom leading to self-sustainability. But in more recent times, the austerity measures favored by the Tories do not play as well in Scotland, helping energize the left-leaning Scottish National Party (SNP). On both sides of the debate, elites are trying to convince voters that Scotland is or is not viable on its own. As a young Scottish mother phrased it, "But aren't we just too wee to survive alone?" (Faiola 2012).

In fact, the Deputy First Minister of Scotland Nicola Sturgeon flatly stated that this was the key battleground of the referendum: "I firmly believe who wins the economic argument will win the referendum" (Johnson 2014). Early in the independence debate, the unionists seemed to be winning that part of the debate. Only 34 percent of Scots believe that the Scottish economy would be stronger outside the UK. 53 percent fear higher taxes if Scotland votes for independence (Settle 2012). More problematically for the Scottish Nationalists, even the voters who think Scotland would be better off are skeptical of independence. A 2014 ScotCen Social Research poll finds that only 52 percent of Scots who think an independent Scotland would make them £500 better off would support it (Neville and Dickie 2014). In contrast, of the 59 percent of Catalan voters think Catalonia would be better off after independence, 89 percent support independence (Centre d'Estudis d'Opinió 2013).

These concerns contribute to the fact that only a minority of Scots currently support full independence (Settle 2012; Whitaker 2012). Depending on the polls, between 25 and 45 percent of Scottish survey respondents support independence. For instance, only 24 percent supported independence in the 2012 Scottish Social Attitudes Survey (SSA) (ScotCen Social Research 2012), but polls taken in April and May 2014 show that 44 percent of Scots are pro-independence, with a steady increase since early 2013 (Curtice 2014).[33] In the end, the "No" vote won the September 2014 independence referendum, with a 55.3 percent to 44.7 percent margin.

Certainly, the 2014 debate over whether Scotland would automatically join the EU, with all the UK opt-outs such as currency union, or whether it would be forced to apply for membership, is a crucial part of the viability story for Scotland (Johnson 2012). In late 2012, the president of the European Commission, Jose Manuel Barroso, seemed to reject the SNP position: "If one part of a country ... wants to become an independent state, of course as an independent state it has to apply to the European membership according to the rules—that is obvious" (*BBC News UK* 2012), but neither Scottish nor Catalan politicians accept this opinion as being the final word on the subject. "Independence in Europe" has long been the centerpiece of the SNP case for independence, but even the pro-EU SNP would have a hard time convincing Scottish voters that the Euro offers more stability than the British pound when beset by crisis.

Tyler Cowen (2011) takes this argument to its theoretical limit: "If you think that the world is now more prone to financial crises (and I do), the optimal size for a nation-state has gone up. Risk-sharing really matters." Or, as Paul Volcker, former US Federal Reserve Chairman (supposedly) exclaimed, "In turbulent times, it's better to be on the bigger boat" (qtd. in Price 2011). The question remains, though, whether the best "bigger boat" is the traditional Westphalian state

---

[33] Contrast this level of support with Catalonia. Nearly 59 percent of Catalan respondents say that they would vote "yes" in a referendum on independence, according to the 2nd wave of the 2013 Political Opinion Barometer (BOP) (Centre d'Estudis d'Opinió 2013).

(e.g., the UK) or a larger regional organization (e.g., the EU). The answer clearly depends on whether the European Union can expand its risk-sharing role, or if the member states must rely on their own political and financial resources to resolve their crises. The Eurozone crisis will have repercussions for the European Union, for the viability of small states, and for the optimal size of states.

Discussion

Outside academia, attention is increasingly focused on the "Balkanization" of Europe (Hundley 2007) or even a "post-national European Union" (Erlanger 2012), led by strong culturally distinct regions like Scotland and Catalonia. Within the context of the EU, great powers are increasingly seen as obsolete, while small states are safe from attack and in an even better economic position than ever before (Hundley 2007). As Erlanger (2012) so clearly states, "The great paradox of the European Union, which is built on the concept of shared sovereignty, is that it lowers the stakes for regions to push for independence."

But if this fiery rhetoric is to have purchase, changes in political behavior must follow. As Horowitz (1985, 5) argues, "Although international conditions cannot create a conflict where one does not exist—for contagion is not the source of ethnic conflict—they can create a setting in which ethnic demands seem timely and realistic." The findings in this book demonstrate a clear and significant effect of European integration on regionalist parties in precisely this manner.

In this book, I evaluate whether supranational integration facilitates or impedes this trend toward fragmentation of traditional states and the political mechanisms through which European integration strengthens regionalist autonomy movements. I find that European integration does strengthen sub-national movements, in the form of regionalist political parties. I also demonstrate that it is the increased viability of small states within the European Union that drives the relationship between integration and regionalist political parties. Because this book provides convincing support for the descriptive and causal inferences, it has implications for both future academic work and regional economic and political regimes. In the future, national political actors must consider the unintended consequence of increased sub-national mobilization when considering deeper regional integration.

Conclusion 161

For Europe, the implications of the book seem clear, even if the future of the European Union is less so. The days of autarky in Europe are gone. Increasing interdependence between member states and between regions will continue, and these interactions will continue to shift the balance of power between central states and regionalist groups. If a "Europe of regions," or a thorough fragmentation of member states, is not likely in the near future, increasing decentralization of authority will continue to threaten state sovereignty from below as European integration and globalization threatens it from above.

APPENDIX A

Regionalist Party Vote Shares, by Country

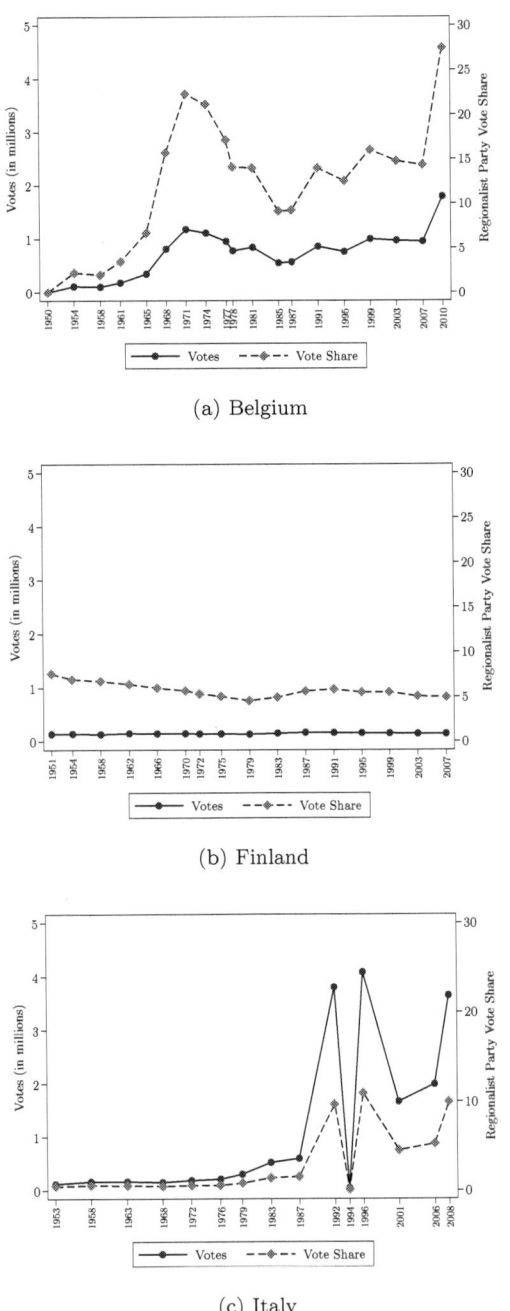

Figure A.1: Regionalist Support in Countries with Large Regionalist Parties (1)

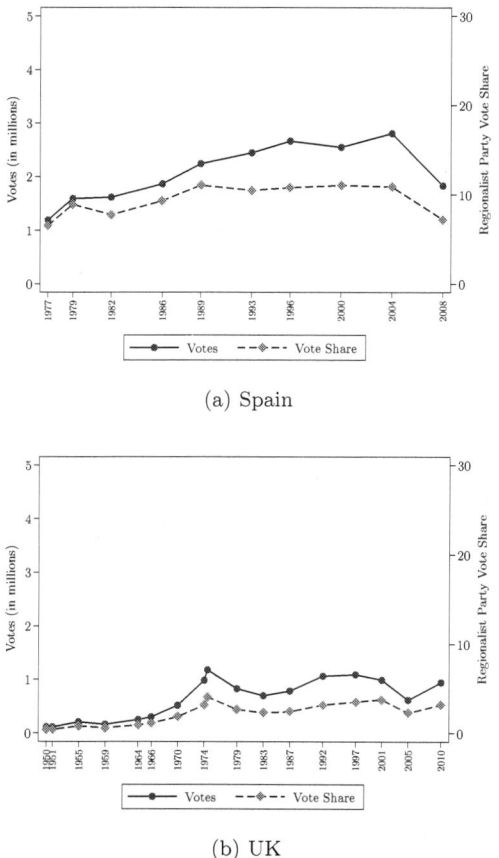

Figure A.2: Regionalist Support in Countries with Large Regionalist Parties (2)

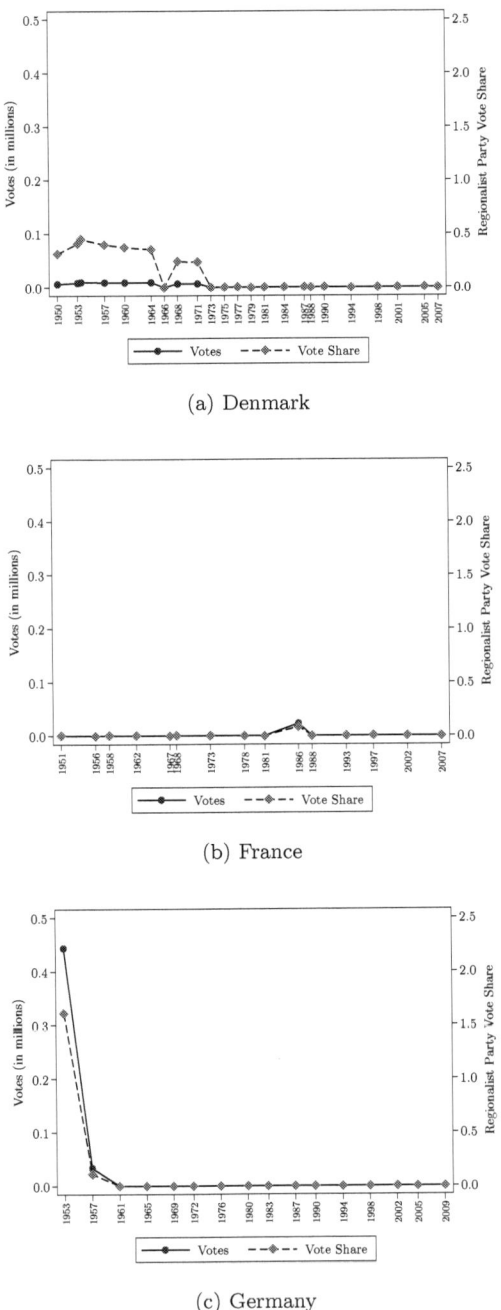

Figure A.3: Regionalist Support in Countries with Small Regionalist Parties

APPENDIX B

Cultural Difference by Language Families

Appendix B. Cultural Difference by Language Families

Region	Language (Language Family)	Classification
Austria		
National	German, standard	Indo-European, Germanic, West, High German, German, Middle German, East Middle German
Burgenland	German, standard (0.10)	Indo-European, Germanic, West, High German, German, Middle German, East Middle German (10)
Karnten	German, standard (0.10)	Indo-European, Germanic, West, High German, German, Middle German, East Middle German (10)
Niederosterreich	German, standard (0.10)	Indo-European, Germanic, West, High German, German, Middle German, East Middle German (10)
Oberosterreich	German, standard (0.10)	Indo-European, Germanic, West, High German, German, Middle German, East Middle German (10)
Salzburg	German, standard (0.10)	Indo-European, Germanic, West, High German, German, Middle German, East Middle German (10)
Steiermark	German, standard (0.10)	Indo-European, Germanic, West, High German, German, Middle German, East Middle German (10)
Tirol	German, standard (0.10)	Indo-European, Germanic, West, High German, German, Middle German, East Middle German (10)
Vorarlberg	German, standard (0.10)	Indo-European, Germanic, West, High German, German, Middle German, East Middle German (10)
Wien	German, standard (0.10)	Indo-European, Germanic, West, High German, German, Middle German, East Middle German (10)

Appendixes 169

Appendix B. Cultural Difference by Language Families

Region	Language (Language Difference)	Classification (Language Family)
Belgium		
National	Dutch	Indo-European, Germanic, West, Low Saxon-Low Franconian, Low Franconian
National	French	Indo-European, Italic, Romance, Italo-Western, Western, Gallo-Iberian, Gallo-Romance, Gallo-Rhaetian, Oïl, French
Vlaams Gewest	Vlaams (0.50)	Indo-European, Germanic, West, Low Saxon-Low Franconian, Low Franconian (2)
Vlaams Gewest	Dutch (0.50)	Indo-European, Germanic, West, Low Saxon-Low Franconian, Low Franconian (2)
Brussels	Dutch (0.50)	Indo-European, Germanic, West, Low Saxon-Low Franconian, Low Franconian (2)
Brussels	French (0.50)	Indo-European, Italic, Romance, Italo-Western, Western, Gallo-Iberian, Gallo-Romance, Gallo-Rhaetian, Oïl, French (2)
Region Wallonne	French (0.50)	Indo-European, Italic, Romance, Italo-Western, Western, Gallo-Iberian, Gallo-Romance, Gallo-Rhaetian, Oïl, French (2)
Denmark		
National	Danish	Indo-European, Germanic, North, East Scandinavian, Danish-Swedish, Danish-Bokmal, Danish
Arhus	Danish (0.10)	Indo-European, Germanic, North, East Scandinavian, Danish-Swedish, Danish-Bokmal, Danish (10)
Bornholm	Skåne (0.167)	Indo-European, Germanic, North, East Scandinavian, Danish-Swedish, Swedish (6)

Continued on next page

Appendix B. Cultural Difference by Language Families (continued)

Region	Language (Language Difference)	Classification (Language Family)
		Denmark (continued)
Bornholm	Danish (0.10)	Indo-European, Germanic, North, East Scandinavian, Danish-Swedish, Danish-Bokmal, Danish (10)
Frederiksborg	Danish (0.10)	Indo-European, Germanic, North, East Scandinavian, Danish-Swedish, Danish-Bokmal, Danish (10)
Fyn	Danish (0.10)	Indo-European, Germanic, North, East Scandinavian, Danish-Swedish, Danish-Bokmal, Danish (10)
Kobenhavn	Danish (0.10)	Indo-European, Germanic, North, East Scandinavian, Danish-Swedish, Danish-Bokmal, Danish (10)
Nordjylland	Danish (0.10)	Indo-European, Germanic, North, East Scandinavian, Danish-Swedish, Danish-Bokmal, Danish (10)
Ribe	Danish (0.10)	Indo-European, Germanic, North, East Scandinavian, Danish-Swedish, Danish-Bokmal, Danish (10)
Ringkobing	Danish (0.10)	Indo-European, Germanic, North, East Scandinavian, Danish-Swedish, Danish-Bokmal, Danish (10)
Roskilde	Danish (0.10)	Indo-European, Germanic, North, East Scandinavian, Danish-Swedish, Danish-Bokmal, Danish (10)
Sonderjylland	Danish (0.10)	Indo-European, Germanic, North, East Scandinavian, Danish-Swedish, Danish-Bokmal, Danish (10)
Staden Kobenhavn	Danish (0.10)	Indo-European, Germanic, North, East Scandinavian, Danish-Swedish, Danish-Bokmal, Danish (10)
Storstrom	Danish (0.10)	Indo-European, Germanic, North, East Scandinavian, Danish-Swedish, Danish-Bokmal, Danish (10)

Appendix B. Cultural Difference by Language Families

Region	Language (Language Difference)	Classification (Language Family)
Denmark (continued)		
Vejle	Danish (0.10)	Indo-European, Germanic, North, East Scandinavian, Danish-Swedish, Danish-Bokmal, Danish (10)
Vestsjællands amt	Danish (0.10)	Indo-European, Germanic, North, East Scandinavian, Danish-Swedish, Danish-Bokmal, Danish (10)
Viborg amt	Danish (0.10)	Indo-European, Germanic, North, East Scandinavian, Danish-Swedish, Danish-Bokmal, Danish (10)
Finland		
National	Finnish	Uralic, Finno-Ugric, Finno-Permic, Finno-Cheremisic, Finno-Mordvinic, Finno-Lappic, Baltic-Finnic, Finnic
Etälä-Suomen lääni	Finnish (0.10)	Uralic, Finno-Ugric, Finno-Permic, Finno-Cheremisic, Finno-Mordvinic, Finno-Lappic, Baltic-Finnic, Finnic (10)
Länsi-Suomen lääni	Finnish (0.10)	Uralic, Finno-Ugric, Finno-Permic, Finno-Cheremisic, Finno-Mordvinic, Finno-Lappic, Baltic-Finnic, Finnic (10)
Itä-Suomen lääni	Finnish (0.10)	Uralic, Finno-Ugric, Finno-Permic, Finno-Cheremisic, Finno-Mordvinic, Finno-Lappic, Baltic-Finnic, Finnic (10)
Oulun lääni	Finnish (0.10)	Uralic, Finno-Ugric, Finno-Permic, Finno-Cheremisic, Finno-Mordvinic, Finno-Lappic, Baltic-Finnic, Finnic (10)
Lappi lääni	Finnish (0.10)	Uralic, Finno-Ugric, Finno-Permic, Finno-Cheremisic, Finno-Mordvinic, Finno-Lappic, Baltic-Finnic, Finnic (10)
Lappi lääni	Saami (0.143)	Uralic, Finno-Ugric, Finno-Permic, Finno-Cheremisic, Finno-Mordvinic, Finno-Lappic, Lappic, Central (7)

Continued on next page

Appendix B. Cultural Difference by Language Families (continued)

Region	Language (Language Difference)	Classification (Language Family)
		Finland (continued)
Åland	Swedish (1)	Indo-European, Germanic, North, East Scandinavian, Danish-Swedish, Swedish (1)
		France
National	French	Indo-European, Italic, Romance, Italo-Western, Western, Gallo-Iberian, Gallo-Romance, Gallo-Rhaetian, Oïl, French
Alsace	Alemannisch (0.50)	Indo-European, Germanic, West, High German, German, Upper German, Alemannic (2)
Aquitaine	Basque, Souletin (1)	Basque (1)
Aquitaine	Gascon (0.143)	Indo-European, Italic, Romance, Italo-Western, Western, Gallo-Iberian, Ibero-Romance, Oc (7)
Auvergne	Auvergnat (0.143)	Indo-European, Italic, Romance, Italo-Western, Western, Gallo-Iberian, Ibero-Romance, Oc (7)
Basse-Normandie	French (0.10)	Indo-European, Italic, Romance, Italo-Western, Western, Gallo-Iberian, Gallo-Romance, Gallo-Rhaetian, Oïl, French (10)
Bourgogne	French (0.10)	Indo-European, Italic, Romance, Italo-Western, Western, Gallo-Iberian, Gallo-Romance, Gallo-Rhaetian, Oïl, French (10)
Bretagne	Breton (0.50)	Indo-European, Celtic, Insular, Brythonic (2)
Centre	French (0.10)	Indo-European, Italic, Romance, Italo-Western, Western, Gallo-Iberian, Gallo-Romance, Gallo-Rhaetian, Oïl, French (10)
Champagne-Ardenne	French (0.10)	Indo-European, Italic, Romance, Italo-Western, Western, Gallo-Iberian, Gallo-Romance, Gallo-Rhaetian, Oïl, French (10)
Corse	Corsican (0.25)	Indo-European, Italic, Romance, Southern, Corsican (4)

Appendix B. Cultural Difference by Language Families

Region	Language (Language Difference)	Classification (Language Family)
		France (continued)
Franche-Comte	French (0.10)	Indo-European, Italic, Romance, Italo-Western, Western, Gallo-Iberian, Gallo-Romance, Gallo-Rhaetian, Oïl, French (10)
Haute-Normandie	French (0.10)	Indo-European, Italic, Romance, Italo-Western, Western, Gallo-Iberian, Gallo-Romance, Gallo-Rhaetian, Oïl, French (10)
Ile-de-France	French (0.10)	Indo-European, Italic, Romance, Italo-Western, Western, Gallo-Iberian, Gallo-Romance, Gallo-Rhaetian, Oïl, French (10)
Languedoc-Roussillon	Languedocien (0.143)	Indo-European, Italic, Romance, Italo-Western, Western, Gallo-Iberian, Ibero-Romance, Oc (7)
Limousin	Limousin (0.143)	Indo-European, Italic, Romance, Italo-Western, Western, Gallo-Iberian, Ibero-Romance, Oc (7)
Lorraine	Luxem-bourgeois (0.50)	Indo-European, Germanic, West, High German, German, Middle German, Moselle Franconian (2)
Mid-Pyrenees	Gascon (0.143)	Indo-European, Italic, Romance, Italo-Western, Western, Gallo-Iberian, Ibero-Romance, Oc (7)
Mid-Pyrenees	Languedocien (0.143)	Indo-European, Italic, Romance, Italo-Western, Western, Gallo-Iberian, Ibero-Romance, Oc (7)
Nord-Pas-de-Calais	Picard (0.10)	Indo-European, Italic, Romance, Italo-Western, Western, Gallo-Iberian, Gallo-Romance, Gallo-Rhaetian, Oïl, French (10)
Pays de la Loire	French (0.10)	Indo-European, Italic, Romance, Italo-Western, Western, Gallo-Iberian, Gallo-Romance, Gallo-Rhaetian, Oïl, French (10)

Continued on next page

Appendix B. Cultural Difference by Language Families (continued)

Region	Language (Language Difference)	Classification (Language Family)
France (continued)		
Picardie	Picard (0.10)	Indo-European, Italic, Romance, Italo-Western, Western, Gallo-Iberian, Gallo-Romance, Gallo-Rhaetian, Oïl, French (10)
Poitou-Charentes	French (0.10)	Indo-European, Italic, Romance, Italo-Western, Western, Gallo-Iberian, Gallo-Romance, Gallo-Rhaetian, Oïl, French (10)
Provence-Alpes-Cote d'Azur	Provencal (0.143)	Indo-European, Italic, Romance, Italo-Western, Western, Gallo-Iberian, Ibero-Romance, Oc (7)
Rhone Alpes	Franco-Provencal (0.10)	Indo-European, Italic, Romance, Italo-Western, Western, Gallo-Iberian, Gallo-Romance, Gallo-Rhaetian, Oïl, Southeastern (10)
Germany		
National	German, Standard	Indo-European, Germanic, West, High German, German, Middle German, East Middle German
Baden-Wurttemberg	Alemannisch (0.167)	Indo-European, Germanic, West, High German, German, Upper German, Allemanic (6)
Bayern [Bavaria]	Bavarian (0.167)	Indo-European, Germanic, West, High German, German, Upper German, Bavarian-Austrian (6)
Berlin	German, Standard (0.10)	Indo-European, Germanic, West, High German, German, Middle German, East Middle German (10)
Berlin	Saxon, Low (0.25)	Indo-European, Germanic, West, Low Saxon-Low Franconian, Low Saxon (4)
Brandenburg	Saxon, Low (0.25)	Indo-European, Germanic, West, Low Saxon-Low Franconian, Low Saxon (4)

Appendix B. Cultural Difference by Language Families

Region	Language (Language Difference)	Classification (Language Family)
		Germany (continued)
Bremen	Saxon, Low (0.25)	Indo-European, Germanic, West, Low Saxon-Low Franconian, Low Saxon (4)
Hamburg	Plautdietsch (0.25)	Indo-European, Germanic, West, Low Saxon-Low Franconian, Low Saxon (4)
Hessen	German, Standard (0.10)	Indo-European, Germanic, West, High German, German, Middle German, East Middle German (10)
Mecklenburg-Vorpommern	Saxon, Low (0.25)	Indo-European, Germanic, West, Low Saxon-Low Franconian, Low Saxon (4)
Niedersachsen	Saxon, Low (0.25)	Indo-European, Germanic, West, Low Saxon-Low Franconian, Low Saxon (4)
Nordrhein-Westfalen	Kolsch (0.143)	Indo-European, Germanic, West, High German, German, Middle German, West Middle German, Ripuarian Franconian (7)
Nordrhein-Westfalen	Westphalien (0.25)	Indo-European, Germanic, West, Low Saxon-Low Franconian, Low Saxon (4)
Rheinland-Pfalz	Main-frankisch (0.143)	Indo-European, Germanic, West, High German, German, Middle German, West Middle German, Moselle Franconian (7)
Rheinland-Pfalz	Pfaelzisch (0.143)	Indo-European, Germanic, West, High German, German, Middle German, West Middle German, Rhenisch Fraconian (7)
Saarland	German, Standard (0.10)	Indo-European, Germanic, West, High German, German, Middle German, East Middle German (10)

Continued on next page

Appendix B. Cultural Difference by Language Families (continued)

Region	Language (Language Difference)	Classification (Language Family)
Germany (continued)		
Sachsen	Saxon, Upper (0.10)	Indo-European, Germanic, West, High German, German, Middle German, East Middle German (10)
Sachsen-Anhalt	Saxon, Upper (0.10)	Indo-European, Germanic, West, High German, German, Middle German, East Middle German (10)
Schleswig-Holstein	Frisian, Northern	Indo-European, Germanic, West, Frisian (4)
Schleswig-Holstein	Saxon, Low (0.25)	Indo-European, Germanic, West, Low Saxon-Low Franconian, Low Saxon (4)
Thüringen	German, Standard (0.10)	Indo-European, Germanic, West, High German, German, Middle German, East Middle German (10)
Greece		
National	Greek	Indo-European, Greek, Attic
Attica	Greek (0.10)	Indo-European, Greek, Attic (10)
Central Greece	Greek (0.10)	Indo-European, Greek, Attic (10)
Central Macedonia	Greek (0.10)	Indo-European, Greek, Attic (10)
Crete	Greek (0.10)	Indo-European, Greek, Attic (10)
East Macedonia and Thrace	Greek (0.10)	Indo-European, Greek, Attic (10)
Epirus	Greek (0.10)	Indo-European, Greek, Attic (10)
Ionian Islands	Greek (0.10)	Indo-European, Greek, Attic (10)
North Aegean	Greek (0.10)	Indo-European, Greek, Attic (10)

Appendix B. Cultural Difference by Language Families

Region	Language (Language Difference)	Classification (Language Family)
Greece (continued)		
Peloponnesos	Greek (0.10)	Indo-European, Greek, Attic (10)
South Aegean	Greek (0.10)	Indo-European, Greek, Attic (10)
Thessaly	Greek (0.10)	Indo-European, Greek, Attic (10)
West Greece	Greek (0.10)	Indo-European, Greek, Attic (10)
West Macedonia	Greek (0.10)	Indo-European, Greek, Attic (10)
Ireland		
National	English	Indo-European, Germanic, West, English
	Gaelic, Irish	Indo-European, Celtic, Insular, Goidelic
Border, Midland, & Western	English (0.10)	Indo-European, Germanic, West, English (10)
	Gaelic, Irish (0.10)	Indo-European, Celtic, Insular, Goidelic (10)
Southern & Eastern	English (0.10)	Indo-European, Germanic, West, English (10)
	Gaelic, Irish (0.10)	Indo-European, Celtic, Insular, Goidelic (10)
Italy		
National	Italian	Indo-European, Italic, Romance, Italo-Western, Italo-Dalmatian
Abruzzo	Italian (Abruzzese) (0.10)	Indo-European, Italic, Romance, Italo-Western, Italo-Dalmatian (10)
Basilicata	Napoletano-Calabrese (0.167)	Indo-European, Italic, Romance, Italo-Western, Italo-Dalmatian (6)
Calabria	Napoletano-Calabrese (0.167)	Indo-European, Italic, Romance, Italo-Western, Italo-Dalmatian (6)

Continued on next page

Appendix B. Cultural Difference by Language Families (continued)

Region	Language (Language Difference)	Classification (Language Family)
Italy (continued)		
Campania	Napoletano-Calabrese (0.167)	Indo-European, Italic, Romance, Italo-Western, Italo-Dalmatian (6)
Emilia-Romagna	Emiliano-Romagnolo (0.20)	Indo-European, Italic, Romance, Italo-Western, Western, Gallo-Iberian, Gallo-Romance, Gallo-Italian (5)
Friuli-Venezia	Friulian (0.20)	Indo-European, Italic, Romance, Italo-Western, Western, Gallo-Iberian, Gallo-Romance, Gallo-Rhaetian, Rhaetian (5)
Lazio	Italian (Laziale) (0.10)	Indo-European, Italic, Romance, Italo-Western, Italo-Dalmatian (10)
Liguria	Ligurian (0.20)	Indo-European, Italic, Romance, Italo-Western, Western, Gallo-Iberian, Gallo-Romance, Gallo-Italian (5)
Lombardia	Lombard (0.20)	Indo-European, Italic, Romance, Italo-Western, Western, Gallo-Iberian, Gallo-Romance, Gallo-Italian (5)
Marche	Italian (Marchigiano) (0.10)	Indo-European, Italic, Romance, Italo-Western, Italo-Dalmatian (10)
Molise	Italian (Molisano) (0.10)	Indo-European, Italic, Romance, Italo-Western, Italo-Dalmatian (10)
Piemonte	Piemontese (0.20)	Indo-European, Italic, Romance, Italo-Western, Western, Gallo-Iberian, Gallo-Romance, Gallo-Italian (5)
Puglia	Italian (Pugliese) (10)	Indo-European, Italic, Romance, Italo-Western, Italo-Dalmatian (10)
Sardegna	Sardinian (0.25)	Indo-European, Italic, Romance, Southern, Sardinian (4)
Sicilia	Sicilian (0.167)	Indo-European, Italic, Romance, Italo-Western, Italo-Dalmatian, Sicilian (6)

Appendix B. Cultural Difference by Language Families

Region	Language (Language Difference)	Classification (Language Family)
Italy (continued)		
Toscana	Italian (Tuscan) (0.10)	Indo-European, Italic, Romance, Italo-Western, Italo-Dalmatian (10)
Trentino-Alto Adige	German (0.50)	Indo-European, Germanic, West, High German, German, Middle German, East Middle German (2)
Umbria	Italian (Umbrian) (0.10)	Indo-European, Italic, Romance, Italo-Western, Italo-Dalmatian (10)
Valle d'Aosta	Walser (0.50)	Indo-European, Germanic, West, High German, German, Upper German, Allemannic (2)
Valle d'Aosta	Franco-Provencal (0.20)	Indo-European, Italic, Romance, Italo-Western, Western, Gallo-Iberian, Gallo-Romance, Gallo-Rhaetian, Oil, Southeastern (5)
Valle d'Aosta	French (0.20)	Indo-European, Italic, Romance, Italo-Western, Western, Gallo-Iberian, Gallo-Romance, Gallo-Rhaetian, Oil, French (5)
Veneto	Venetian (0.20)	Indo-European, Italic, Romance, Italo-Western, Western, Gallo-Iberian, Gallo-Romance, Gallo-Italian (5)
Netherlands		
National	Dutch	Indo-European, Germanic, West, Low Saxon-Low Franconian, Low Franconian
Drenthe	Drents (0.20)	Indo-European, Germanic, West, Low Saxon-Low Franconian, Low Saxon (5)
Friesland	Frisian, Western (0.25)	Indo-European, Germanic, West, Frisian (4)

Continued on next page

Appendix B. Cultural Difference by Language Families (continued)

Region	Language (Language Difference)	Classification (Language Family)
		Netherlands (continued)
Gelderland	Achterhoeks (0.20)	Indo-European, Germanic, West, Low Saxon-Low Franconian, Low Saxon (5)
Groningen	Gronings (0.20)	Indo-European, Germanic, West, Low Saxon-Low Franconian, Low Saxon (5)
Flevoland	Dutch (0.10)	Indo-European, Germanic, West, Low Saxon-Low Franconian, Low Franconian (10)
Limburg	Dutch (0.10)	Indo-European, Germanic, West, Low Saxon-Low Franconian, Low Franconian (10)
Noord-Brabant	Dutch (0.10)	Indo-European, Germanic, West, Low Saxon-Low Franconian, Low Franconian (10)
Noord-Holland	Dutch (0.10)	Indo-European, Germanic, West, Low Saxon-Low Franconian, Low Franconian (10)
Overijssel	Sallands (0.20)	Indo-European, Germanic, West, Low Saxon-Low Franconian, Low Saxon (5)
Utrecht	Dutch (0.10)	Indo-European, Germanic, West, Low Saxon-Low Franconian, Low Franconian (10)
Zeeland	Vlaams (0.10)	Indo-European, Germanic, West, Low Saxon-Low Franconian, Low Franconian (10)
Zuid-Holland	Dutch (0.10)	Indo-European, Germanic, West, Low Saxon-Low Franconian, Low Franconian (10)

Appendix B. Cultural Difference by Language Families

Region	Language (Language Difference)	Classification (Language Family)
Portugal		
National	Portuguese	Indo-European, Italic, Romance, Italo-Western, Western, Gallo-Iberian, Ibero-Romance, West Iberian, Portuguese-Galician
Madeira	Portuguese (0.10)	Indo-European, Italic, Romance, Italo-Western, Western, Gallo-Iberian, Ibero-Romance, West Iberian, Portuguese-Galician (10)
Azores	Portuguese (0.10)	Indo-European, Italic, Romance, Italo-Western, Western, Gallo-Iberian, Ibero-Romance, West Iberian, Portuguese-Galician (10)
Alentejo	Portuguese (0.10)	Indo-European, Italic, Romance, Italo-Western, Western, Gallo-Iberian, Ibero-Romance, West Iberian, Portuguese-Galician (10)
Lisboa	Portuguese (0.10)	Indo-European, Italic, Romance, Italo-Western, Western, Gallo-Iberian, Ibero-Romance, West Iberian, Portuguese-Galician (10)
Centro	Portuguese (0.10)	Indo-European, Italic, Romance, Italo-Western, Western, Gallo-Iberian, Ibero-Romance, West Iberian, Portuguese-Galician (10)
Algarve	Portuguese (0.10)	Indo-European, Italic, Romance, Italo-Western, Western, Gallo-Iberian, Ibero-Romance, West Iberian, Portuguese-Galician (10)
Norte	Portuguese (0.10)	Indo-European, Italic, Romance, Italo-Western, Western, Gallo-Iberian, Ibero-Romance, West Iberian, Portuguese-Galician (10)
Spain		
National	Spanish	Indo-European, Italic, Romance, Italo-Western, Western, Gallo-Iberian, Ibero-Romance, West Iberian, Castilian
Andalucía	Spanish (0.10)	Indo-European, Italic, Romance, Italo-Western, Western, Gallo-Iberian, Ibero-Romance, West Iberian, Castilian (10)

Continued on next page

Appendix B. Cultural Difference by Language Families (continued)

Region	Language (Language Difference)	Classification (Language Family)
Spain (continued)		
Aragon	Aragonese (0.167)	Indo-European, Italic, Romance, Italo-Western, Western, Pyrenean-Mozarabic, Pyrenean (6)
Asturias	Asturian (0.111)	Indo-European, Italic, Romance, Italo-Western, Western, Gallo-Iberian, Ibero-Romance, West Iberian, Asturo-Leonese (9)
Canarias	Spanish (0.10)	Indo-European, Italic, Romance, Italo-Western, Western, Gallo-Iberian, Ibero-Romance, West Iberian, Castilian (10)
Cantabria	Spanish (0.10)	Indo-European, Italic, Romance, Italo-Western, Western, Gallo-Iberian, Ibero-Romance, West Iberian, Castilian (10)
Castilla–La Mancha	Spanish (0.10)	Indo-European, Italic, Romance, Italo-Western, Western, Gallo-Iberian, Ibero-Romance, West Iberian, Castilian (10)
Castilla y Leon	Spanish (0.10)	Indo-European, Italic, Romance, Italo-Western, Western, Gallo-Iberian, Ibero-Romance, West Iberian, Castilian (10)
Cataluna	Catalan-Valencian-Balear (0.125)	Indo-European, Italic, Romance, Italo-Western, Western, Gallo-Iberian, Ibero-Romance, East Iberian (8)
Extremadura	Extremaduran (0.10)	Indo-European, Italic, Romance, Italo-Western, Western, Gallo-Iberian, Ibero-Romance, West Iberian, Castilian (10)
Galicia	Galician (0.111)	Indo-European, Italic, Romance, Italo-Western, Western, Gallo-Iberian, Ibero-Romance, West Iberian, Portuguese-Galician (9)
Islas Baleares	Catalan-Valencian-Balear (0.125)	Indo-European, Italic, Romance, Italo-Western, Western, Gallo-Iberian, Ibero-Romance, East Iberian (8)
La Rioja	Spanish (0.10)	Indo-European, Italic, Romance, Italo-Western, Western, Gallo-Iberian, Ibero-Romance, West Iberian, Castilian (10)

Appendix B. Cultural Difference by Language Families

Region	Language (Language Difference)	Classification (Language Family)
Spain (continued)		
Madrid	Spanish (0.10)	Indo-European, Italic, Romance, Italo-Western, Western, Gallo-Iberian, Ibero-Romance, West Iberian, Castilian (10)
Murcia	Spanish (0.10)	Indo-European, Italic, Romance, Italo-Western, Western, Gallo-Iberian, Ibero-Romance, West Iberian, Castilian (10)
Navarra	Basque (1)	Basque (1)
Pais Vasco	Basque (1)	Basque (1)
Valenciana	Catalan-Valencian-Balear (0.125)	Indo-European, Italic, Romance, Italo-Western, Western, Gallo-Iberian, Ibero-Romance, East Iberian (8)
Sweden		
National	Swedish	Indo-European, Germanic, North, East Scandinavian, Danish-Swedish, Swedish
Stockholms lan	Swedish (0.10)	Indo-European, Germanic, North, East Scandinavian, Danish-Swedish, Swedish (10)
Uppsala lan	Swedish (0.10)	Indo-European, Germanic, North, East Scandinavian, Danish-Swedish, Swedish (10)
Sodermanlands lan	Swedish (0.10)	Indo-European, Germanic, North, East Scandinavian, Danish-Swedish, Swedish (10)
Ostergotlands lan	Swedish (0.10)	Indo-European, Germanic, North, East Scandinavian, Danish-Swedish, Swedish (10)
Orebro lan	Swedish (0.10)	Indo-European, Germanic, North, East Scandinavian, Danish-Swedish, Swedish (10)

Continued on next page

Appendix B. Cultural Difference by Language Families (continued)

Region	Language (Language Difference)	Classification (Language Family)
		Sweden (continued)
Vastmanlands lan	Swedish (0.10)	Indo-European, Germanic, North, East Scandinavian, Danish-Swedish, Swedish (10)
Blekinge lan	Swedish (0.10)	Indo-European, Germanic, North, East Scandinavian, Danish-Swedish, Swedish (10)
Skåne lan	Skåne (0.143)	Indo-European, Germanic, North, East Scandinavian, Danish-Swedish, Swedish (7)
Varmlands lan	Swedish (0.10)	Indo-European, Germanic, North, East Scandinavian, Danish-Swedish, Swedish (10)
Dalarnas lan	Swedish (0.10)	Indo-European, Germanic, North, East Scandinavian, Danish-Swedish, Swedish (10)
Gavleborgs lan	Swedish (0.10)	Indo-European, Germanic, North, East Scandinavian, Danish-Swedish, Swedish (10)
Vasternorrlands lan	Swedish (0.10)	Indo-European, Germanic, North, East Scandinavian, Danish-Swedish, Swedish (10)
Jamtlands lan	Jamska (0.25)	Indo-European, Germanic, North, West Scandinavian (4)
Vasterbottens lan	Swedish (0.10)	Indo-European, Germanic, North, East Scandinavian, Danish-Swedish, Swedish (10)
Norrbottens lan	Swedish (0.10)	Indo-European, Germanic, North, East Scandinavian, Danish-Swedish, Swedish (10)
Jonkopings lan	Swedish (0.10)	Indo-European, Germanic, North, East Scandinavian, Danish-Swedish, Swedish (10)

Appendix B. Cultural Difference by Language Families

Region	Language (Language Difference)	Classification (Language Family)
		Sweden (continued)
Kronobergs lan	Swedish (0.10)	Indo-European, Germanic, North, East Scandinavian, Danish-Swedish, Swedish (10)
Kalmar lan	Swedish (0.10)	Indo-European, Germanic, North, East Scandinavian, Danish-Swedish, Swedish (10)
Gotlands lan	Swedish (0.10)	Indo-European, Germanic, North, East Scandinavian, Danish-Swedish, Swedish (10)
Hallands lan	Swedish (0.10)	Indo-European, Germanic, North, East Scandinavian, Danish-Swedish, Swedish (10)
Vastra Gotalands	Swedish (0.10)	Indo-European, Germanic, North, East Scandinavian, Danish-Swedish, Swedish (10)
		United Kingdom
National	English	Indo-European, Germanic, West, English
London	English (0.10)	Indo-European, Germanic, West, English (10)
South East	English (0.10)	Indo-European, Germanic, West, English (10)
South West	Cornish (0.50)	Indo-European, Celtic, Insular, Brythonic (2)
West Midlands	English (0.10)	Indo-European, Germanic, West, English (10)
North West	English (0.10)	Indo-European, Germanic, West, English (10)
North East	English (0.10)	Indo-European, Germanic, West, English (10)
Yorkshire and the Humber	English (0.10)	Indo-European, Germanic, West, English (10)

Continued on next page

Appendix B. Cultural Difference by Language Families (continued)

Region	Language (Language Difference)	Classification (Language Family)
United Kingdom (continued)		
East Midlands	English (0.10)	Indo-European, Germanic, West, English (10)
East of England	English (0.10)	Indo-European, Germanic, West, English (10)
Wales	Welsh (0.50)	Indo-European, Celtic, Insular, Brythonic (2)
Scotland	Gaelic, Scots (0.50)	Indo-European, Celtic, Insular, Goidelic (2)
Scotland	Scots (0.20)	Indo-European, Germanic, West, English (5)
Northern Ireland	Gaelic, Irish (0.50)	Indo-European, Celtic, Insular, Goidelic (2)

Notes: Coding based on *Ethnologue* (SIL International 2006) Language Family data and the coding procedure described in Fearon and Laitin (2000) and Fearon and van Houten (2002)

APPENDIX C

Incidence and Success

IN THIS APPENDIX, I present alternative specifications for the main models from Chapter 3. First, I consider the incidence models and then the alternative success models. Finally, I present a Heckman selection model that combines the two separate models.

The robustness across these various specifications offer considerable confidence in the key result, namely that European integration has a significant and positive effect on the incidence and electoral success of regionalist parties in western Europe.

C.1 INCIDENCE

C.1.1 ALTERNATIVE CONTROLS

In Table C.1, I present several models with different control variables. In Table C.1 columns 1–3, I consider the base model with and without the strategic party variables. In the main model, Party Accommodation is statistically significant but Party Divergence is not. In the second column, I exclude both party variables with no change to the other coefficients. Separately, each variable behaves in the same way as the base model (i.e., Party Accommodation is significant, while Party Divergence is not.).

Next, I reconsider decentralization. In the main model, the curvilinear effect is not supported: neither variable is statistically significant. In Table C.1 column 5 (RAI), I drop the squared term, but the Regional Authority Index is still not significant.[1]

---

[1] In other specifications, I tried different operationalizations of decentralization but the results are not robust. With Regional Governance Index (Hooghe and Marks 2001), for instance, I do find a curvilinear effect, with an inverted-U shape (incidence increasing at lower levels, then declining beyond a certain point). While these findings are intriguing and certainly warrant more investigation, the crucial component for this project is that in each of these models, European integration

As discussed in the earlier part of Chapter 3, economic variables are theoretically important in the study of regionalist parties, but empirical issues impede their use in long time-series analysis, as noted by Brancati (2014). Regardless, in Table C.1 column 6, I include economic difference and relative GDP/capita to test regional integration in a shorter time series and with political economic controls.[2] Economic Difference has no statistically significant effect on the incidence of regionalist parties. Again, economic difference measures the difference between the GDP per capita of the region and the average GDP of the country. So, poor or rich regions would score high on Economic Difference. Interestingly, Relative GDP per capita does affect where regionalist parties compete. Table C.1 column 6 illustrates that it is in richer regions that regionalist parties compete.[3] The combination of these two variables suggest that it is not simply difference that drives regionalist parties to compete, but relative wealth.

Notably, even with the reduced N and inclusion of the economic variables, the EU coefficient is still significant and positive.

In Table C.1 column 7 (ENP), I include a measure for effective number of parties.[4] A simple argument would be that if more parties compete in an election, then the marketplace would be crowded. Thus, high ENP should reduce the incidence of new parties. In the next column, I include turnout, partly as a proxy to capture a degree of protest vote.[5] Neither variable

maintains a significant, positive effect on probability of incidence.

[2] Specifically, EconDif=abs(RelGDP-100) where relative regional GDP (RelGDP) is simply the ratio of regional GDP per capita to national GDP * 100. So a region that has the same GDP per capita as the country would have a 100. A relatively poor region (Andalusia) would score below 100 ($\sim$ 74) while a relatively rich region (Basque) would score higher ($\sim$ 128) on the RelGDP variable. On the Economic Difference measure, both regions have relatively high scores (26 and 28, respectively).

[3] Given more cross-national survey data sampled at the regional level, it would be interesting to compare egocentric and sociotropic economic evaluations across Europe. The objective wealth variable shows that richer regions support regionalist parties more; however, using individual-level voting models, Lancaster and Lewis-Beck (1989) find that subjective perceptions of a deteriorating economic situation contributed to support for regionalist parties.

[4] The formula for effective number of parties [ENP] is as follows:

$$1/\sum_{i=1}^{n}(v_i)^2$$

or the inverse of the sum of the squared vote share of all the parties in the district election. This index has been widely used in comparative politics, for both ethnic fragmentation and effective number of political parties, since being popularized by Laakso and Taagepera (1979).

[5] Potentially, voter opinions on issues may be driving the vote for regionalist parties. While available studies demonstrate that left/right ideology has no effect on support for regionalist parties (Lancaster and Lewis-Beck 1989, 35), views on particular issues may affect vote choice. (Lancaster and Lewis-Beck 1989, 38) find that when a voter is dissatisfied with a national party's economic policy, they will

achieves statistical significance but the EU variable remains stable.

Finally, I considered a simpler version of the Language Difference variable. I simply dichotomized the variable so that regions above the mean receive a 1 while the regions below the mean receive a 0. In this final model of Table C.1, Language Difference matters and the EU variable is robust.

C.1.2 Alternative Specifications

As discussed in the main chapter, these data present several statistical problems, particularly regarding time. Beck, Katz, and Tucker (1998) argue for a new and fairly simple way to treat the temporal dependence problems common in binary cross-sectional time-series data. Recognizing that binary cross-sectional time-series data are actually grouped duration or event history data, Beck, Katz, and Tucker (1998, 1261) (BKT) propose adding either a series of dummy variables or splines to a standard logit or probit analysis to correct for temporal dependence. In these data, temporal dependence seems obvious: whether a regionalist political party competes in a particular election depends on the electoral history of that party. Once a party enters competition at one election, it is easier to compete in future elections.

Unfortunately, the bias from duration dependence is potentially significant. Per Beck, Katz, and Tucker (1998, 1263), standard logit and probit can underestimate variability by 50 percent or more. To test whether there is temporal independence, I included the temporal dummies and conducted a standard likelihood ratio test (Beck, Katz, and Tucker 1998, 1269). After confirming the existence of temporal dependence, I include the temporal dummies in Model 3 of Table C.2.[6]

Adding numerous temporal dummies is not necessarily ideal, though, because the loss of degrees of freedom can affect the precision of the estimates. So Beck, Katz, and Tucker (1998, 1721) prefer to use natural cubic splines to correct for duration dependence, expecting no significant difference for the explanatory variable coefficients.[7] The base model in Table C.2, which is also the main model in Table 3.2, presents the results from the BKT spline model.

---

be more likely to vote for a regional party. Since survey data for regions across the time series of this sample are unavailable, I include turnout to proxy for voter discontent with the government in an attempt to control for this variable's effect.

[6] Using BTSCS in Stata (Tucker 1999), I created the temporal dummies to correct for duration dependence. Basically, the program creates a series of dummy variables equal to the maximum number of events since the last incidence. In these data, the temporal dummies extend to 19 elections. These dummies equal 1 if the event occurs at that time point, and 0 otherwise. In other words, if a party does not compete until the 5th election, $k_1 - k_4$ and $k_6 - k_{19} = 0$, but $k_5 = 1$. The technique is described and justified in detail in Beck, Katz, and Tucker (1998).

[7] Tucker's software, BTSCS, also creates the temporal splines from the data (Tucker 1999).

Table C.1: Robustness Checks for Incidence—Variables

	Base model	Party 1	Party 2	Party 3	RAI	Econ model	ENP	Turnout	Diff Lang
Supranational Governance Index	5.28*** (0.55)	5.64*** (0.51)	5.28*** (0.53)	5.54*** (0.53)	5.34*** (0.57)	1.75*** (0.43)	5.09*** (0.55)	5.43*** (0.62)	4.77*** (0.57)
Language Difference	3.69** (1.17)	3.85** (1.18)	3.69** (1.16)	3.85** (1.18)	3.68** (1.14)	2.54* (1.02)	3.73** (1.25)	3.76** (1.16)	
Party Accommodation	0.08* (0.03)		0.08* (0.03)		0.08** (0.03)		0.08* (0.03)	0.08* (0.03)	0.12*** (0.03)
Party Divergence	-0.00 (0.00)			-0.00 (0.00)	-0.00 (0.00)		-0.00 (0.00)	-0.00 (0.00)	-0.00 (0.00)
District Magnitude	-0.01* (0.01)	-0.01* (0.01)	-0.01* (0.01)	-0.01* (0.01)	-0.01* (0.01)		-0.02** (0.00)	-0.01* (0.01)	-0.01** (0.00)
Regional Authority Index	0.01 (0.10)	0.02 (0.10)	0.01 (0.10)	0.01 (0.10)	-0.03 (0.03)		-0.01 (0.10)	0.00 (0.10)	-0.02 (0.10)
Regional Authority Index^2	-0.00 (0.00)	-0.00 (0.00)	-0.00 (0.00)	-0.00 (0.00)			-0.00 (0.00)	-0.00 (0.00)	-0.00 (0.00)
Elections since Last Incidence	-2.13*** (0.29)	-2.12*** (0.27)	-2.14*** (0.29)	-2.05*** (0.27)	-2.13*** (0.29)	-2.16*** (0.26)	-2.17*** (0.30)	-2.11*** (0.29)	-2.32*** (0.27)
Economic Difference						0.00 (0.01)			
Relative GDP/capita						0.01* (0.01)			
Effective # of Parties							0.20 (0.15)		
Turnout								0.01 (0.01)	
Different Language									1.53*** (0.29)
Constant	-1.31 (0.70)	-1.29 (0.72)	-1.40* (0.69)	-1.15 (0.73)	-1.18* (0.47)	-0.99 (0.53)	-2.05** (0.66)	-1.99 (1.45)	-1.01 (0.68)
BKT Splines	Yes	Yes	Yes	Yes	Yes	Yes	Yes	Yes	Yes
Pseudo R^2	0.54	0.56	0.54	0.54	0.54	0.58	0.54	0.54	0.53
N	2627	2740	2627	2627	2627	1271	2627	2627	2627

* $p \leq 0.05$, ** $p \leq 0.01$, *** $p \leq 0.001$

This particular dataset presents an additional complication. While most event history analysis only has one "failure" per unit, political parties can compete in multiple elections, and in fact should be expected to do so more frequently if they have an electoral history. Following Beck, Katz and Tucker's (1998, 1272) advice, I test the model with a control variable which counts the number of previous events. This variable does not change the substantive results of the models, though as expected it does weaken the statistical significance of some of the variables in a way similar to what lagged dependent variables would do.

In Table C.2 Model 4, I include a conditional fixed effects logit. By incorporating a fixed effects model, we assume away any unit effects and can focus on the European Union variable less fearful of omitted regional variables, such as relative wealth. But the presence of fixed effects limits the ability to explore all the explanatory variables, since language difference varies across region but not over time. Also, the fixed effects significantly diminish the degrees of freedoms in the model and they ignore information from those regions that either always or never have competitive regional political parties. Nevertheless, I include the fixed effects model in Table C.2 and in Table 3.2 simply to test the main explanatory variable for robustness in the presence of fixed effects. As discussed in the main chapter, the EU variable is still robust in a fixed effects model.

In some ways, introducing a lagged dependent variable, or an autoregressive term, seems an intuitive way to deal with the problems inherent in this dataset. It allows for explicit modeling of the dynamic nature of the dependent variable (Keele and Kelly 2006). The lagged dependent variable is a powerful predictor of future performance and in fact may even swamp the coefficients of other variables (Achen 2000). If there are omitted variables in the model, the lagged dependent variable will likely pick up some of their effects because the variables are part of the equation to explain the lagged dependent variable itself. Achen (2000) argues convincingly against relying too much on lagged dependent variables, but as Achen (2000, 25) notes, "The point is simply that autoregressive terms cannot be used to control for serial correlation without taking account of their impact on other coefficients." In other words, if the explanatory variables of interest appear statistically insignificant, the result is not necessarily damning. Nevertheless, the case against lagged dependent variables implies that including one makes a tougher test for any explanatory variables of interest.[8] As long as it makes it harder and not easier for explanatory variables to attain statistical significance, then it is a valuable model to run to control for time-series issues. I include a lagged dependent variable, with robust standard errors, in a fixed effects model in Table C.2, column 5.

---

[8] Keele and Kelly (2006, 4) contend that lagged dependent variable models have been much maligned in recent years and that the potential bias associated with them is often trivial, at worst.

Table C.2: Robustness Checks for Incidence—Specifications (1)

	Base model	Pre-fail	BKT Temporal	FE	FE (LDV)
Supranational Governance Index	5.28***	2.17*	5.36***	5.42***	3.09*
	(0.55)	(0.85)	(0.60)	(1.21)	(1.25)
Language Difference	3.69**	2.86**	3.97**		
	(1.17)	(0.94)	(1.22)		
Party Accommodation	0.08*	0.00	0.06	−0.07	−0.02
	(0.03)	(0.04)	(0.04)	(0.07)	(0.07)
Party Divergence	−0.00	−0.01**	−0.01	0.01	0.01
	(0.00)	(0.00)	(0.00)	(0.01)	(0.01)
District Magnitude	−0.01*	−0.03*	−0.01*		
	(0.01)	(0.01)	(0.01)		
Regional Authority Index	0.01	0.11	0.00	−0.03	0.04
	(0.10)	(0.10)	(0.10)	(0.21)	(0.20)
Regional Authority Index^2	−0.00	−0.01	−0.00	−0.00	−0.00
	(0.00)	(0.00)	(0.00)	(0.01)	(0.01)
Elections since Last Incidence	−2.13***	−1.57***	0.06		
	(0.29)	(0.30)	(0.03)		
# of Previous Events		0.50***			
		(0.13)			
Lagged Dependent Variable					1.37***
					(0.25)
Constant	−1.31	−1.81**	−8.82***		
	(0.70)	(0.58)	(0.98)		
BKT Splines	Yes	Yes	No	No	No
BKT Temporal Dummies	No	No	Yes	No	No
Pseudo R^2	0.54	0.60	0.56	0.13	0.19
N	2627	2627	2627	572	572

* $p \leq 0.05$, ** $p \leq 0.01$, *** $p \leq 0.001$

Table C.3: Robustness Checks for Incidence—Specifications (2)

	Base model	RE Probit	RE Probit (LDV)
SupraGovIndex	5.28***	2.56***	1.17*
	(0.55)	(0.49)	(0.47)
Language Difference	3.69**	9.33***	5.38***
	(1.17)	(1.33)	(0.99)
Party Accommodation	0.08*	−0.02	0.01
	(0.03)	(0.03)	(0.03)
Party Divergence	−0.00	0.01	0.00
	(0.00)	(0.00)	(0.00)
District Magnitude	−0.01*	−0.07	−0.06
	(0.01)	(0.04)	(0.04)
Regional Authority Index	0.01	0.09	0.12
	(0.10)	(0.08)	(0.07)
Regional Authority Index^2	−0.00	−0.00	−0.00
	(0.00)	(0.00)	(0.00)
Elections since Last Incidence	−2.13***		
	(0.29)		
Lagged Dependent Variable			1.36***
			(0.16)
Constant	−1.31	−5.75***	−4.15***
	(0.70)	(0.52)	(0.51)
lnsig2u		2.00***	0.87**
		(0.20)	(0.28)
BKT Splines	Yes	No	No
Pseudo R^2	0.54		
Log Likelihood	−472.10	−410.29	−375.40
N	2627	2627	2627

* $p \leq 0.05$, ** $p \leq 0.01$, *** $p \leq 0.001$

While we can test the robustness of the EU variable with a fixed effects model, we cannot evaluate properly the effects of time-invariant variables, such as language difference. To do so, I use random effects probit in the RE Probit model in Table C.3. This model utilizes information from both the within-unit and between-unit models to yield coefficients and uncertainty estimates. These models are typically more appropriate when there are more units than time points, which is not true in this case where the two are nearly equal. Thus, I do not rely on these estimates to interpret the results, but simply to test the EU result for robustness.

In discussing the results in the main text, I rely on the base model and the fixed effects model because they are the most theoretically appropriate for this particular dataset. This decision is supported by the fit and model comparison statistics. Though it had a slightly weaker R^2 and Bayesian Information Criteria statistic than the lagged dummy variable and the random effects probit, the statistical justification for this model is stronger. But the robustness of the EU variable across these various specifications, each solving and creating their own statistical issues, should provide significant confidence in the main result.

C.1.3 Sensitivity Analysis

Finally, I consider the possibility that a particular country is driving the result. In Table C.4, I use the Fixed Effects model to evaluate the robustness of the EU variable after excluding the few countries with significant regionalist party presence one by one. After excluding Belgium, Finland, Italy, Spain, and even the UK, the EU variable remains robust.

C.2 Success

C.2.1 Alternative Controls

The second main dependent variable, regionalist party vote share, shares similar statistical concerns about temporal and spatial dependence; however, since vote share is not dichotomous but has a nearly continuous range, we can bypass some of the problems with the incidence variable.

First, I considered alternative control variables. Similar to Table C.1, I consider the strategic party variables in isolation as well as together in Table C.5, columns 2–4. The only interesting change occurs in the EU variable, which has a p-value of 0.058 in the base model (thereby achieving statistical significance at the $p \leq 0.10$ level and barely missing the $p \leq 0.05$ level) but a p-value of 0.037 in the model without party variables (thereby achieving statistical significance at the more traditional $p \leq 0.05$ level). In the final column, I exchanged Language Difference for the dummy variable discussed above (Language Difference). The results are robust.

In the remaining columns of Table C.1, I included other variables, such as district magnitude (to control for electoral rules) and turnout (as discussed above). Also, I tested decentralization without a squared term and find a similar substantive effect to the base model (i.e., more decentralization is associated with more success). The EU variable does not retain its significance in these models.

Given the small N in these models and the interrelated nature of many of these variables (especially with the time and country effects included),[9] the instability is not surprising though it highlights even more the dramatic effect of cultural heterogeneity which retains significance regardless of controls. Instead of over-specifying the model and pushing these data to their limits, I consider alternative model specifications to better manage the relatively small N and many alternative controls.

---

[9]To be clear, the number of observations is not especially small, but with the cross-sectional time-series aspects of the data alongside fixed effects, the degrees of freedom are something to keep in mind when evaluating the models.

Table C.4: Robustness Checks for Incidence—Excluding Countries

	FE model	No Belgium	No Finland	No Italy	No Spain	No UK
Supranational Governance Index	5.42***	4.55***	5.64***	4.95**	4.72***	5.51***
	(1.21)	(1.30)	(1.28)	(1.53)	(1.37)	(1.26)
Party Accommodation	−0.07	−0.10	−0.21**	0.16	−0.02	−0.11
	(0.07)	(0.08)	(0.08)	(0.08)	(0.07)	(0.07)
Party Divergence	0.01	0.01	0.01	0.02*	0.01	0.01
	(0.01)	(0.01)	(0.01)	(0.01)	(0.01)	(0.01)
Regional Authority Index	−0.03	0.05	−0.28	−0.41	0.02	0.00
	(0.21)	(0.23)	(0.25)	(0.26)	(0.21)	(0.22)
Regional Authority Index^2	−0.00	−0.00	0.01	0.01	−0.00	−0.00
	(0.01)	(0.01)	(0.01)	(0.01)	(0.01)	(0.01)
Pseudo R^2	0.13	0.13	0.13	0.11	0.10	0.13
N	572	521	542	292	492	555

* $p \leq 0.05$, ** $p \leq 0.01$, *** $p \leq 0.001$

Table C.5: Robustness Checks for Success—Variables

	Base model	Party 1	Party 2	Party 3	D Mag	RAI	Turnout	Diff Lang
Supranational Governance Index	24.43†	26.48*	24.38†	23.80†	24.43†	16.07	16.73	24.89†
	(12.86)	(12.65)	(12.85)	(12.86)	(12.86)	(13.44)	(12.33)	(14.07)
Language Difference	36.09***	37.90***	36.11***	36.19***	36.09***	40.24***	34.44***	
	(5.15)	(5.11)	(5.15)	(5.11)	(5.15)	(5.23)	(4.95)	
Party Accommodation	0.10		0.13		0.10	-0.18	0.08	0.28
	(0.33)		(0.30)		(0.33)	(0.33)	(0.32)	(0.37)
Party Divergence	-0.01			-0.01	-0.01	0.02	0.01	-0.01
	(0.04)			(0.03)	(0.04)	(0.04)	(0.03)	(0.04)
Effective # of Parties	-1.38*	-1.13*	-1.37*	-1.40*	-1.38*	-1.22*	-1.07†	-1.78*
	(0.59)	(0.53)	(0.59)	(0.58)	(0.59)	(0.58)	(0.58)	(0.69)
Regional Authority Index	-0.56	-0.47	-0.54	-0.52	-0.56	1.75***	-0.99	-1.09
	(0.76)	(0.71)	(0.77)	(0.74)	(0.76)	(0.32)	(0.75)	(0.90)
Regional Authority Index^2	0.12***	0.12***	0.12**	0.12***	0.12***		0.12***	0.18***
	(0.04)	(0.03)	(0.04)	(0.03)	(0.04)		(0.03)	(0.04)
Belgium	-33.16***	-33.90***	-33.21***	-33.01***	-17.35***	-36.81***	-20.40***	-39.88***
	(3.67)	(3.38)	(3.66)	(3.66)	(4.57)	(3.76)	(5.22)	(4.22)
Denmark	-3.34	-3.82	-3.48	-3.49	7.85*	-7.91**	1.16	-4.51
	(2.52)	(2.45)	(2.58)	(2.49)	(3.34)	(2.77)	(2.61)	(2.78)
France	-31.50***	-32.52***	-31.75***	-31.45***		-39.75***	-24.69***	-30.77***
	(7.52)	(7.63)	(7.50)	(7.52)		(8.03)	(7.39)	(4.83)
Germany	-48.90***	-48.90***	-48.99***	-48.66***	-19.94*	-43.32***	-35.37***	-74.76***
	(5.73)	(5.60)	(5.69)	(5.57)	(8.86)	(6.04)	(6.84)	(4.38)
Italy	-15.41***	-16.52***	-15.44***	-15.60***	15.26*	-22.30***	-4.80	-23.24***
	(3.39)	(3.10)	(3.42)	(3.26)	(7.07)	(2.91)	(4.49)	(3.78)
Spain	-18.68***	-19.45***	-18.63***	-18.96***	-2.51	-25.07***	-12.59***	-19.56***
	(3.62)	(3.35)	(3.56)	(3.43)	(4.66)	(3.35)	(3.87)	(3.91)
UK	-17.85***	-18.46***	-17.88***	-17.87***	13.65†	-19.63***	-15.63***	-18.86***
	(2.85)	(2.74)	(2.84)	(2.83)	(7.69)	(3.10)	(2.80)	(3.31)
District Magnitude					2.55***			
					(0.61)			
Turnout							-0.50***	
							(0.13)	
Different Language								12.99***
								(2.07)
Decade Dummies	Yes	Yes	Yes	Yes	Yes	Yes	Yes	Yes
Constant	13.19**	11.77**	12.81**	13.67***	-20.87*	9.44*	48.74***	20.78***
	(4.61)	(4.02)	(4.36)	(4.33)	(9.44)	(4.48)	(11.23)	(5.54)
R^2	0.69	0.69	0.69	0.69	0.69	0.68	0.70	0.63
N	345	374	345	345	345	345	345	345

† $p \leq 0.10$, * $p \leq 0.05$, ** $p \leq 0.01$, *** $p \leq 0.001$

C.2.2 SPECIFICATION DISCUSSION

Following the discussion in Section C.1.2, I evaluated Regionalist Party vote share using fixed effects and random effects models in Table C.6 and Table C.7.

First, in the fixed effects model, several control variables drop as expected (e.g., Language Difference and country dummies). But regardless of the other controls included in Table C.6, the EU variable remains robust and, in fact, achieves statistical significance at the $p \leq 0.01$ or $p \leq 0.001$ levels. Thus, controlling for fixed effects of the regions, these data support a statistically significant finding for European integration.

The Random Effects models demonstrate a similar story. Rather than reducing the significance of European integration, utilizing fixed or random effects actually highlights the EU's significance. Random Effects models are not the most appropriate statistical model for these data, but they do allow for the testing of Language Difference alongside the EU. Regardless, the continued robustness is a strong sign for the main theoretical proposition.

C.2.3 SENSITIVITY ANALYSIS

In the final set of models focusing on vote share presented in Table C.8, I conduct sensitivity analysis by excluding each country one by one. Given the already small N and the fixed effects approach, this model is a tough test of the theory. In the "No Belgium" model, the variable does not achieve statistical significance even though it does maintain the positive sign as predicted by the theory. Nevertheless, except for the model excluding Belgium, the EU variable remains statistically significant.

Table C.6: Robustness Checks for Success—Specifications (1)

	Base model	FE 1	FE 2	FE 3
Supranational Governance Index	24.43†	12.76***	14.56***	24.48**
	(12.86)	(2.53)	(3.55)	(7.94)
Language Difference	36.09***			
	(5.15)			
Party Accommodation	0.10		0.21	0.14
	(0.33)		(0.20)	(0.21)
Party Divergence	−0.01		0.02	0.02
	(0.04)		(0.02)	(0.02)
Effective # of Parties	−1.38*		0.69	0.11
	(0.59)		(0.49)	(0.51)
Regional Authority Index	−0.56		−0.33	−0.47
	(0.76)		(0.43)	(0.42)
Regional Authority Index^2	0.12***		−0.01	0.02
	(0.04)		(0.02)	(0.02)
Fifties	−0.96			−2.64
	(2.94)			(2.03)
Sixties	0.54			−1.68
	(2.65)			(1.91)
Seventies	5.35*			2.17
	(2.35)			(1.39)
Nineties	−4.44			−0.85
	(3.41)			(2.07)
Oughts	−16.82**			−6.82*
	(5.38)			(3.20)
Belgium	−33.16***			
	(3.67)			
Denmark	−3.34			
	(2.52)			
France	−31.50***			
	(7.52)			
Germany	−48.90***			
	(5.73)			
Italy	−15.41***			
	(3.39)			
Spain	−18.68***			
	(3.62)			
UK	−17.85***			
	(2.85)			
Constant	13.19**	13.34***	13.57***	13.38***
	(4.61)	(0.72)	(2.93)	(3.44)
R^2	0.69	0.07	0.10	0.17
N	345	374	345	345

† $p \leq 0.10$, * $p \leq 0.05$, ** $p \leq 0.01$, *** $p \leq 0.001$

Table C.7: Robustness Checks for Success—Specifications (2)

	Base model	RE 1	RE 2	RE 3
Supranational Governance Index	24.43†	12.06***	11.92***	24.13**
	(12.86)	(2.53)	(3.52)	(8.36)
Language Difference	36.09***		41.14***	45.82***
	(5.15)		(7.23)	(6.15)
Party Accommodation	0.10		0.15	0.07
	(0.33)		(0.20)	(0.22)
Party Divergence	−0.01		0.01	0.01
	(0.04)		(0.02)	(0.02)
Effective # of Parties	−1.38*		0.32	−0.40
	(0.59)		(0.48)	(0.51)
Regional Authority Index	−0.56		−0.58	−0.72
	(0.76)		(0.42)	(0.44)
Regional Authority Index^2	0.12***		0.02	0.05*
	(0.04)		(0.02)	(0.02)
Fifties	−0.96			−3.02
	(2.94)			(2.14)
Sixties	0.54			−1.82
	(2.65)			(2.01)
Seventies	5.35*			2.56†
	(2.35)			(1.47)
Nineties	−4.44			−1.41
	(3.41)			(2.18)
Oughts	−16.82**			−8.48*
	(5.38)			(3.36)
Belgium	−33.16***			−22.54**
	(3.67)			(6.98)
Denmark	−3.34			−1.33
	(2.52)			(10.30)
France	−31.50***			−30.47***
	(7.52)			(7.45)
Germany	−48.90***			−16.78†
	(5.73)			(9.47)
Italy	−15.41***			−12.85*
	(3.39)			(5.07)
Spain	−18.68***			−10.73*
	(3.62)			(5.45)
UK	−17.85***			−22.14***
	(2.85)			(6.40)
Constant	13.19**	7.86**	−2.40	9.63†
	(4.61)	(2.46)	(4.22)	(5.74)
R^2	0.69			
R^2 Within		0.07	0.09	0.16
R^2 Between		0.05	0.30	0.54
R^2 Overall		0.01	0.37	0.62
N	345	374	345	345

† $p \leq 0.10$, * $p \leq 0.05$, ** $p \leq 0.01$, *** $p \leq 0.001$

Table C.8: Robustness Checks for Success—Excluding Countries

	FE model	No Belgium	No Finland	No Italy	No Spain	No UK
Supranational Governance Index	24.48**	10.36	35.64**	30.17***	25.76**	19.92*
	(7.94)	(8.50)	(11.03)	(7.56)	(9.34)	(9.05)
Party Accommodation	0.14	−0.16	0.35	0.17	0.00	0.29
	(0.21)	(0.25)	(0.29)	(0.21)	(0.23)	(0.24)
Party Divergence	0.02	0.02	0.03	−0.02	0.01	0.04
	(0.02)	(0.02)	(0.03)	(0.03)	(0.02)	(0.03)
Effective # of Parties	0.11	0.26	0.16	1.07	−0.38	−0.20
	(0.51)	(0.56)	(0.55)	(0.67)	(0.59)	(0.54)
Regional Authority Index	−0.47	−0.55	0.14	−0.70	−0.58	−0.82
	(0.42)	(0.47)	(0.48)	(0.43)	(0.45)	(0.62)
Regional Authority Index^2	0.02	0.02	−0.01	0.04	0.02	0.05
	(0.02)	(0.03)	(0.03)	(0.02)	(0.03)	(0.03)
Fifties	−2.64	−4.03†	−2.94	−2.86	−2.08	−0.53
	(2.03)	(2.13)	(2.79)	(2.16)	(2.13)	(2.30)
Sixties	−1.68	−2.92	−2.18	−1.57	−1.01	−0.56
	(1.91)	(2.08)	(2.43)	(2.15)	(2.00)	(2.09)
Seventies	2.17	−1.12	2.59	1.98	3.46*	3.15†
	(1.39)	(1.52)	(1.61)	(1.47)	(1.60)	(1.62)
Nineties	−0.85	2.56	−2.26	−5.58*	1.00	−0.56
	(2.07)	(2.17)	(2.61)	(2.29)	(2.49)	(2.25)
Oughts	−6.82*	−1.20	−9.56*	−9.86**	−3.65	−8.57*
	(3.20)	(3.42)	(4.05)	(3.22)	(4.13)	(3.58)
Constant	13.38***	17.36***	5.37	13.68***	15.60***	15.09***
	(3.44)	(3.68)	(4.39)	(3.82)	(3.93)	(4.10)
R^2	0.17	0.16	0.23	0.25	0.21	0.12
N	345	301	297	232	279	286

† $p \leq 0.10$, * $p \leq 0.05$, ** $p \leq 0.01$, *** $p \leq 0.001$

In the following section, I consider two final alternative specifications.

C.3 Combined Incidence and Success Models

In the main chapter and above, I conduct separate tests for incidence and success. Most studies simply ignore the incidence stage and focus on explaining vote share; thus, analyzing both dependent variables is an important step forward for the literature on regionalist parties. However, if you instead just include all the 0s in the dependent variable, there is a continuous variable with 96 percent of the cases at 0. Using the same Fixed Effects model as in column 4 of Table C.6 but with the new combined dependent variable, the EU variable achieves statistical significance with a p-value of 0.011.

A final alternative model would be a Heckman two-step selection model, with the first stage as incidence and the second stage as success. Heckman (1979) focuses on a problem where a researcher might be interested in the effect of an independent variable, but the sample is truncated in a non-random way. In this case, I am interested in the effect of regional integration on regionalist party success, but the vote share variable is necessarily censored in those places where regionalist parties do not compete. This two-stage sequence only becomes a statistical problem if the unmeasured factors influencing the selection equation are correlated with the unmeasured factors affecting the success variable. In other words, it is a type of sample selection bias, which can be treated as an omitted variable problem (Heckman 1979). In this case, that seems a likely scenario.[10]

I present these results in Table C.9.

In the Heckman selection model, the first stage is simply whether a region has a regionalist party or not. The second stage then examines the effects of the independent variables on success, controlling for the first stage.[11]

Rather than focus on the coefficients, I present the marginal effects graph in Figure C.1.[12] This predicted value graph illustrates a comparable effect for European integration as found in the base models. In general, I focus on the incidence and success models rather than the selection model because, in general, selection models are more sensitive to its assumptions (e.g., normality) than OLS and other models. Nevertheless, that the effect of European integration is robust to a Heckman model provides confidence in the results.

---

[10] In the selection model in Table C.9, the Wald test of independent equations indicates that the correlation is quite significant.

[11] For the Heckman model, the exclusion restriction is met by including a variable in the selection equation that does not appear in the outcome variable. Also, the Heckman model is estimated using the two-step estimator rather than the full information maximum likelihood estimator because the two-step is considered more robust.

[12] For these graphs, I used the **margins** and **marginsplot** commands in Stata.

Table C.9: Heckman Selection Model (2-step)

	OLS		Heckman	
RPP Vote Share				
Supranational Governance Index	24.43†	(12.86)	17.46	(13.06)
Language Difference	36.09***	(5.15)	27.50***	(3.99)
Party Accommodation	0.10	(0.33)	0.24	(0.35)
Party Divergence	−0.01	(0.04)	0.01	(0.04)
Effective # of Parties	−1.38*	(0.59)	−1.66**	(0.57)
Regional Authority Index	−0.56	(0.76)	−0.65	(0.66)
Regional Authority Index^2	0.12***	(0.04)	0.13***	(0.03)
Sixties	1.50	(2.23)	1.58	(3.10)
Seventies	6.31*	(2.67)	5.72†	(3.07)
Eighties	0.96	(2.94)	1.55	(3.22)
Nineties	−3.49	(4.97)	−4.95	(5.20)
Oughts	−15.86*	(7.07)	−17.48*	(7.01)
Belgium	−33.16***	(3.67)	−34.31***	(3.39)
Denmark	−3.34	(2.52)	−3.06	(4.74)
France	−31.50***	(7.52)	−24.52***	(6.81)
Germany	−48.90***	(5.73)	−49.74***	(7.89)
Italy	−15.41***	(3.39)	−14.34***	(3.25)
Spain	−18.68***	(3.62)	−18.37***	(3.28)
UK	−17.85***	(2.85)	−19.41***	(2.90)
Constant	12.23**	(4.04)	22.86***	(4.85)
RPP Dummy				
Supranational Governance Index			2.90***	(0.31)
Language Difference			2.08***	(0.22)
Party Accommodation			0.04*	(0.02)
Party Divergence			−0.00	(0.00)
District Magnitude			−0.01*	(0.00)
Regional Authority Index			0.03	(0.03)
Regional Authority Index^2			−0.00	(0.00)
Elections since Last Incidence			−1.21***	(0.11)
Spline 1			−0.13***	(0.02)
Spline 2			0.03***	(0.01)
Spline 3			−0.00	(0.00)
Constant			−0.78***	(0.17)
lambda			−6.77***	(1.44)
rho			−0.53	
sigma			12.74	
N	345		2627	

† $p \leq 0.10$, * $p \leq 0.05$, ** $p \leq 0.01$, *** $p \leq 0.001$

C.4 Discussion

In this statistical appendix, my main goal is to evaluate the robustness of the key statistical finding. In nearly all the models presented, the effect is consistent. Using a variety of specifications and assumptions, European integration exerts a statistically significant and positive effect on regionalist parties, at both the incidence and success stages.

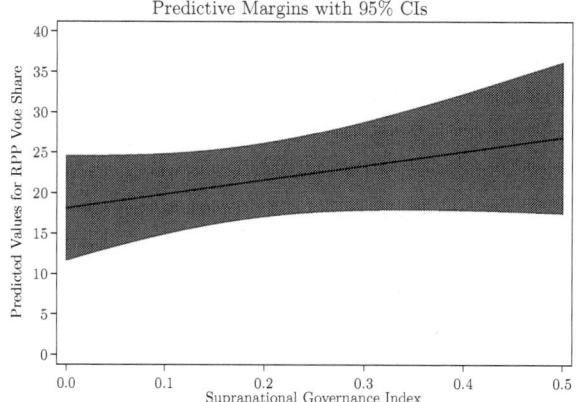

Figure C.1: Predicted Vote Shares, by European Integration Heckman Selection Model

APPENDIX D

Survey Questions

For 1979, I use the following questions to determine actual voting positions:
"30a. Did you vote in the recent Referendum on Devolution for Scotland?
IF YES Did you vote 'Yes' or 'No'?
IF NO Did you favour the 'Yes' side or the 'No' side?" [v315]

For 1997, I use the following questions:
"6a) The questions asked in the Referendum are set out on this card. How did you vote on the first question?" [refvote]

If the respondent did not vote, the survey followed up with this question:
"7a) The questions asked in the Referendum are set out on this card. If you had voted, how would you have voted on the first question?" [nvrefvote]

For both questions, I group spoiled ballots, would not vote, refused to answer, and don't knows into the don't know category. In the tables in Chapter 5, actual voting numbers include those who either voted for or favored (or voted against or opposed) the referendum in the "Yes" (or "No") category.

To determine attitudes toward devolution, I used the following question on the 1979 survey:
"31a) Here are a number of suggestions which have been made about different ways of governing Scotland. Can you tell me which one comes closest to your own view?

1. No devolution or Scottish Assembly of any sort.

2. Have Scottish Committees of the House of Commons come up to Scotland for their meetings.

3. An elected Scottish Assembly which would handle some Scottish affairs and would be responsible to Parliament at Westminster.

Appendixes

   4. A Scottish Parliament which would handle most Scottish affairs, including many economic affairs, leaving the Westminster Parliament responsible for defence, foreign policy and international economic policy.
   5. A completely independent Scotland with a Scottish Parliament.
   8. DK" [v322]

Following Dardanelli (2005*b*), I group "No devolution" and Scottish Committees as status quo and the Scottish Assembly and Scottish parliament options as devolution.

For 1997, I use the following survey question:
   "21a) Which of these statements comes closest to your view?
   1. Scotland should become independent, separate from the UK and the European Union.
   2. Scotland should become independent, separate from the UK but part of the EU.
   3. Scotland should remain part of the UK, with its own elected parliament which has some taxation powers.
   4. Scotland should remain part of the UK, with its own elected parliament which has no taxation powers.
   5. Scotland should remain part of the UK without an elected parliament.
   8. (Don't know)" [srrefvw1]

All questions and survey responses are drawn from the 1979 Scottish Election Study and the 1997 Scottish Devolution Study (Miller and Brand 1981; Jowell, Heath, and Curtice 1998).

References

Achen, Christopher H. 2000. "Why Lagged Dependent Variables Can Suppress the Explanatory Power of Other Independent Variables." Presented at the Annual Meeting of the Political Methodology Section of the American Political Science Association, 20–22 July, UCLA.

Alesina, Alberto and Enrico Spolaore. 1997. "On the Number and Size of Nations." *Quarterly Journal of Economics* 112.4 (November): 1027–1056.

Alesina, Alberto and Enrico Spolaore. 2003. *The Size of Nations*. Cambridge, MA: MIT Press.

Alesina, Alberto, Enrico Spolaore, and Romain Wacziarg. 2000. "Economic Integration and Political Disintegration." *American Economic Review* 90.5 (December): 1276–1296.

Alesina, Alberto and Romain Wacziarg. 1998. "Openness, Country Size and Government." *Journal of Public Economics* 69: 305–321.

Allardt, Erik. 1979. *Implications of the Ethnic Revival in Modern Industrialized Society*. Societas Scientiarium Fennica.

Allen, David. 1996. "Cohesion and Structural Adjustment." In *Policy-Making in the European Union*, ed. Helen Wallace and William Wallace. 3rd ed. New York: Oxford University Press, 209–233.

Anderson, Benedict. 1983. *Imagined Communities: Reflections on the Origin and Spread of Nationalism*. London: Verso.

Anderson, James and Liam O'Dowd. 1999. "Contested Borders: Globalization and Ethno-national Conflict in Ireland." *Regional Studies* 33.7: 681–696.

Anderson, Malcolm. 2000. *States and Nationalism in Europe since 1945*. New York: Routledge.

Aspinwall, Mark. 2002. "Preferring Europe: Ideology and National Preferences on European Integration." *European Union Politics* 3.1 (March): 81–111.

Assembly of European Regions. 1996. *Declaration on Regionalism in Europe*. Strasbourg, France: Assembly of European Regions.

BBC News Europe. 2012. "Huge Turnout for Catalan Independence Rally." *BBC News World Europe* 11 September. http://bbc.in/1ufMHqx. Last accessed: 12 December 2012.

BBC News UK. 2012. "Scottish Independence: EC's Barroso Says New States Need 'Apply to Join EU'." *BBC News UK* 10 December. http://bbc.in/1x6DXVT. Last accessed: 14 December 2012.

Beck, Nathaniel, Jonathan N. Katz, and Richard Tucker. 1998. "Taking Time Seriously: Time-Series-Cross-Section Analysis with a Binary Dependent Variable." *American Journal of Political Science* 42.4 (October): 1260–1288.

Becker, Gary. 2005. "Why Small has Become Beautiful." *The Becker-Posner Blog*. 17 April http://www.becker-posner-blog.com/2005/04/why-small-has-become-beautiful-becker.html. Last accessed: 1 May 2007.

Begg, H.M. and J.A. Stewart. 1971. "The Nationalist Movement in Scotland." *Journal of Contemporary History* 6.1 (Nationalism and Separatism): 135–152.

Beramendi, Pablo. 2012. *The Political Geography of Inequality: Regions and Redistribution*. New York: Cambridge University Press.

Berger, Suzanne. 1977. "Bretons and Jacobins: Reflections on French Regional Ethnicity." In *Ethnic Conflict in the Western World*, ed. Milton J. Esman. Ithaca, NY: Cornell University Press, 159–178.

Bildt, Carl. 2012. Twitter.com. 12 September http://twitter.com/carlbildt/status/245969622145302528. Last accessed: 13 December 2012.

Birch, A.H. 1977. *Political Integration and Disintegration in the British Isles*. Boston: Allen & Unwin.

Birch, Anthony H. 1978. "Minority Nationalist Movements and Theories of Political Integration." *World Politics* 30.3 (April): 325–344.

Blimes, Randall J. 2006. "The Indirect Effect of Ethnic Heterogeneity on the Likelihood of Civil War Onset." *Journal of Conflict Resolution* 50.4 (August): 536–547.

Bolton, Patrick and Gerard Roland. 1997. "The Breakup of Nations: A Political Economy Analysis." *Quarterly Journal of Economics* 112.4 (November): 1057–1090.

Brancati, Dawn. 2004. "The Regionalization of Party Systems under Decentralization." Paper presented at the Micro-Foundations of Federal Institutional Stability conference, 30 April–1 May, Duke University.

Brancati, Dawn. 2008. "The Origins and Strengths of Regional Parties." *British Journal of Political Science* 38.1 (January): 135–159.

Brancati, Dawn. 2014. "Another Great Illusion: The Advancement of Separatism through Economic Integration." *Political Science Research and Methods* 2.1 (April): 69–95.

Brigevich, Anna. 2011. "Identity, Attachment to Europe, and Decentralization in the French Regions." Paper presented at the 12th Biennial International Conference of the European Union Studies Association, 3–5 March, Boston.

Brinegar, Adam P. and Seth K. Jolly. 2004. "Integration: Using the Eurobarometer to Measure Support." In *Public Opinion and Polling Around the World*, ed. John G. Geer. ABC-CLIO, 497–503.

Brinegar, Adam P. and Seth K. Jolly. 2005. "Location, Location, Location: National Contextual Factors and Public Support for European Integration." *European Union Politics* 6.2 (June): 155–180.

Brinegar, Adam P., Seth K. Jolly, and Herbert Kitschelt. 2004. "Varieties of Capitalism and Political Divides Over European Integration." In *European Integration and Political Conflict*, ed. Gary Marks and Marco R. Steenbergen. New York: Cambridge University Press, 62–92.

Brown, Alice, David McCrone, and Lindsay Patterson. 1999. *The Scottish Electorate. The 1997 General Election and Beyond.* St. Martin's Press, Inc.

Budge, Ian, Hans-Dieter Klingemann, Andrea Volkens, Judith Bara, and Eric Tanenbaum. 2001. *Mapping Policy Preferences. Estimates for Parties, Electors, and Governments 1945-1998.* New York: Oxford University Press.

Bureau, Dominique and Paul Champsaur. 1992. "Fiscal Federalism and European Economic Unification." *American Economic Review* 82.2 (May): 88–92.

Caramani, Daniele. 2000. *The Societies of Europe. Elections in Western Europe since 1815. Electoral Results by Constituencies.* Eds. Peter Flora, Franz Kraus and Franz Rothenbacher. New York: Grove's Dictionaries.

Caramani, Daniele. 2004. *The Nationalization of Politics: The Formation of National Electorates and Party Systems in Western Europe.* Cambridge, UK: Cambridge University Press.

Carey, Sean. 2002. "Undivided Loyalties. Is National Identity an Obstacle to European Integration?" *European Union Politics* 3.4: 387–413.

Carrell, Severin. 2011. "Salmond Hails 'Historic' Victory as SNP Secures Holyrood's First Ever Majority." *The Guardian* 6 May. http://gu.com/p/2zqaq/stw. Accessed: 20 July 2011.

Carrubba, Clifford J. 2001. "The Electoral Connection in European Union Politics." *Journal of Politics* 63.1: 141–158.

Casella, Alessandra and Jonathan S. Feinstein. 2002. "Public Goods in Trade: On the Formation of Markets and Jurisdictions." *International Economic Review* 43.2 (May): 437–461.

Centre d'Estudis d'Opinió. 2013. *Political Opinion Barometer, 2nd Wave 2013.* Barcelona, November 2013. BOP 723 [Data de consulta: 21 de març de 2013].

Chacha, Mwita. 2013. "Regional Attachment and Support for European Integration." *European Union Politics* 14.2 (June): 206–227.

Cinnirella, Marco. 2000. "Britain: A History of Four Nations." In *European Nations and Nationalism: Theoretical and Historical Perspectives*, ed. Louk Hagendoorn et al. Brookfield, VT: Ashgate Publishing Ltd, 37–66.

Connor, Walker. 1977. "Ethnonationalism in the First World: The Present in Historical Perspective." In *Ethnic Conflict in the Western World*, ed. Milton J. Esman. Ithaca, NY: Cornell University Press, 19–45.

Connor, Walker. 2001. "From a Theory of Relative Economic Deprivation towards a Theory of Relative Political Deprivation." In *From a Theory of Relative Economic Deprivation towards a Theory of Relative Political Deprivation*, ed. Michael Keating and John McGarry. New York: Oxford University Press, 114–133.

Cowen, Tyler. 2011. "One Reason Why Independence for Scotland Would Be a Bad Idea." *Marginal Revolution*. 8 May. http://bit.ly/1zHoRcA. Last accessed: 29 July 2011.

Crowley, John. 2000. "France: The Archetype of a Nation-State." In *European Nations and Nationalism: Theoretical and Historical Perspectives*, ed. Louk Hagendoorn et al. Brookfield, VT: Ashgate Publishing Ltd., 67–106.

Curtice, John. 2013. "Who Supports and Opposes Independence—and Why?" *Economic and Social Research Council*. (15 May). http://bit.ly/1xuDgtg. Last accessed: 28 March 2014.

Curtice, John. 2014. "Poll of Polls: 8 May." *What Scotland Thinks*. (11 May). http://blog.whatscotlandthinks.org/2014/05/poll-of-polls-8-may/. Last accessed: 14 May 2014.

da Silva, Milton M. 1975. "Modernization and Ethnic Conflict: The Case of the Basques." *Comparative Politics* 7.2 (January): 227–251.

Dardanelli, Paolo. 2001. "The Europeanisation of Regionalisation: European Integration and Public Support for Self-Government in Scotland 1979/1997." *Queen's Papers on Europeanisation* 5.

Dardanelli, Paolo. 2005a. *Between Two Unions. Europeanisation and Scottish Devolution*. New York: Manchester University Press.

Dardanelli, Paolo. 2005b. "Democratic Deficit or the Europeanisation of Secession? Explaining the Devolution Referendums in Scotland." *Political Studies* 53: 320–342.

Dardanelli, Paolo. 2014. "European Integration, Party Strategies, and State Restructuring: A Comparative Analysis." *European Political Science Review* 6.2 (May): 213–236.

de Miguel, Carolina. 2011. "The Geography of Economic Inequality, Institutions and Party System Territorialization." (August 22). Available at SSRN: http://ssrn.com/abstract=1915225 or http://dx.doi.org/10.2139/ssrn.1915225.

De Vries, Catherine E. and Erica Edwards. 2009. "Taking Europe to its Extremes: Extremist Parties and Public Euroscepticism." *Party Politics* 15.1: 5–28.

de Winter, Lieven. 1998. "Conclusion: A Comparative Analysis of the Electoral, Office and Policy Success of Ethnoregionalist Parties." In *Regionalist Parties in Western Europe*, ed. Lieven de Winter and Huri Türsan. New York: Routledge, 204–247.

de Winter, Lieven. 2001. "The Impact of European Integration on Ethnoregionalist Parties." WP núm. 195. Institut de Ciències Polítiques i Socials.

de Winter, Lieven and Huri Türsan, eds. 1998. *Regionalist Parties in Western*

Europe. New York: Routledge.
de Winter, Lieven and Margarita Gomez-Reino Cachafeiro. 2002. "European Integration and Ethnoregionalist Parties." *Party Politics* 8.4: 483–503.
de Winter, Lieven, Margarita Gómez-Reino, and Peter Lynch, eds. 2006. *Autonomist Parties in Europe: Identity Politics and the Revival of the Territorial Cleavage.* Vols. 1 & 2. Barcelona: Institut de Ciències Poltiques i Socials (ICPS).
Denver, David. 2002. "Voting in the 1997 Scottish and Welsh Devolution Referendums: Information, Interests and Opinions." *European Journal of Political Research* 41: 827–843.
Dion, Stephane. 1996. "Why is Secession Difficult in Well-Established Democracies? Lessons from Quebec." *British Journal of Political Science* 26.2 (April): 269–283.
Donadio, Rachel. 2012. "Supporters of Bailout Claim Victory in Greek Election." *The New York Times* 17 June. http://nyti.ms/MGXDYO. Last accessed: 13 December 2012.
Drèze, Jacques. 1993. "Regions of Europe: A Feasible State, to Be Discussed." *Economic Policy* 8.17 (October): 265–307.
Easterly, William and Ross Levine. 1997. "Africa's Growth Tragedy: Policies and Ethnic Divisions." *Quarterly Journal of Economics* 112.4 (November): 1203–1250.
Edwards, Jeremy. 1993. "Discussion of Jacques Drèze's Regions of Europe." *Economic Policy* 8.17 (October): 290–293.
Elias, Anwen. 2008. "From Euro-enthusiasm to Euro-scepticism? A Reevaluation of Minority Nationalist Party Attitudes Towards European Integration." *Regional & Federal Studies* 18.5 (October): 557–581.
Elias, Anwen. 2009. *Minority Nationalist Parties and European Integration.* New York: Routledge.
Erlanger, Steven. 2012. "Europe's Richer Regions Want Out." *The New York Times* 6 October. http://nyti.ms/RIqwKg. Last accessed: 13 December 2012.
Esman, Milton J. 1977a. "Introduction." In *Ethnic Conflict in the Western World*, ed. Milton J. Esman. Ithaca, NY: Cornell University Press, 11–18.
Esman, Milton J. 1977b. "Perspectives on Ethnic Conflict in Industrialized Societies." In *Ethnic Conflict in the Western World*, ed. Milton J. Esman. Cornell University Press, 371–390.
Esman, Milton J. 1977c. "Scottish Nationalism, North Sea Oil, and the British Response." In *Ethnic Conflict in the Western World*, ed. Milton J. Esman. Ithaca, NY: Cornell University Press, 251–286.
Esman, Milton J., ed. 1977d. *Ethnic Conflict in the Western World.* Ithaca, NY: Cornell University Press.
European Commission. 2002. "Action Plan for Skills and Mobility." http://bit.ly/1yYELhx. Last accessed: 29 July 2011.
European Commission. 2006. *Employment in Europe 2006.* Luxembourg: Office for Official Publications of the European Communities. http://

digitalcommons.ilr.cornell.edu/intl/32. Last accessed: 29 July 2011.
European Union. 2010. "Nomenclature of Territorial Units for Statistics—NUTS Statistical Regions of Europe." http://epp.eurostat.ec.europa.eu/portal/page/portal/nuts_nomenclature/introduction. Last accessed: 1 August 2011.
Eurostat. 2004. *Regional Statistics (REGIO)*. Data Service & Information. NewCronos database.
Faiola, Anthony. 2012. "Scotland Moves Toward Vote on Independence." *The Washington Post* 25 February. http://wapo.st/11kiCPV. Last accessed: 19 December 2012.
Fazal, Tanisha M. and Ryan D. Griffiths. 2014. "Membership Has Its Privileges: The Changing Benefits of Statehood." *International Studies Review* 16.1 (March): 79–106.
Fearon, James D. and David D. Laitin. 2000. "Ordinary Language and External Validity: Specifying Concepts in the Study of Ethnicity." Presented at the Meeting of the Laboratory in Comparative Ethnic Processes (LiCEP), 20–22 October, University of Pennsylvania.
Fearon, James D. and David D. Laitin. 2003. "Ethnicity, Insurgency, and Civil War." *American Political Science Review* 97.1 (February): 75–90.
Fearon, James D. and Pieter van Houten. 2002. "The Politicization of Cultural and Economic Difference. A Return to the Theory of Regional Autonomy Movements." Presented at the Fifth Meeting of the Laboratory in Comparative Ethnic Processes (LiCEP), 10–11 May, Stanford University.
Fitjar, Rune Dahl. 2010. *The Rise of Regionalism: Causes of Regional Mobilisation in Western Europe*. London: Routledge.
Gabel, Matthew. 1998a. "Public Support for European Integration: An Empirical Test of Five Theories." *Journal of Politics* 60.2 (May): 333–354.
Gabel, Matthew J. 1998b. *Interests and Integration. Market Liberalization, Public Opinion, and European Union*. Ann Arbor, MI: The University of Michigan Press.
Gabel, Matthew and Kenneth Scheve. 2007a. "Estimating the Effect of Elite Communications on Public Opinion Using Instrumental Variables." *American Journal of Political Science* 51.4 (October): 1013–1028.
Gabel, Matthew and Kenneth Scheve. 2007b. "Mixed Messages. Party Dissent and Mass Opinion on European Integration." *European Union Politics* 8.1: 37–59.
Gallagher, Michael, Michael Laver, and Peter Mair. 2006. *Representative Government in Modern Europe*. 4th ed. New York: McGraw Hill.
Gallagher, Michael, Michael Laver, and Peter Mair. 2011. *Representative Government in Modern Europe*. 5th ed. New York: McGraw Hill.
Gallagher, Tom. 1991. "The SNP Faces the 1990s." In *Nationalism in the 1990s*, ed. Tom Gallagher. Edinburgh: Polygon.
Garrett, Geoffrey and Jonathan Rodden. 2003. "Globalization and Fiscal Decentralization." In *Governance in a Global Economy*, ed. Miles Kahler

and David A. Lake. Princeton: Princeton University Press, 87–109.

Gelman, Andrew. 2005. "The Secret Weapon." http://andrewgelman.com/2005/03/07/the_secret_weap/ (7 March 2005). Last accessed: 24 June 2009.

Ghai, Yash. 1998. "The Structure of the State: Federalism and Autonomy." In *Democracy and Deep-Rooted Conflict: Options for Negotiators*, ed. Peter Harris and Ben Reilly. Stockholm, Sweden: International Institute for Democracy and Electoral Assistance (IDEA), 155–167.

Gordin, Jorge P. 2001. "The Electoral Fate of Ethnoregionalist Parties in Western Europe: A Boolean Test of Extant Explanations." *Scandinavian Political Studies* 24.2: 149–170.

Gourevitch, Peter Alexis. 1979. "The Reemergence of "Peripheral Nationalisms": Some Comparative Speculations on the Spatial Distribution of Political Leadership and Economic Growth." *Comparative Studies in Society and History* 21.3 (July): 303–322.

Goyal, Sanjeev and Klaas Staal. 2004. "The Political Economy of Regionalism." *European Economic Review* 48: 563–593.

Haas, Ernst B. 1958. *The Uniting of Europe: Political, Social and Economic Forces, 1950–1957*. 2004 ed. Notre Dame, IN: University of Notre Dame Press.

Habyarimana, James, Macartan Humphreys, Daniel N. Posner, and Jeremy M. Weinstein. 2007. "Why Does Ethnic Diversity Undermine Public Goods Provision?" *American Political Science Review* 101.4 (November): 709–725.

Haesly, Richard. 2001. "Euroskeptics, Europhiles and Instrumental Europeans: European Attachment in Scotland and Wales." *European Union Politics* 2.1: 81–102.

Harvie, Christopher and Peter Jones. 2000. *The Road to Home Rule*. Edinburgh: Polygon.

Hearl, Derek J., Ian Budge, and Bernard Pearson. 1996. "Distinctiveness of Regional Voting: A Comparative Analysis Across the European Community (1979-1993)." *Electoral Studies* 15.2: 167–182.

Hechter, Michael. 1975. *Internal Colonialism: The Celtic Fringe in British National Development*. Berkeley, CA: University of California Press.

Hechter, Michael. 2000. *Containing Nationalism*. New York: Oxford University Press.

Heckman, James. 1979. "Sample Selection Bias as a Specification Error." *Econometrica* 47: 153–161.

Heiberg, Marianne. 1989. *The Making of the Basque Nation*. Cambridge University Press.

Hepburn, Eve. 2007. *The New Politics of Autonomy. Territorial Strategies and the Uses of European Integration by Political Parties in Scotland, Bavaria, and Sardinia 1979-2005*. Ph.D. Thesis. Florence, Italy: European University Institute.

Hepburn, Eve. 2008. "The Rise and Fall of a 'Europe of the Regions'."

Regional & Federal Studies 18.5 (October): 537–555.
Hepburn, Eve. 2010. *Using Europe: Territorial Party Strategies in a Multi-Level System.* Manchester University Press.
Hepburn, Eve and Anwen Elias. 2011. "Dissent on the Periphery? Island Nationalisms and European Integration." *West European Politics* 34.4 (July): 859–882.
Hirschman, Albert O. 1970. *Exit, Voice, and Loyalty.* Cambridge, MA: Harvard University Press.
Hobsbawm, Eric J. 1990. *Nations and Nationalism Since 1780.* 2nd ed. New York: Cambridge University Press.
Hooghe, Liesbet. 1992. "Nationalist Movements and Social Factors: a Theoretical Perspective." In *The Social Origins of Nationalist Movements: The Contemporary West European Experience*, ed. John Coakley. London: Sage Publications, 22–44.
Hooghe, Liesbet and Gary Marks. 2001. *Multi-Level Governance and European Integration.* Lanham, MD: Rowman and Littlefield Publishers.
Hooghe, Liesbet and Gary Marks. 2003. "Unraveling the Central State, but How? Types of Multi-level Governance." *American Political Science Review* 97.2 (May): 233–244.
Hooghe, Liesbet and Gary Marks. 2004. "Does Identity or Economic Rationality Drive Public Opinion on European Integration?" *PS: Political Science and Politics* 37.3 (July): 415–420.
Hooghe, Liesbet and Gary Marks. 2005. "Calculation, Community and Cues. Public Opinion on European Integration." *European Union Politics* 6.4: 419–443.
Hooghe, Liesbet and Gary Marks. 2009. "A Postfunctionalist Theory of European Integration: From Permissive Consensus to Constraining Dissensus." *British Journal of Political Science* 39.1 (January): 1–23.
Hooghe, Liesbet, Gary Marks, and Arjan H. Schakel. 2010. *The Rise of Regional Authority: A Comparative Study of 42 Democracies (1950-2006).* London: Routledge.
Hooghe, Liesbet, Gary Marks, and Carole J. Wilson. 2004. "Does Left/Right Structure Party Positions on European Integration?" In *European Integration and Political Conflict*, ed. Gary Marks and Marco R. Steenbergen. New York: Cambridge University Press, 120–140.
Hooghe, Liesbet, Ryan Bakker, Anna Brigevich, Catherine de Vries, Erica Edwards, Gary Marks, Jan Rovny, Marco Steenbergen, and Milada Vachudova. 2010. "Reliability and Validity of Measuring Party Positions: The Chapel Hill Expert Surveys of 2002 and 2006." *European Journal of Political Research* 49.5: 687–703.
Hoppe, Marcus. 2007. "Sub-State Nationalism and European Integration: Constructing Identity in the Multi-Level Political Space of Europe." *Journal of Contemporary European Research* 1.2: 13–28.
Horowitz, Donald. 1981. "Patterns of Ethnic Separatism." *Comparative Studies in Society and History* 23.2 (April): 165–195.

Horowitz, Donald. 1985. *Ethnic Groups in Conflict*. Berkeley, CA: University of California Press.

Horowitz, Donald. [1985] 2000. *Ethnic Groups in Conflict*. 2nd edition ed. Berkeley, CA: University of California Press.

Hug, Simon. 2001. *Altering Party Systems: Strategic Behavior and the Emergence of New Political Parties in Western Democracies*. Ann Arbor: University of Michigan Press.

Hundley, Tom. 2007. "In New EU, Smaller is Better." *Chicago Tribune* (23 March): 1–13.

Jensen, Christian B. and Jae-Jae Spoon. 2010. "Thinking Locally, Acting Supranationally: Niche Party Behaviour in the European Parliament." *European Journal of Political Research* 49: 174–201.

Johnson, Simon. 2012. "European Commission: Separate Scotland Forced to Reapply for EU Membership." *The Telegraph* 12 September. http://fw.to/SJCdDxg. Last accessed: 13 December 2012.

Johnson, Simon. 2014. "Nicola Sturgeon: Economy Will Decide Independence Referendum." *The Telegraph* 3 January. http://fw.to/AAQJgxl. Last accessed: 30 March 2014.

Jolly, Seth K. 2007. "The Europhile Fringe? Regionalist Party Support for European Integration." *European Union Politics* 8.1 (February): 109–130.

Jolly, Seth K. 2014. "Strange Bedfellows: Public Support for the EU Among Regionalists." In *Emerging Europeans and the Challenges of Ethnoregionalism, Religion, and New Nationalism*, ed. Andrew C. Gould and Anthony M. Messina. New York: Cambridge University Press.

Jowell, R., A. Heath, and J.K. Curtice. 1998. *Scottish and Welsh Referendum Studies, 1997*. Colchester, Essex: UK Data Archive [distributor]. SN: 3952.

Keating, Michael. 1988. *State and Regional Nationalism: Territorial Politics and the European State*. New York: Harvester Wheatsheaf.

Keating, Michael. 1995. "Europeanism and Regionalism." In *The European Union and the Regions*, ed. J. Barry Jones and Michael Keating. New York: Oxford University Press, 1–23.

Keating, Michael. 1998. *The New Regionalism in Western Europe: Territorial Restructuring and Political Change*. Edward Elgar Pub.

Keating, Michael. 2001a. *Nations Against the State. The New Politics of Nationalism in Quebec, Catalonia and Scotland*. 2nd ed. Palgrave.

Keating, Michael. 2001b. "Nations without States: The Accommodation of Nationalism in the New State Order." In *Minority Nationalism and the Changing International Order*, ed. Michael Keating and John McGarry. New York: Oxford University Press, 19–43.

Keating, Michael. 2009. *The Independence of Scotland: Self-Government and the Shifting Politics of Union*. Oxford: Oxford University Press.

Keating, Michael and John McGarry. 2001. "Introduction." In *Minority Nationalism and the Changing International Order*, ed. Michael Keating and John McGarry. New York: Oxford University Press, 1–15.

Keele, Luke and Nathan J. Kelly. 2006. "Dynamic Models for Dynamic

Theories: The Ins and Outs of Lagged Dependent Variables." *Political Analysis* 14 (Spring): 186–205.
Kelley, Judith G. 2004. *Ethnic Politics in Europe: The Power of Norms and Incentives*. Princeton, NJ: Princeton University Press.
Keman, Hans. 2007. "Experts and Manifestos: Different Sources — Same Results for Comparative Research?" *Electoral Studies* 26.1: 76–89.
Keohane, Robert O. 1984. *After Hegemony: Cooperation and Discord in the World Political Economy*. Princeton, NJ: Princeton University Press.
King, Gary, Michael Tomz, and Jason Wittenberg. 2000. "Making the Most of Statistical Analyses: Improving Interpretation and Presentation." *American Journal of Political Science* 44.2 (April): 347–361.
Kitschelt, Herbert. 1989. *The Logics of Party Formation. Ecological Politics in Belgium and West Germany*. Ithaca, NY: Cornell University Press.
Kitschelt, Herbert. 1995. *The Radical Right in Western Europe*. Ann Arbor: The University of Michigan Press.
Kurzer, Paulette. 1997. "Decline or Preservation of Executive Capacity? Political and Economic Integration Revisited." *Journal of Common Market Studies* 35.1 (March): 31–56.
Laakso, Markku and Rein Taagepera. 1979. "'Effective' Number of Parties: A Measure with Application to Western Europe." *Comparative Political Studies* 12.1 (April): 3–27.
Lago, Ignacio and Ferran Martínez. 2011. "Why New Parties?" *Party Politics* 17.1: 3–20.
Laible, Janet. 2001. "Nationalism and a Critique of European Integration: Questions from the Flemish Parties." In *Minority Nationalism and the Changing International Order*, ed. Michael Keating and John McGarry. Oxford University Press, 223–245.
Lancaster, Thomas D. and Michael S. Lewis-Beck. 1989. "Regional Vote Support: the Spanish Case." *International Studies Quarterly* 33.1 (March): 29–43.
Lane, Jan-Erik and Svante O Ersson. 1999. *Politics and Society in Western Europe*. 4th ed ed. London: Sage Publications.
LeDuc, Lawrence, Richard G. Niemi, and Pippa Norris. 1996. "Introduction: The Present and Future of Democratic Elections." In *Comparing Democracies: Elections and Voting in Global Perspective*, ed. Lawrence LeDuc, Richard G. Niemi, and Pippa Norris. London: Sage Publications, 1–49.
Levi, Margaret and Michael Hechter. 1985. "A Rational Choice Approach to the Rise and Decline of Ethnoregional Political Parties." In *New Nationalisms of the Developed West*, ed. Ronald Rogowski and Edward A. Tiryakian. Boston, MA: Allen & Unwin, 128–146.
Liang, Christina Schori, ed. 2007. *Europe for the Europeans: The Foreign and Security Policy of the Populist Radical Right*. Ashgate Publishing Ltd.
Lijphart, Arend. 1977. "Political Theories and the Explanation of Ethnic Conflict in the Western World: Falsified Predictions and Plausible Postdictions." In *Ethnic Conflict in the Western World*, ed. Milton J. Esman.

Ithaca, NY: Cornell University Press, 46–64.
Lindsay, Isobel. 1991. "The SNP and the Lure of Europe." In *Nationalism in the 1990s*, ed. Tom Gallagher. Edinburgh: Polygon.
Linz, Juan J. 1973. "Early State-Building and Late Peripheral Nationalisms Against the State: the Case of Spain." In *Building States and Nations*, ed. S. N. Eisenstadt and Stein Rokkan. Beverly Hills, CA: Sage Publications.
Lipset, Seymour Martin and Stein Rokkan. 1967. "Cleavage Structures, Party Systems, and Voter Alignments." In *Party Systems and Voter Alignments: Cross-National Perspectives*, ed. Seymour Martin Lipset and Stein Rokkan. Free Press, 1–64.
Lynch, Peter. 1996. *Minority Nationalism and European Integration*. Cardiff: University of Wales Press.
Lynch, Peter. 1998. "Co-operation Between Regionalist Parties at the Level of the European Union." In *Regionalist Parties in Western Europe*, ed. Lieven de Winter and Huri Türsan. New York: Routledge, 190–203.
Lynch, Peter. 2009. "From Social Democracy back to No Ideology?—The Scottish National Party and Ideological Change in a Multi-level Electoral Setting." *Regional and Federal Studies* 19.4–5: 619–637.
Lynch, Peter and Lieven de Winter. 2008. "The Shrinking Political Space of Minority Nationalist Parties in an Enlarged Europe of the Regions." *Regional and Federal Studies* 18.5: 583–606.
Marks, Gary. 2004. "Conclusion: European Integration and Political Conflict." In *European Integration and Political Conflict*, ed. Gary Marks and Marco R. Steenbergen. New York: Cambridge University Press, 235–259.
Marks, Gary and Carole Wilson. 2000. "The Past in the Present: A Cleavage Theory of Party Response to European Integration." *British Journal of Political Science* 30.3 (July): 433–459.
Marks, Gary, Carole Wilson, and Leonard Ray. 2002. "National Political Parties and European Integration." *American Journal of Political Science* 46.3: 585–594.
Marks, Gary and Liesbet Hooghe. 2000. "Optimality and Authority: A Critique of Neoclassical Theory." *Journal of Common Market Studies* 38.5 (December): 795–816.
Marks, Gary, Liesbet Hooghe, Marco R. Steenbergen, and Ryan Bakker. 2007. "Cross-Validating Data on Party Positioning on European Integration." *Electoral Studies* 26.1: 23–38.
Marks, Gary, Liesbet Hooghe, Moira Nelson, and Erica Edwards. 2006. "Party Competition and European Integration in East and West. Different Structure, Same Causality." *Comparative Political Studies* 39 (March): 155–75.
Marks, Gary and Marco R Steenbergen, eds. 2004. *European Integration and Political Conflict*. New York: Cambridge University Press.
McAdam, Doug. 1982. *Political Process and the Development of Black Insurgency, 1930-1970*. Chicago: University of Chicago Press.
McCrone, D., A. Brown, P. Surridge, and K. Thomson. 1997. *British Gen-*

eral Election Study: Scottish Election Survey, 1997. 2nd ICPSR version. London, England: Social and Community Planning Research [producer], 1998. Colchester, England: The Data Archive/Ann Arbor, MI: Inter-university Consortium for Political and Social Research [distributors], 2000. doi:10.3886/ICPSR02617.

McCrone, David. 2001. *Understanding Scotland: The Sociology of a Nation.* 2nd ed. New York: Routledge.

McCrone, David and Bethan Lewis. 1999. "The Scottish and Welsh Referendum Campaigns." In *Scotland and Wales: Nations Again?*, ed. Bridget Taylor and Katarina Thomson. Cardiff: University of Wales Press, 17–40.

McDonnell, Duncan. 2014. "Lega Nord's Euroscepticism Represents Political Opportunism rather than a Deeply-held Ideological Stance Similar to UKIP." *LSE's EUROPP Blog.* 6 May http://bit.ly/1qaxB9X. Last accessed: 6 May 2014.

McLaren, Lauren M. 2002. "Public Support for the European Union: Cost/Benefit Analysis or Perceived Cultural Threat?" *Journal of Politics* 64.2 (May): 551–566.

McMillan, Joyce. 1996. "Scotland's Quiet Nationalism." In *Europe's New Nationalism: States and Minorities in Conflict*, ed. Richard Caplan and John Feffer. New York: Oxford University Press.

Meadwell, Hudson and Pierre Martin. 1996. "Economic Integration and the Politics of Independence." *Nations and Nationalism* 2.1: 67–87.

Meguid, Bonnie M. 2005. "Competition Between Unequals: The Role of Mainstream Party Strategy in Niche Party Success." *American Political Science Review* 99.3 (August): 347–360.

Meguid, Bonnie M. 2008. *Party Competition between Unequals: Strategies and Electoral Fortunes in Western Europe.* New York: Cambridge University Press.

Miguel, Edward. 2003. "Tribe or Nation: Nation-Building and Public Goods in Kenya versus Tanzania." Presented at the Duke University Comparative Politics Workshop, 20 October, Durham NC.

Mill, John Stuart. [1861] 1998. *Utilitarianism, On Liberty, Considerations on Representative Government.* Ed. Geraint Williams. London: Everyman.

Miller, W.L. and J.A. Brand. 1981. *Scottish Election Study, 1979.* Colchester, Essex: UK Data Archive [distributor]. SN: 1604.

Mitchell, James. 1996. *Strategies for Self-Government. The Campaigns for a Scottish Parliament.* Edinburgh: Polygon.

Mitchell, James, David Denver, Charles Pattie, and Hugh Bochel. 1998. "The 1997 Devolution Referendum in Scotland." *Parliamentary Affairs* 51.2 (April): 166–181.

Monnet, Jean. 1962. "A Ferment of Change." *Journal of Common Market Studies* 1.1: 203–211.

Moore, Margaret. 2001. "Globalization, Cosmopolitanism, and Minority Nationalism." In *Minority Nationalism and the Changing International Order*, ed. Michael Keating and John McGarry. New York: Oxford University

Press, 44–60.
Moravcsik, Andrew. 1998. *The Choice for Europe: Social Purpose and State Power from Messina to Maastricht.* Cornell University Press.
Mulholland, Hélène and Matthew Tempest. 2006. "Majority in Scotland Wants Independence, Says Poll." *The Guardian* 2 November. http://gu.com/p/pcp3/stw. Last accessed: 28 July 2011.
Neville, Sarah and Mure Dickie. 2014. "Scotland's Poorer More Likely to Favour Independence." *Financial Times* 21 January. http://on.ft.com/1fa717j. Last accessed: 30 March 2014.
Newhouse, Joseph. 1997. "Europe's Rising Regionalism." *Foreign Affairs* 76.1 (January/February): 67–84.
Nielsen, Francois. 1980. "The Flemish Movement in Belgium after World War II: A Dynamic Analysis." *American Sociological Review* 45: 76–94.
Nielsen, Francois. 1985. "Toward a Theory of Ethnic Solidarity in Modern Societies." *American Sociological Review* 50: 133–149.
Norris, Pippa. 2005. *Radical Right: Voters and Parties in the Electoral Market.* New York: Cambridge University Press.
Olson, Anna M. 2011. "Linking the EU to Its Citizens—Regions as Interest Representatives in Brussels." Paper presented at the 12th Biennial International Conference of the European Union Studies Association, 3–5 March, Boston.
Olzak, Susan. 1983. "Contemporary Ethnic Mobilization." *Annual Review of Sociology* 9: 355–374.
Olzak, Susan. 2006. *The Global Dynamics of Racial and Ethnic Mobilization.* Stanford, CA: Stanford University Press.
Pereira, Juan Montabes, Carmen Ortega Villodres, and Enrique G. Pérez Nieto. 2003. "Electoral Systems and Electoral Success of Regionalist Parties in Western Europe." Presented at the ECPR Joint Sessions, 28 March–2 April, Edinburgh, Scotland.
Pittock, Murray G. H. 2001. *Scottish Nationality.* New York: Palgrave.
Posner, Daniel N. 2004. "Measuring Ethnic Fractionalization in Africa." *American Journal of Political Science* 48.4 (October): 849–863.
Price, Adam. 2011. "Small Is Cute, Sexy, and Successful: Why Independence for Wales and Other Countries Makes Economic Sense." *Harvard Kennedy School Review: 2011 Edition* http://bit.ly/1uNjmcg. Last accessed: 17 December 2012.
Ragin, Charles C. 1979. "Ethnic Political Mobilization: The Welsh Case." *American Sociological Review* 44.4 (August): 619–635.
Ragin, Charles C. 1987. *The Comparative Method: Moving Beyond Qualitative and Quantitative Strategies.* Berkeley, CA: University of California Press.
Ray, Leonard. 1999. "Measuring Party Orientations Towards European Integration: Results from an Expert Survey." *European Journal of Political Research* 36: 283–306.
Ray, Leonard. 2004. "Don't Rock the Boat: Expectations, Fears, and Oppo-

sition to EU-level Policy-Making." In *European Integration and Political Conflict*, ed. Gary Marks and Marco R. Steenbergen. New York: Cambridge University Press, 51–61.

Reid, T.R. 2000. "EU's Potential Lifts Scots' Hope of Independence; Separatists Look to Continent." *The Washington Post* 12 December: A01.

Roessingh, Martijn A. 1996. *Ethnonationalism and Political Systems in Europe: A State of Tension*. Amsterdam: Amsterdam University Press.

Rüdig, Wolfgang. 1990. *Explaining Green Party Development. Reflections on a Theoretical Framework*. Glasgow, Scotland: Strathclyde Papers on Government and Politics, No. 71.

Rudolph, J. R. and R. J. Thompson. 1985. "Ethnoterritorial Movements and the Policy Process: Accommodating Nationalist Demands in the Developed World." *Comparative Politics* 17.3 (April): 291–311.

Rudolph Jr., Joseph R. 1977. "Ethnic Sub-States and the Emergent Politics of Tri-Level Interaction in Western Europe." *The Western Political Quarterly* 30.4 (December): 537–557.

Scharpf, Fritz. 1996. "Negative and Positive Integration in the Political Economy of European Welfare States." In *Governance in the European Union*, ed. Gary Marks, Fritz W. Scharpf, Philippe C. Schmitter, and Wolfgang Streeck. Sage, 15–39.

Scheinman, Lawrence. 1977. "The Interfaces of Regionalism in Western Europe: Brussels and the Peripheries." In *Ethnic Conflict in the Western World*, ed. Milton J. Esman. Ithaca, NY: Cornell University Press, 65–80.

Schmitt, Hermann and Evi Scholz. 2005. *Mannheim Eurobarometer Trend File, 1970-2002*. Mannheim, Germany: Mannheimer Zentrum fur Europaische Sozialforschung and Zentrum fur Umfragen, Methoden und Analysen [producers], 2005. Cologne, Germany: Zentralarchiv fur Empirische Sozialforschung/Ann Arbor, MI: Inter-university Consortium for Political and Social Research [distributors], 2005-12-06.

Schumacher, Gijs. 2012. "Election Report: 2012 Netherlands Parliamentary Elections—An Unexpected Outcome." *The Monkey Cage*. 13 September http://bit.ly/1hLCJgh. Last accessed: 13 December 2012.

ScotCen Social Research. 2012. *Scottish Social Attitudes Survey, 2012*. [computer file]. 2nd Edition. Colchester, Essex: UK Data Archive [distributor], September 2013. SN: 7338.

Scottish National Party. 1947. *Policy of the Scottish National Party*. Scottish National Party.

Scottish National Party. 1949. *Constitution and Rules of the Scottish National Party*. Scottish National Party.

Scottish National Party. 1974a. *Getting Together. General Election Manifesto—February 1974*. 4th ed. Scottish National Party.

Scottish National Party. 1974b. *It's Time... Supplement to the Election Manifesto of the Scottish National Party—September 1974*. 4th ed. Scottish National Party.

Scottish National Party. 1974c. *SNP & You. Aims & Policy of the Scottish*

National Party. 4th ed. Scottish National Party.
Scottish National Party. 1976. *Scotland's Future. S.N.P. Manifesto*. Scottish National Party.
Scottish National Party. 1979. *Return to Nationhood. Manifesto for the General Election*. Scottish National Party.
Scottish National Party. 1983. *Choose Scotland—The Challenge of Independence. Manifesto for the General Election*. Scottish National Party.
Scottish National Party. 1987. *Play the Scottish Card. Manifesto for the General Election*. Scottish National Party.
Scottish National Party. 1990. *Scotland's Future—Independence in Europe. Manifesto for the Regional Elections*. Scottish National Party.
Scottish National Party. 1992. *Independence in Europe—Make It Happen Now. Manifesto for the Regional Elections*. Scottish National Party.
Scottish National Party. 1997. *Yes We Can. Win the Best for Scotland. Manifesto for the General Election*. Scottish National Party.
Scottish National Party. 1999. *Manifesto for Scottish Parliament Elections*. Scottish National Party.
Scottish National Party. 2001. *We Stand for Scotland. Manifesto for the General Election*. Scottish National Party.
Scottish National Party. 2003. *The Complete Case for a Better Scotland. Manifesto for the Scottish Election*. Scottish National Party.
Scottish National Party. 2005a. *If Scotland Matters to You Make It Matter in May. Manifesto Core for the General Election*. Scottish National Party.
Scottish National Party. 2005b. *If Scotland Matters to You Make It Matter in May. Manifesto Magazine for the General Election*. Scottish National Party.
Scottish National Party. 2010. *Elect a Local Champion. Manifesto 2010*. Scottish National Party. http://bit.ly/snp2010manifesto. Last accessed: 18 December 2012.
Selb, Peter and Sandrine Pituctin. 2010. "Methodological Issues in the Study of New Parties' Entry and Electoral Success." *Party Politics* 16.2: 147–170.
Settle, Michael. 2012. "Voters Fear Economic Impact of Independence." *Herald Scotland* 16 September. http://bit.ly/1vu0r8m. Last accessed: 13 December 2012.
SIL International. 2006. "Ethnologue—Languages of the World." http://www.ethnologue.com (March 24, 2006).
Sillars, Jim. 1986. *Scotland. The Case for Optimism*. Polygon.
Sillars, Jim. 2011. "It's Time to Ditch EU, Alex." *Scotsman* 20 December. http://bit.ly/sillars2011. Last accessed: 17 December 2012.
Sorens, Jason. 2004. "Globalization, Secessionism, and Autonomy." *Electoral Studies* 23: 727–752.
Sorens, Jason. 2005. "The Cross-Sectional Determinants of Secessionism in Advanced Democracies." *Comparative Political Studies* 38.3 (April): 324–326.
Spendzharova, Aneta B. and Milada Anna Vachudova. 2012. "Catching Up?

Consolidating Liberal Democracy in Bulgaria and Romania after EU Accession." *West European Politics* 35.1: 39–58.

Spoon, Jae-Jae. 2011. *Political Survival of Small Parties in Europe*. Ann Arbor: University of Michigan Press.

Steenbergen, Marco and Gary Marks. 2007. "Evaluating Expert Surveys." *European Journal of Political Research* 46.3: 347–366.

Steenbergen, Marco R. and Bradford S. Jones. 2002. "Modeling Multilevel Data Structures." *American Journal of Political Science* 46.1 (January): 218–237.

Steenbergen, Marco R., Erica E. Edwards, and Catherine E. de Vries. 2007. "Who's Cueing Whom? Mass-Elite Linkages and the Future of European Integration." *European Union Politics* 8.1: 13–35.

Sullivan, Kevin. 2008. "Bailout's Toll Is Higher in Scotland." *The Washington Post* 16 October. http://wapo.st/11kk7xz. Accessed: 29 July 2011.

Surridge, Paula and David McCrone. 1999. "The 1997 Scottish Referendum Vote." In *Scotland and Wales: Nations Again?*, ed. Bridget Taylor and Katarina Thomson. Cardiff: University of Wales Press, 41–64.

Taggart, Paul. 1998. "A Touchstone of Dissent: Euroscepticism in Contemporary Western European Party Systems." *European Journal of Political Research* 33: 363–388.

Taggart, Paul and Aleks Szczerbiak. 2004. "Contemporary Euroscepticism in the Systems of the European Union Candidate States of Central and Eastern Europe." *European Journal of Political Research* 43.1 (January): 1–27.

Tatham, Michaël and Michael W. Bauer. 2011. "Not necessarily supranationalists? Regio-crats and the European Commission." Paper presented at the 6th ECPR General Conference, 25–27 August, University of Iceland, Iceland.

Tavits, Margit. 2006. "Party System Change. Testing a Model of New Party Entry." *Party Politics* 12.1: 99–119.

Taylor, Bridget, John Curtice, and Katarina Thomson. 1999. "Introduction and Conclusions." In *Scotland and Wales: Nations Again?*, ed. Bridget Taylor and Katarina Thomson. Cardiff: University of Wales Press, xxiii–xlii.

The Economist. 2005. "Spain's Rowdy Regions." *The Economist* (6 October).

The Economist. 2010. "An artificial kingdom moves closer to its end." *The Economist* (14 June).

The Economist. 2011a. "Charlemagne. Ceci n'est plus un pays." *The Economist* (23 July): 52.

The Economist. 2011b. "Charlemagne. How much closer a union?" *The Economist* (30 July): 50.

The Economist. 2012. "Europe's Next Independent State?" *The Economist* (22 September) http://econ.st/OI1iY8. Last accessed: 17 December 2012.

Tiebout, Charles. 1956. "A Pure Theory of Local Expenditures." *The Journal of Political Economy* 64.5 (October): 416–424.

Tilly, Charles. 1975. "Reflections on the History of European State-Making." In *The Formation of National States in Western Europe*, ed. Charles Tilly. Princeton, NJ: Princeton University Press, 3–83.

Tisdall, Simon. 2012. "Separation Anxiety: The State of Independence Movements in Europe." *The Guardian* 13 September. http://gu.com/p/3adfx/stw. Last accessed: 13 December 2012.

Tomz, Michael, Jason Wittenberg, and Gary King. 2003. "CLARIFY: Software for Interpreting and Presenting Statistical Results." Software. http://gking.harvard.edu/ (April 24, 2007).

Treisman, Daniel. 2007. *The Architecture of Government: Rethinking Political Decentralization*. New York: Cambridge University Press.

Tronconi, Filippo. 2006. "Ethnic Identity and Party Competition. An Analysis of the Electoral Performance of Ethnoregionalist Parties in Western Europe." *World Political Science Review* 2.2: 137–163.

Tucker, Richard. 1999. "BTSCS: A Binary Time-Series-Cross-Section Data Analysis Utility." Software. http://www.prio.org/Data/Stata-Tools/ (April 29, 2005).

Vachudova, Milada Anna. 2005. *Europe Undivided: Democracy, Leverage, and Integration After Communism*. Oxford: Oxford University Press.

van Amersfoort, Hans and Jan Mansvelt Beck. 2000. "Institutional Plurality: A Way Out of the Basque Conflict?" *Journal of Ethnic and Migration Studies* 26.3 (July): 449–467.

van Houten, Pieter. 2000. *Regional Assertiveness in Western Europe. Political Constraints and the Role of Party Competition*. Ph.D. Thesis. Chicago: University of Chicago.

van Houten, Pieter. 2003. "Globalization and Demands for Regional Autonomy in Europe." In *Governance in a Global Economy*, ed. Miles A. Kahler and David Lake. Princeton, NJ: Princeton University Press, 110–135.

Van Morgan, Sydney A. 2006. "Plaid Cymru—The Party of Wales: the New Politics of Welsh Nationalism at the Dawn of the 21st Century." In *Autonomist Parties in Europe: Identity Politics and the Revival of the Territorial Cleavage*, ed. Lieven de Winter, Margarita Gómez-Reino, and Peter Lynch. Vol. 1. Barcelona: Institut de Ciències Polítiques i Socials (ICPS), 253–283.

Volkens, Andrea, Onawa Lacewell, Sven Regel, Henrike Schultze, and Annika Werner. 2010. "The Manifesto Data Collection. Manifesto Project (MRG/CMP/MARPOR)." http://manifestoproject.wzb.eu/ (6 May, 2011).

Volkens, Hans-Dieter Klingemann Andrea, Judith Bara, Ian Budge, and Michael McDonald. 2006. *Mapping Policy Preferences II. Estimates for Parties, Electors, and Governments in Eastern Europe, European Union and OECD 1990–2003*. New York: Oxford University Press.

Whitaker, Andrew. 2012. "Scottish Independence: No Sign of Surge in Scots' Support." *Scotsman* 17 September. http://bit.ly/1tmvU4U. Last accessed: 13 December 2012.

Wilson, Andrew. 2003. *Moving Scotland Beyond the Subsidy Myth. Why Economic Growth is What Matters*. Scottish National Party.

Wittman, Donald. 2000. "The Wealth and Size of Nations." *The Journal of Conflict Resolution* 44.6 (December): 868–884.

Young, Robert. 2012. "The Inconvenient Truth about Seceding States." *The New York Times* 1 November. http://nyti.ms/1tmvXxN. Last accessed: 17 December 2012.

Young, Robert A. 1992. "Does Globalization Make an Independent Quebec More Viable?" In *Federalism in Peril: National Unity, Individualism, Free Markets, and the Emerging Global Economy*, ed. A. R. Riggs and Tom Velk. Vancouver: Fraser University Press, 121–134.

Index

Adenauer, Konrad, 1
African Union, 2, 155
Amsterdam, Treaty of, 66n24
Andalusia, 21
Andalusian Party, 21, 94
anti-EU sentiment, 112. *See also* Euroskepticism
APT, *See* Association for Trieste
Aragon, 21, 78
Aragonese League, 21
Aragonese Regionalist Party, 21
ASEAN, 2, 155
Assembly of European Regions, 68
assimilation, 8, 11
Association for Trieste, 20
Austria, 70, 107, 110, 168
autarky, 125, 155, 161
autonomy movements
  cultural autonomy, 16, 46
  European integration, 89, 150
  homogenous preference, 47
  modernization, 35
  regionalism, 7
  separatism, 16
  support for, 52
  Viability Theory, 3

bailouts, 43n15, 157
Balearic Islands, 21
balkanization, 160
Barcelona, 149
Barroso, Jose Manuel, 159
Bavarian Party, 20

Basque country
  economic interests, 37, 146
  Euro crisis, 149
  European Union, support for, 97, 120
  industrialization, 17, 146
  language difference, 58
  regionalist movements, 1
  regionalist parties, 21, 52, 71
Basque Left, 21
Basque Nationalist Party, 21, 94
Basque Solidarity, 21, 94
Bavaria, 20, 70
Belgian ID21, 93n4
Belgium
  European integration, 105
  European Parliament, 105
  European Union, 97
  Heckman selection model, 202
  language families, 169
  markets, 105
  party family, 107, 110
  regionalist parties, 19
  regionalist party incidence, 69–70
  regionalist party success, 83, 196, 198–199
  2010 elections, 129
  vote share, 164
BNG (Galician Nationalist Bloc), 114
Bretagne, 77
Breton Democratic Union, 20
Bretons, 46
Brittany, 20
Brown, Gordon, 158

Bureau of Unrepresented European Nations, 38
business interests, 140

Calabria, 78
Canarian Coalition, 21, 94
Canarian Independent Groupings, 21
Canaries, 21
capitalism, 34
Catalan Convergence and Union, 22, 94, 101, 105
Catalan Republican Left, 22, 94
Catalonia
  economic interests, 158
  Euro-enthusiasm, 51
  independence, 159
  language difference, 58
  population, 149, 155
  regionalist movement, 2
  regionalist parties, 22
  regionalist party incidence, 71
Celtic language, 146. See also language families
center-periphery, 52
centralization, 157
centrist parties, 98
Chapel Hill Expert Survey, 10, 92, 93n4, 95, 103, 117, 128
Christian Social Union of Bavaria (CSU), 19
cleavages, 15, 18, 52, 90, 100, 103, 153
Committee of the Regions, 117
Common Fisheries Policy, 115, 116, 119
communications revolution, 35
Comparative Manifesto Project, 61, 62, 93, 95
Condorcet, Nicolas de, 1
conservative party family, 96, 111
Conservatives, 137, 139, 145
Convergence and Union. See Catalan Convergence and Union
Cornwall, 22
Corsica, 20, 92, 120

Council of Ministers, 118
cross-party coordination, 140
cultural heterogeneity, 147, 194
Cunningham Amendment, 126, 137

de Wever, Bart, 149
decentralization
  advantages of, 37
  deeper integration, 11
  hypothesis, 81
  mainstream parties, 78
  new party entry, 63
  party position, 62–63
  political decentralization, 64
  political opportunity structure, 154
  public support, 123
  regionalist movement goals, 2
  regionalist party incidence, 187
  Scottish referenda, 5
  state sovereignty, 161
deeper European integration
  centralization, 123
  homogenization, 123
  influence on support for regionalist parties, 52
  regionalist party incidence, 67, 85
  regionalist party success, 67
  Scottish support for autonomy, 126
  sub-national mobilization, 148, 160
  See also European integration
defense spending, 44
Democratic Convergence of Navarre, 22
Democratic Front of Francophones, 19
Denmark
  Heckman selection model, 202
  language families, 169–171
  regionalist parties, 20
  regionalist party incidence, 69–70
  regionalist party success, 83, 196, 198–199
  vote share, 166
détente, 35

devolution
 elite cues, 39n7
 ethno-national aspirations, 64
 European integration, 124
 expected support for, 141
 preference orderings, 142
 public perception, 141
 public support, 138, 147
 referendum, 6, 125, 134
 Scotland, 136, 137n20, 138–139, 152
 survey questions, 204
 Think Twice campaign, 140
 voting positions, 138
district magnitude
 Heckman selection model, 202
 regionalist party incidence, 75, 192–193, 195
 regionalist party success, 65, 79–80, 196, 198–199

economic classes, 136
economic crisis, 150
economic differences, 77, 188
economic dislocation, 51, 136, 152
economic integration, 2, 40, 103
economic interests, 60, 129
economic variables, 73n33
effective number of parties, 82, 83, 188, 196, 198–202
effective number of parties formula, 81n46, 188n3
Electoral Coalition of Left in Catalonia, 22
electoral laws, 61
electoral support, by party family, 106
elite cues, 124–129, 131–133, 136, 149, 152
energy resources, 115. See also oil
ethnic conflict, 154
ethnic distinctiveness, 16
ethnic divisions, 1. See also European identity; national identity; regional identity
ethnic fragmentation, 40, 81n46
ethnic mobilization, 34n1, 156

ethnic peripheral nationalist, 13
ethnicity, 16n6
ethnoregional, 13
ethnoregionalist, 13, 16–17
ethnoterritorial, 13
EU-14, 9, 14n1, 24n13, 55, 68, 70, 73
EU-15, 46, 73
Euro crisis, 12, 149, 157
Euro, 50, 67n25
Euro-enthusiasm, 92, 117, 119. See also Europhile
European Charter for Regional and Minority Languages, 38
European Commission, 46n17
European Council on Foreign Relations, 3
European Court of Justice, 38
European Economic Community, 1
European Free Alliance, 38, 120
European identity, 1, 11, 49, 90–91
European integration
 autonomy, 6
 casual inference, 50
 conditions for regionalist groups, 3
 descriptive inference, 50
 devolution, 124
 disadvantages for large states, 41
 economic interests, 124
 European Parliament, 103
 explanatory variable, 50
 free trade area, 9
 globalization, 8
 internal market, 103
 monetary union, 9
 multi-level governance, 1
 negative integration, 91
 neoclassical theory, 44
 party families, 91
 party position, 92, 108
 political space, functional space, 39
 positive integration, 91
 preferences, 45
 regionalist mobilization, 2, 53
 regionalist party incidence, 72
 regionalist party success, 82, 84, 151

regionalist party support, 3–4, 151, 153
regionalist mobilization, 53
role of states, 44
salience, 101, 103
small state viability, 9
sovereignty, 161
sub-national autonomy movements, 54, 86
sub-national mobilization, 9
treaties, 50
viability of independence, 124
See also deeper European integration
European Parliament, 105, 118
European Union
  access to world community, 38
  autonomy movements, 37
  economic dislocation, 89
  expected support for, 131
  free trade area, 39, 42, 48
  globalization, 37, 48
  independence, 149
  instrumental support, 125
  integration as threat to regionalists, 123
  left/right cleavage, 99
  mobility, 33
  multi-culturalism, 90
  party position, 51
  party strategy, 145
  protectionism, 33
  public support, 123
  regional organization, 159
  regionalist mobilization, 2
  regionalist party incidence, 4
  regulatory policy, 42
  salience, 102
  security, 41
  small state viability, 3
  structural funds, subsidies, 43
  support by income, 130
  support by occupation, 130
  support by party, 97–98, 111, 131n11
  support by political interest, 130
  supranational structure, 7
  trade forums, 42
European Union, Treaty of, 66n24
Europhiles, 87–88, 90, 92, 96, 119
Euroskepticism
  degrees of, 88
  government parties, 98
  Lega Nord, 97n8
  party strategy, 5, 90, 96, 152
  regionalist mobilization, 49
  regionalist parties' supporters, 87–88
  Scottish National Party, 114
  separatism, 117
  United Kingdom, 119
  Viability Theory, 49n20
Eurotrepid, 96
Eurozone, 160
exit option, 46–47. *See also* regionalist mobility
extreme left, 109, 112

federalism, 64, 91, 156
Finland
  language families, 171–172
  party family, 107, 110
  regionalist parties, 20
  regionalist party incidence, 69–70
  vote share, 164
fishing interests, 115–117
Flanders, 1, 19, 158
Flemish Interest, 94
Flemish People's Union, 19, 93n4, 94, 101
formula, effective number of parties, 81n46, 188n3
fragmentation, 160–161
France
  Heckman selection model, 202
  homogenous preference, 46
  language families, 172-174
  party family, 107, 110
  regionalist parties, 20
  regionalist party incidence, 4, 69

INDEX 229

regionalist party success, 83, 196, 198–199
vote share, 166
Francophone Democratic Front, 94, 101
free trade, 42, 85, 116
fringe parties, 95, 109, 111–112

Gabel model, 129n9
GAL/TAN, 100–101
Galicia, 22, 92
Galician Nationalist Bloc, 22, 94
Germany
    Heckman selection model, 202
    language families, 174–176
    party family, 107, 110
    regionalist parties, 20
    regionalist party incidence, 4, 69–70
    regionalist party success, 83, 196, 198–199
    vote share, 166
globalization, 12, 16n7, 43, 156, 161
government participation, 106
Greece, 43n15, 70, 107, 110, 157, 176–177
Greens, 96
group identity, 16

Heckman selection model, 81n44, 187, 201
Herri Batasuna
    European Union, 97, 105
    Euroskepticism, 111, 120
    left wing parties, 99
    regionalist party success, 81
    vote share, 94
heterogeneous states, 89
Hobsbawm, Eric, 1
hypotheses, 67, 88–92, 105, 151

immigration, 8, 51
incidence. *See* regionalist party incidence
independence, 2. *See also* separatism

industrial rationalization, 35
Initiative for Catalonia, 93n4, 94
instrumental Europeans, 119
International Monetary Fund, 38
intra-party dissent, 102n12, 115
Ireland, 22, 38, 70, 107, 110, 177
Irish Independence, 22
isolationism, 114
Italy
    economic issues, 158
    Heckman selection model, 202
    language difference, 58, 78
    language families, 177–179
    party family, 107, 110
    regionalist parties, 20
    regionalist party incidence, 69–71
    regionalist party success, 83, 196, 198–199
    vote share, 164

labor mobility, 116
labor skill levels, 129
Labour, 137n20, 145
language classification, 58
language difference
    capital language, 57n6
    changes over time, 76
    determinant of regionalist parties, 56
    Heckman selection model, 202
    random effects model, 197
    regionalist party incidence, 75, 192–193, 195
    regionalist party success, 83, 196, 198–199
    standard deviation, 82
    Western Europe, 59
language difference values, 58
language families, 57–58, 167
language, historical, 57–58
language, regional, 85
latent regionalism, 16
League for Southern Action (LAM), 20
left/right ideology, 105–106

Lega Nord
  anti-EU sentiments, 105
  Euro-enthusiasm, 102
  European Union, 100
  Euroskepticism, 10, 97n8, 120
  labor mobility, 47
  political-economic preferences, 58
  regional identity, 125
  regionalist party, 19–20
  right-wing parties, 99
  vote share, 25, 94
Leonard, Mark, 3
Lisbon, Treaty of, 66n24
List Dedecker, 19
List, Friedrich, 36
Luxembourg, 9n1, 14n1, 24n13, 55n3, 73

Maastricht, 50, 77
mainstream parties, 61–62, 96, 154
major parties, 8
market integration, 157
markets, 3, 7, 41–42
Marx, Karl, 1
Mas i Gavarró, Artur, 149
Mebyon Kernow, 22, 24, 71
Member of the European Parliament, 88, 103, 120
MEP. *See* Member of the European Parliament
Mercosur, 2, 155
Merger Treaty, 66n24
Mill, John Stuart, 37
mininationalist, 13
minority nationalist, 13, 80, 155
minority, 139
mobility, 47, 49. *See also* regionalist mobility
modernization theory, 34
monetary union, 85, 159–160
Monnet, Jean, 1
Movement for Autonomies, 20
multi-level governance
  centralization, 39
  European integration, 88

federalism, 157
globalization, 12
mobilization, 48n19
party position, 66, 154
party strategy, 15, 87
small state viability, 7

NAFTA, 37n5
National and Supranational Governance scale, 66
national elections, 5, 55, 68–69, 73n45, 81, 153
national fragmentation, 150
National Front, 97
national identity, 1, 124–125, 128, 147
national parties, 19, 62n19
Nationalists and Independent nationalists, 22
nationalism, 34
nation-state, 3
NATO, 44
Navarre, 22, 37
Netherlands, 70, 107, 110, 179–180
New Flemish Alliance (N-VA), 19, 93n4, 94, 98–99, 101–102, 104–105, 149
new party entry, 61–62, 150, 155, 189
Nice, Treaty of, 66n24
niche parties, 65
Nomenclature of Territorial Units for Statistics (NUTS), 23n12, 68
Northern Ireland, 22, 57n5, 71
Northern League. *See* Lega Nord
Norway, 42n13
NUTS. *See* Nomenclature of Territorial Units for Statistics
N-VA. *See* New Flemish Alliance

oil, 31n15, 114, 158
optimal size of states, 3, 7, 33, 39, 45, 150, 160

Parti Autonomiste Breton, 51
party accommodation
  decentralization, 62, 78
  Heckman selection model, 202

Index

mainstream parties, 81
regionalist party incidence, 75, 187, 192–193, 195
regionalist party success, 82, 83, 196, 198–199
party competition, 15, 153
party cues. *See* elite cues
party divergence
  Heckman selection model, 202
  left/right cleavage, 61
  regionalist party incidence, 75, 187, 192–193, 195
  regionalist party success, 82–83, 196, 198–199
party family
  agrarian, 107, 110
  Christian Democratic, 107, 110
  conservative, 107, 110
  Euro-enthusiasm, 92
  European integration, 91
  European Union, 127
  Europhile, 120
  Euroskepticism, 96
  extreme right, 107, 110
  Green, 107, 110
  intra-family variation, 96
  left/right cleavage, 107, 110
  liberal, 107, 110
  Protestant, 107, 110
  regionalist, 107, 110
  Social Democratic, 107, 110
  support for European Union, 131n11
party manifestos, 51, 61, 115. *See also* Comparative Manifesto Project
Party of Wales. *See* Plaid Cymru
party position
  European integration, 103
  European Union, 51, 147, 154
  independence, 6, 51
party strategy, 60, 149
peripheral nationalist, 13, 15
peripheral regionalist, 13
permanent minorities, 90, 139
Plaid Cymru, 23, 81, 91, 93–94, 127

political behavior, 160
political dynamics, 150
political entrepreneurs, 8
political independence, 89
political institutions, 63
political integration, 1, 103
political opportunity structure, 136, 151, 154
political parties, 8, 14. *See also* party family; new party entry
political representation, demand for, 56
Portugal, 107, 110, 181
post-functionalist theory of integration, 124
preference orderings, 141–142, 144, 147
preferences
  distinct, 46
  divergent, 59, 82
  effects on autonomy movements, 47
  heterogeneity, 55–56, 60, 151
  homogenous, 46
  ideological, 46
  language, 46
  mobility, 46
  political-economic preferences, 59
  regional identity, 125
  regionalist mobilization, 46
  regionalist movements, 45
  regionalist parties, 48
pro-Europe, 152. *See also* Europhile
Progressives for the Balearic Islands, 21
proportional representation, 64–65
PSd'Az. *See* Sardinian Action Party
public goods, 40, 41n12, 42
public opinion, 124, 127–128, 152
public sector policy, 63
Pujol, Jordi, 51

Quebec, 37n5

radical left parties, 96
radical right parties, 53, 55, 90, 96, 108–109, 125

Rapid Response Centre, 42
referendum, 125, 134, 136, 158. *See also* Scotland
regional attachments, 132n12
Regional Authority Index
   decentralization, 64
   Heckman selection model, 202
   regionalist party incidence, 75, 192–193, 195
   regionalist party success, 83, 196, 198–199
regional citizens, 11
regional identity, 34, 124–125
regional integration, 1–2, 156, 188
regional movements, 35–36. *See also* regionalist movements
regional party, in contrast to regionalist party, 16n5
regional, 13
regionalism, 2, 7, 16
regionalist autonomy movements, 113, 136
regionalist challenges, 149
regionalist identity, 128
regionalist mobilization
   decentralization, 82
   dependent variable, 50
   European integration, 4, 8, 33, 150
   European Union, 2
   globalization, 33
   language difference, 78
   modernization, 34
regionalist movements, 2, 60, 149
regionalist parties
   classification, 18
   cleavages, 15
   decision to compete, 8
   deeper integration, 9–10
   EU membership, 67
   European Union, support for, 89
   Euroskepticism, 10
   exit option, 47
   goals, 17
   group identity, 35–36
   language difference, 58
   objective trait, 35
   party positions toward EU, 10
   supporters, 126, 128, 131–132, 147
   tactics, 133
   vote share, 25, 30–33, 163
   See also regionalist party incidence; regionalist party success
regionalist party family variable, 109
regionalist party family, 7, 13, 124
regionalist party identification, 148
regionalist party incidence
   alternative controls, 187
   combined models, 201
   comparative analysis, 153
   by country, 24
   by decade, 26–28
   decision to compete, 80
   hypothesis, 54
   rise of, 29
   specifications, 192
   variables, 190
   vote share, 80
regionalist party success
   cleavages, 153
   combined models, 201
   cultural difference, 55
   decentralization, 64
   European integration, 151
   hypothesis, 54
   party position, 87
   preferences, 48
   specifications, 198
   variables, 196
relative GDP per capita, 77, 188
Republican Left of Catalonia, 22
Republican Labour, 22
Republican, 22
Republican Clubs, 22
right wing parties, 92
right/left ideological score, 61
Rome, Treaty of, 50, 66n24, 77, 114

Salmond, Alex, 6, 122n25
Salvini, Matteo, 103
Sardinia, 20, 120

Index

Sardinian Action Party (PSd'Az), 20, 23n10, 94
Schleswig Party, 20
Schleswig-Holstein, 20, 71
Scotland
  access to world community, 38
  bailout, 158
  decentralization, 2, 5
  devolution, 136, 141, 143, 152
  economic issues, 158
  European integration, 11, 126
  European Union, 134
  homogenous preference, 46
  identity, 37
  independence, 11, 205
  language difference, 57n5
  party identification, 135n16
  politicization of regional movements, 35n2, 35
  population, 155
  preference orderings, 141–142
  referendum, 11, 118, 125, 136, 144, 158–159
  referendum positions by class, 146–147
  regionalist parties, 23
  regionalist party incidence, 71
  security concerns, 44
  small state viability, 150
  sub-state national movements, 1
Scottish Assembly, 204
Scottish Labour Party, 23
Scottish Militant Labour, 23
Scottish National Party
  access to markets, 43
  austerity measures, 158
  economic well-being, 60
  electoral support, 31n15
  EU support across GAL/TAN, 101
  European Union, 11, 89, 113, 127, 152
  Euroskepticism, 120
  founding, 5
  goals, 17
  independence, 91, 116
  mainstream parties, 79
  national elections, 23
  party position, 10, 11, 51, 112, 148
  peak vote share, 94
  Scottish Parliament, 155
  strategy toward EU, 119
  supporters, 135, 140, 145
  unemployment, 43
Scottish Parliament, 12, 137n20, 138n21, 140, 144, 155, 205
Scottish Socialist Alliance, 23
Scottish Socialist Party, 23
secession, 48, 126, 148
secessionist movements, 39n7, 156
security concerns, 35, 37, 41, 44
self-government, 136–137
sensitivity analysis, 194
separatism, 41n11
Sicily, 78
Sillars, Jim, 51, 89, 116, 117n23, 122n25
Single European Act, 66n24, 115
single-member district system, 65
Sinn Féin, 22, 93n5, 99
small state viability
  Catalonia, 150
  cost-benefit approach, 156
  economic viability, 37
  European Union, 6, 12
  globalization, 156
  oil, 31n15
  Scotland, 134, 150
Social Democratic and Labour Party, 22, 94
social democratic parties, 91
Socialist Party of Andalusia, 21
Sons of Cornwall, 22. *See also* Mebyon Kernow
South Schleswig Voters' Union, 20
South Tyrol, 20, 71
South Tyrolean People's Party (SVP), 20, 94, 114
Southern Jutland, 20
sovereignty, 87, 90, 113–114, 161
Soviet Union, 35, 44

Spain
    exception to support for EU, 97
    Heckman selection model, 202
    language difference, 58, 78
    language families, 181–183
    party family, 107, 110
    regionalist parties, 21
    regionalist party incidence, 4, 69–71
    regionalist party success, 83, 196, 198–199
    vote share, 165
stateless nationalist, 13
states
    economies of scale, 39, 41
    heterogeneity within, 3, 39–40
    markets, size of, 42
    optimal size, 3, 7, 33, 39, 45, 150, 160
    public goods, 41
security concerns, 44
structural funds, 43, 43n15
Sturgeon, Nicola, 158
sub-national autonomy movements, 121
sub-national conflicts, 34
sub-national governance, 88
sub-national mobilization, 148, 160
sub-national movements, 63, 151
sub-national regionalist, 13
sub-national units, 44
sub-state identification, 128
sub-state nationalist, 1, 7, 11, 13, 52, 65
sub-state regions, 150
success. See regionalist party success
supranational governance, 88
Supranational Governance Index, 66, 76–77, 83–84
supranational integration, 148, 150, 160
supranational organization, 121
survey questions, 204
Sweden, 70, 107, 110, 183–185
Swedish People's Party, 20, 94, 101

Tartan tax, 137n20
tax-varying authority, 140, 144
territorial autonomy, 39, 120
territorial claims, 16
territorialized party systems, 59n11
Think Twice campaign, 140
Tories, 116, 158
trade barriers, 48. *See also* free trade
trade missions, 38
traditional states, challenge to authority, 38
treaties, 38, 50, 66n24, 77
Trentino Alto Adige, 77
Trieste, 20

UKIP, 103
Union of Canarian People, 21
Union of Corsican People, 20
Union of the Navarrese People, 22
United Kingdom
    Heckman selection model, 202
    language families, 185-186
    party family, 107, 110
    regionalist parties, 22
    regionalist party incidence, 4, 15, 69–70
    regionalist party success, 83, 196, 198–199
    vote share, 165
    Westphalian state, 159
United Left, 93n4
United People, 21

Valdostian Union, 21
Valencia Union, 22, 94
Valencia, 22
Viability Theory
    casual inference, 50
    centralization, 125
    descriptive inference, 50
    Euro-enthusiasm, 10, 88, 120
    European integration, 10, 86, 127, 151
    European Union, 5, 11
    Euroskepticism, 49n20

INDEX 235

   new parties, 8
   political environment, 55
   regionalist mobilization, 4
   regionalist party supporters, 134
   Scottish Parliament, 12
   Scottish referendum, 144, 147
   small state viability, 3
   sub-national mobilization, 7, 148
viability, perceptions of, 136
Vlaams Beiang. *See* Vlaams Blok
Vlaams Blok, 19, 97, 99–100, 120, 125
Volker, Paul, 159
vote positions, actual, 204
vote share
   correlation with government participation, 108
   by country, 163
   European integration, 85
   national elections, 80
   peak, 93–94
   predicted vote shares, 203
   regionalist parties, 84
voter policy preferences, 53, 90
voting behavior, 147

Wales, 2, 23, 37, 44, 71, 92
Wallonia, 19
Walloon parties, 149
Walloon Rally, 19
Welsh Republican Movement, 23
Western Europe, 4, 14
Wilson, Gordon, 89

Yes to Navarre campaign, 22